THE IDEA OF HUMAN RIGHTS

THE IDEA OF
HUMAN RIGHTS

CHARLES R. BEITZ

OXFORD
UNIVERSITY PRESS

OXFORD

UNIVERSITY PRESS

Great Clarendon Street, Oxford OX2 6DP
United Kingdom

Oxford University Press is a department of the University of Oxford.
It furthers the University's objective of excellence in research, scholarship,
and education by publishing worldwide. Oxford is a registered trade mark of
Oxford University Press in the UK and in certain other countries

First published 2009
First published in paperback 2011
Reprinted 2013

British Library Cataloguing in Publication Data
Data available

Library of Congress Cataloging in Publication Data
Data available

ISBN 978-0-19-960437-1

For Ann,
and for Caroline and Stephan

Contents

Chapter 5 A Fresh Start

Chapter 6 Normativity

Chapter 7 International Concern

Chapter 8 Conclusion

Abbreviations

Core international human rights instruments (with dates entered into force)

CAT	Convention against Torture and other Cruel, Inhuman or Degrading Treatment or Punishment (1987)
CEDAW	Convention on the Elimination of all Forms of Discrimination against Women (1981)
CERD	Convention on the Elimination of all Forms of Racial Discrimination (1969)
CRC	Convention on the Rights of the Child (1990)
ICCPR	International Covenant on Civil and Political Rights (1976)
ICESCR	International Covenant on Economic, Social and Cultural Rights (1976)
UDHR	Universal Declaration of Human Rights (adopted 1948)

Preface

I began to write a book about human rights almost thirty years ago, in the innocence of a first sabbatical. But after reading and thinking for most of a year, I concluded that human rights was not a good subject for political philosophy. For one thing, the disputed questions seemed mostly to be artifacts of the Cold War; for all their political significance, they did not seem to involve very interesting philosophical problems. Moreover, the idea of a human right as it was expressed in international doctrine seemed to have been stretched beyond what might plausibly be accepted as a legacy of philosophically respectable thought about fundamental rights. Human rights seemed more like the expression of a conception of social justice. But in that case the topic of real interest would be the idea of social and perhaps global justice, not that of human rights. Feeling unable to get a grip, I turned to other things.

That might not have been a mistake then, but it would be today. In the intervening years the language of human rights has become the common idiom of social criticism in global politics. That there should be wide acceptance of global critical standards for domestic political institutions is one part of what people mean when they speak of a "human rights revolution" in the last several decades. Another is that violations or threatened violations of these standards within a society might reasonably be taken as a justification for remedial or preventive action by outside agents. One need not deny that international humanitarian action has a longer history to recognize that these facts mark a watershed in the history of global normative order.

The problem is that, although the idea and language of human rights have become increasingly prominent in public discourse, it has not become any more clear what kinds of objects human rights are supposed to be, why we should believe that people have them, or what follows from this belief for political practice. Perhaps this should not be surprising, but it is still a problem for anyone inclined to believe that our political ideas should have some clear and distinct significance in our thinking about how to act. This is especially so when the ideas play such a central role in framing public concerns of great importance.

One kind of contribution political theory can make to our broader intellectual life is to discipline our references to these important ideas. In the case of human rights, there is also more: for once we understand what a commitment to international human rights is a commitment *to*, we see that it can be a demanding commitment and potentially at odds with other and more familiar political values—for example, those associated with toleration, cultural identity, and self-government. So a theory of human rights faces a double challenge: not only to clarify the meaning and grounds of human rights but also to illuminate the ways we might bring them into some reasonable relationship with other values with which they might conflict.

What makes these challenges especially difficult is that "human rights" names not so much an abstract normative idea as an emergent political practice. Those interested in the theory of human rights are not at liberty to interpret this idea in whatever way best suits their philosophical commitments. Human rights is a public enterprise and those who would interpret its principles must hold themselves accountable to its public aims and character. So it seems that an engagement with the idea of a human right must therefore also engage with the nature and purposes of the public enterprise. That, in itself, is a challenge, since the enterprise is complicated both doctrinally and politically and so much of what has been written about it tends to be distorted by either celebratory or skeptical predilections.

This, anyway, is the thought that motivates this book. I have come to appreciate its implications only gradually. One result is that the position I sketch in this book differs in some ways from what I have said in papers on human rights written in the last several years.[1] So although parts of the book are based on these papers, it is also revisionary. This is particularly true about the character of discursive practices, the kinds of normativity of which

[1] "Human Rights as a Common Concern," *American Political Science Review* 95 (2001): 269-82; "What Human Rights Mean," *Daedalus* 132 1 (winter 2003): 36-46; "Human Rights and *The Law of Peoples*," in *The Ethics of Assistance: Morality and the Distant Needy*, ed. Deen Chatterjee (Cambridge: Cambridge University Press, 2004), 193-214; "Protections against Poverty in the Practice of Human Rights," in *The Theory and Politics of Socio-economic Human Rights*, ed. Thomas Pogge (UNESCO, forthcoming).

human rights are capable, the significance of actual and potential convergence among cultural moral codes, and the relationship between human rights and the distinct ideas of social and global justice. I hope that the conception of human rights presented in the book is more plausible than that found in the earlier papers.

The long, disjointed history of this project means that I have accumulated unusually many debts, certainly more than I can recall and acknowledge. For comments, criticisms, and instructive conversations I am grateful to Elizabeth Ashford, Brian Barry, Allen Buchanan, Joshua Cohen, Heather Collister, Ryan Davis, Michael Doyle, Kristen Hessler, James Griffin, Amy Gutmann, George Kateb, Benedict Kingsbury, Stephen Macedo, Jamie Mayerfeld, Liam Murphy, Hans Oberdiek, Susan Moller Okin, Thomas Pogge, John Rawls, Joseph Raz, Nancy Rosenblum, Rahul Sagar, Thomas Scanlon, Samuel Scheffler, Henry Shue, Lawrence Simon, Marion Smiley, John Tasioulas, Robert Taylor, Dennis Thompson, Thomas Weiss, and Deborah Yashar. David Miller, Mathias Risse, Leif Wenar, and two anonymous readers for Oxford University Press provided exceptionally detailed and helpful comments on a draft of the manuscript. Risse and Wenar helped again later. Dominic Byatt has been the kind of editor every author should wish for: he grasped the aspirations of this book more clearly than I did and his gentle editorial suggestions have improved the manuscript throughout. I am grateful, too, for the attention and questions of members of the academic audiences to whom I presented my ideas about human rights in various stages of gestation. Although I could not be more aware of the book's shortcomings, I know it is much better than it would have been without this copious help.

My first academic leave, when I began work on this subject, was made possible by the Rockefeller Foundation and Swarthmore College. No such investments can have taken longer to bear fruit. Since I returned to the subject, I have been supported by the Guggenheim Foundation, Bowdoin College, and Princeton University. I enjoyed the hospitality of the Warden and Fellows of Merton College, Oxford, and the University of Oxford Department of Politics and International Relations, and of the Institute for International Law and Justice at New York University School of Law during a sabbatical when I drafted much of the book. I finished most of the final revisions during a subsequent leave at Stanford University, where I was a guest of the Global Justice Program. I thank all of these institutions for their generosity.

I

Introduction

THE doctrine of human rights is the articulation in the public morality of
world politics of the idea that each person is a subject of global
concern. It does not matter what a person's spatial location might be or
which political subdivision or social group the person might belong
to. Everyone has human rights, and responsibilities to respect and protect
these rights may, in principle, extend across political and social boundaries.
The propagation and diffusion of this idea are among the most impressive of
the legacies of World War II. To adopt Richard Rorty's phrase, human
rights have become "a fact of the world" with a reach and influence that
would astonish the framers of the international human rights project.[1]
Today, if the public discourse of peacetime global society can be said to
have a common moral language, it is that of human rights.

1. Why there is a problem

This book is a contribution to the political theory of human rights. It is
stimulated by two observations. The first is that human rights has become an
elaborate international practice. Since the end of World War II, this practice
has developed on several fronts: in international law, in global and regional
institutions, in the foreign policies of (mostly liberal-democratic) states, and
in the activities of a diverse and growing array of nongovernmental organizations (NGOs) and networks. The practice has become more conspicuous
politically since the end of the Cold War as the scope of human rights

---

[1] Richard Rorty, "Human Rights, Rationality, and Sentimentality," in *On Human Rights: The
Oxford Amnesty Lectures 1993*, ed. Stephen Shute and Susan Hurley (New York: Basic Books,
1993), 134.

doctrine has expanded and the human, political, and material resources devoted to the protection and advancement of human rights have multiplied. Participants in this practice take its central moral ideas with great seriousness. Many are empowered by them. Some risk their lives for them. Its beneficiaries and potential beneficiaries regard the practice as a source of hope.

The other observation is that the discourse and practice of human rights can also evoke a disabling skepticism, even among those who admire its motivating ideas. I do not mean the radical skepticism reflected in a wholesale rejection of morality or the more limited skepticism underlying a refusal to accept what we ordinarily regard as moral considerations as reasons for action in global political life. I mean a skepticism about human rights that might be embraced in one or another form even by those who are not alienated from morality in general or global political morality in particular. This kind of skepticism consists of a disparagement of human rights as grounds of political action. It can take various forms and may be encouraged by some elements of the human rights enterprise itself: for example, the indistinctness of the range of interests protected by human rights, the difficulty of seeing contemporary human rights doctrine as significantly "universal," the elasticity of the permissions to interfere that human rights seem to generate, and the potential costs of acting consistently to protect human rights against abuse and to promote adherence to them.

One reason to take up the political theory of human rights is to see how successfully this kind of skepticism can be resisted. This is an important reason, but not the only reason. Even when regarded sympathetically, the practice of human rights is bound to seem puzzling. It is unclear, for example, whether the objects called "human rights" within this practice are in any familiar sense *rights* and why certain standards but not others should count as human rights. It is not clear what responsibilities attach to human rights, on which agents these responsibilities fall, and what kinds of reasons should motivate these agents to care about them. It is not clear why a practice that aims to protect individual persons against various threats should assign responsibilities primarily to states rather than to other kinds of agents. It is not even clear why one should regard human rights as grounds of *international* action at all: one might, instead, regard them as standards whose security within a society is the exclusive responsibility of that society's government. The more clearly we appreciate the substantive scope of international human rights doctrine and the variety of practical purposes for which appeal to human rights is actually made, the more difficult it is to assimilate them to any familiar moral idea. Even a friend of human rights may be left wondering if the enterprise represents anything morally coherent. One might be tempted to regard it, instead, as no more than an unstable construction, explicable only historically.

2. Forms of skepticism

enforcement

Skepticism about human rights comes in many forms. Some philosophers believe it is part of the idea of a right that there should be some mechanism in place for its effective enforcement. But international human rights practice notoriously lacks a standing capacity to enforce many of the rights listed in the major treaties, and even when an enforcement capacity exists, it usually applies selectively and often only at the sufferance of those states against which it might be used. To make matters worse, it is not even clear how we should conceive of "enforcement" in relation to some of the requirements of human rights doctrine. What, for example, would it mean to "enforce" the right to an adequate standard of living?[2] It is possible, of course, to imagine policy measures that would ensure the satisfaction of this right, but it is unclear that the enjoyment of the right can sensibly be "enforced" in the same way as the enjoyment of more familiar rights. If one thinks that genuine rights must be effectively enforceable, then one might be encouraged to believe, as Raymond Geuss suggests, that the idea of a human right "is an inherently vacuous concept."[3]

Another kind of skepticism, perhaps related, arises from the belief that the satisfaction of at least some human rights is not feasible under existing or readily foreseeable social conditions. It is not always clear how this belief should be understood: the thought might be that the resources required to protect or satisfy a right are not available, or that the opportunity cost of devoting resources to this purpose is unreasonably great, or that the right can only be satisfied under institutional or cultural conditions that cannot easily be brought about. The motivating idea in all three cases is that a value

---

[2] International Covenant on Economic, Social and Cultural Rights (ICESCR), art. 11(1).

[3] Raymond Geuss, *History and Illusion in Politics* (Cambridge: Cambridge University Press, 2001), 144. He continues: "Perhaps if we repeat claims about natural rights long enough and loudly enough, and pass enough resolutions, people will stop doing various horrible things to each other. Indeed, perhaps they may, but perhaps not."

cannot count as a right if there is no agent who can be held to be under a duty to satisfy it. If one accepts this idea and some version of the belief that the satisfaction of at least some human rights is not feasible or would be unreasonably costly, then one might conclude that at least some human rights recognized in international doctrine cannot be real rights. Values of this kind state aspirations for the future but do not generate reasons for action in the present.[4] Their status is analogous to Hobbes's laws of nature in the state of nature: they "bind to a desire that they should take place" but not necessarily "to the putting them in act."[5]

Two other forms of skepticism arise from doubt about the idea that human rights can be "universal" in any significant way. The most straightforward interpretation of this idea is that human rights apply to everyone or are claimable by everyone. Skepticism arises when we consider why this might be the case. It is frequently said that human rights belong to persons "as such" or "solely in virtue of their humanity." As we shall see, it is not obvious what this idea amounts to, but for the moment we might say that a right belongs to persons "as such" if the ground or justification of the right appeals to features that persons possess regardless of their contingent relationships or social setting. The skeptic holds that no plausible interpretation of this idea will yield a conception of human nature sufficiently robust to justify any practically interesting catalog of rights. An extreme version of this type of skepticism holds that nothing "called a human right can be derived from human nature" because the behavioral dispositions we actually observe in human beings are too diverse and conflicting to allow for any coherent generalization.[6] A more moderate position holds that the interests that are in fact shared by all human beings are too few to provide a foundation for any but the most elemental prohibitions—for example, of murder, torture, severe material deprivation. The reference to "interests" is essential: the skeptical idea is not that people do not *agree* about human rights (this, too, is a skeptical idea, but it is a different idea). It is, rather, that human beings taken in abstraction from the contingencies of their historical and social circumstances do not share sufficiently many desires or needs to justify more

---

[4] Many people have held views of this kind. An early example can be found in Arthur Holcombe's trenchant critique of the draft of the Universal Declaration in *Human Rights in the Modern World* (New York: New York University Press, 1948). A familiar source is Maurice Cranston, *What Are Human Rights?*, rev. edn. (London: Bodley Head, 1973), ch. 8.

[5] Thomas Hobbes, *Leviathan* [1651], ed. E. Curley (Indianapolis: Hackett, 1994), ch. 15, para. 36.

[6] John O. Nelson, "Against Human Rights," *Philosophy* 65 (1990), 345.

than a very short list of standards.[7] The result of accepting this idea is not a wholesale skepticism about human rights but rather a skepticism about international human rights doctrine as it exists today: its scope will appear to extend well beyond what might reasonably be seen as rights belonging to human beings "as such."

We get another kind of skepticism from the thought that human rights can be "universal" in a morally significant sense only if they are acceptable from all moral and cultural points of view. This is different from the idea that genuine human rights must belong to human beings "as such:" any relationship between the catalogs of rights that satisfy this standard and those that are acceptable all around would be contingent. One might be attracted to the latter idea by recognition that human rights violations can serve as triggers for international interference in the society where the violations take place together with the belief that it would be objectionably paternalistic to interfere in defense of values not actually shared within that society's culture.[8] It is a commonplace that some of the norms found in the main international treaties conflict with elements of some of the major social-moral codes found in the world (consider, for example, provisions requiring equal treatment of men and women or those calling for equal individual rights to participate in politics). If human rights are supposed to describe a basis of intersocietal or intercultural agreement, then again it will appear that international doctrine overreaches. So we arrive by another route at the view that genuinely "universal" human rights are relatively few.[9]

A fifth form of skepticism results from combining this last thought with a view about the influence of the disparities of power found in global politics on human rights doctrine and practice. Modern human rights doctrine originated in Europe and the US, and while it is sometimes overlooked that smaller states, mostly outside of Europe, played a substantial role in the

[7] This idea is found in H. L. A. Hart's analysis of "the minimal content of natural law" in *The Concept of Law* (Oxford: Clarendon Press, 1961), ch. 9.2, though without reference to human rights.

[8] The canonical expression of this idea is the "Statement on Human Rights" of the Executive Board of the American Anthropological Association, *American Anthropologist*, NS 49 (1947): 539-43. The statement no longer represents the position of the Association. See American Anthropological Association, Committee on Human Rights, "Declaration on Anthropology and Human Rights" [1999], http://www.aaanet.org/stmts/humanrts.htm (consulted September 2, 2008).

[9] Chris Brown, "Universal Human Rights," in *Human Rights in Global Politics,* ed. Tim Dunne and Nicholas J. Wheeler (Cambridge: Cambridge University Press, 1999), 119. Of course, someone could share the view that human rights represent particularistic values without becoming a skeptic as characterized here. Richard Rorty's view is an example; see "Human Rights, Rationality, and Sentimentality," 117-19.

genesis of the postwar human rights regime, it is unlikely that there would have been either a declaration or treaties without the active engagement of the wartime great powers. In the subsequent history of international efforts to protect human rights, strong states have been largely immune from political and military interference to protect human rights. Moreover, there is a record of powerful countries relying on human rights as public rationales for measures whose primary purposes were unrelated to and occasionally incompatible with these rationales. And even when powerful actors have been authentically concerned to protect human rights, their attention has usually been directed at regions where they have strategic interests and diverted from those where they do not. Taking these facts together, it may seem that the impact of disparities of political power has been to distort both the content and the application of human rights doctrine in ways that serve the interests of powerful actors at the expense of others. At the limit, human rights may appear to be a mechanism of domination rather than an instrument of emancipation. This perception can argue for a more-or-less radical reshaping of the content of human rights doctrine as well as a resistance to international efforts to enforce its requirements.[10]

There are also other kinds of skepticism, including a pragmatic form that proceeds from the empirical judgment that neither acceptance of human rights treaty obligations nor international efforts at enforcement appreciably affect state behavior.[11] But this is enough to illustrate the variety of reasons why someone might doubt the meaningfulness of human rights talk or the practical significance or value of international human rights practice. I have only gestured at the details of these views. Perhaps a more careful formulation would reveal ways that each view is vulnerable to criticism. But I do not believe that skepticism of these forms is effectively refuted piecemeal. One seldom makes headway by showing that views like these depend on mistaken premises and bad arguments; the views simply reappear in more sophisticated forms. One does better to seek a constructive explanation of

---

[10] For variations of this view, see Tony Evans, *The Politics of Human Rights*, 2nd edn. (London: Pluto Press, 2005), ch. 2; Makau Mutua, *Human Rights: A Political and Cultural Critique* (Philadelphia: University of Pennsylvania Press, 2002), 10-38; and David Kennedy, *The Dark Side of Virtue: Reassessing International Humanitarianism* (Princeton: Princeton University Press, 2004), 3-36. These writers are not equally skeptical about human rights.

[11] E.g. Jack L. Goldsmith and Eric A. Posner, *The Limits of International Law* (New York: Oxford University Press, 2005), ch. 4, and Emilie M. Hafner-Burton and Kiyoteru Tsutsui, "Justice Lost! The Failure of International Human Rights Law to Matter Where Needed Most," *Journal of Peace Research* 44 (2007): 407-25.

the subject-matter that causes the force of skeptical doubts to weaken. One aim of this book is to see whether international human rights practice is susceptible to such an explanation.

3. Approach

We can think of practical principles for various arenas of conduct in one of two ways. We might think of them as inferences from some higher-level ideas or principles of broader scope, adapted to take account of the particularities of the arena of immediate interest. Or we can think of them as principles constructed for this arena, taking account of an unsystematic array of ethical and practical considerations, brought into a relationship whose reasonableness is judged by their coherence, fitness for purpose, and capacity to account for pre-reflective judgments of which we feel confident. Each way of thinking has implications for various aspects of the principles in question: for example, their substantive content, their scope of application, the range and type of considerations that may properly enter into their justification.

This distinction can be found in thinking about human rights.[12] Some philosophers have conceived of human rights as if they had an existence in the moral order that can be grasped independently of their embodiment in international doctrine and practice—for example, as "natural rights" or their secular successors, as fundamental moral rights possessed by all human beings "as such" or "solely in virtue of their humanity," or as conditions for social institutions about which all the world's social moral codes agree. These possibilities are not mutually exclusive. The usual view is that international human rights—that is, the objects referred to as "human rights" in international doctrine and practice—express and derive their authority from some such deeper order of values. For those who accept some variation of this kind of view, the task of a theorist of international human rights is to discover and describe the deeper order of values and judge the extent to which international doctrine conforms to it.

[12] Describing a similar distinction among approaches to human rights, James Griffin uses the terms "top–down" and "bottom–up." He characterizes his own approach to human rights as "bottom–up" but, for reasons I shall suggest (§ 10), it seems to me to be a sophisticated application of the approach described in this paragraph: *On Human Rights* (Oxford: Oxford University Press, 2008), 29.

I shall argue that it is a mistake to think about international human rights in this way. These familiar conceptions are question-begging in presuming to understand and criticize an existing normative practice on the basis of one or another governing conception that does not, itself, take account of the functions that the idea of a human right is meant to play, and actually does play, in the practice. As we shall see, they are also at odds with the historical development of international human rights doctrine. Its authors disowned the thought that human rights are the expression of any single conception of human nature or human good or of any but the most general understanding of the purposes of human social organization. They took it as an inelimin-able fact that people would differ about these matters. They therefore aspired to a doctrine that could be endorsed from many contemporary moral, religious, and cultural points of view and that was suited to be implemented by means distinctive to characteristically modern forms of social organization. The approach that takes human rights as the expression of a received philosophical idea risks missing this feature of international human rights.

I want to explore a different approach, one we might describe as practical. It aims to exploit the observation that the human rights enterprise is a global practice. The practice is both discursive and political. As a first approxima-tion, we might say that it consists of a set of norms for the regulation of the behavior of states together with a set of modes or strategies of action for which violations of the norms may count as reasons. The practice exists within a global discursive community whose members recognize the prac-tice's norms as reason-giving and use them in deliberating and arguing about how to act. These norms are expressed in the main international human rights instruments—the Universal Declaration of 1948 and the major treaties intended to give legal effect to its provisions—though, as we shall see, these formulations are open to interpretation and revision within the practice. The discursive community in which the practice resides is global and consists of a heterogeneous group of agents, including the governments of states, international organizations, participants in the processes of international law, economic actors such as business firms, members of nongovernmental organizations, and participants in domestic and transnational political net-works and social movements. The approach I shall explore tries to grasp the concept of a human right by understanding the role this concept plays within the practice. Human rights claims are supposed to be reason-giving for various kinds of political action which are open to a range of agents. We focused on ac

understand the concept of a human right by asking for what kinds of actions, in which kinds of circumstances, human rights claims may be understood to give reasons.[13]

I will have more to say about the details of the practice of human rights later. Here, I note two qualifications. First, in holding that the practice consists of norms which are widely recognized within a discursive community, I do not mean to say that there is agreement within the community about the scope and content of the system of norms taken as a whole, about the weights that should be attached to the reasons for action supplied by these norms, or about how conflicts among human rights, or between human rights and other values, should be resolved. Indeed, as we shall see, it is not only an inevitable but also a functionally significant aspect of the practice of human rights that its norms serve as much to frame disagreement as agreement. The practice is constituted as a practice not by agreement about the content of the norms or the practical conclusions to which one is committed by accepting them, but rather by acceptance of a distinctive class of norms as sources of reasons—though not necessarily as decisive reasons—for an array of modes of action. We rely on the practice for an understanding of the discursive roles of human rights, not (or anyway not directly) to delineate their scope or content.

The other qualification is that the practice of human rights is emergent. It is unlike more settled and longstanding normative practices such as might be found, say, in a mature legal system. In mature social practices, there is fairly wide agreement within the community about the actions that are appropriate in response to failures to adhere to the practice's norms. This agreement is sustained over time by traditions of judgment about the appropriateness of these responses.[14] But human rights practice is not a mature social practice. There is disagreement about all its main elements—for example, about the content of its norms, the eligible means for their application and enforcement, the distribution of responsibilities to

---

[13] On the understanding of normative concepts in discursive practices, see Robert Brandom, *Articulating Reasons: An Introduction to Inferentialism* (Cambridge, MA: Harvard University Press, 2000), ch. 2, and Stephen C. Angle, *Human Rights and Chinese Thought* (Cambridge: Cambridge University Press, 2002), 27-39. Also instructive is John R. Searle's account of the progression from "social fact" to "institutional fact" in *The Construction of Social Reality* (New York: Free Press, 1995), 88 ff. Searle's brief remarks about human rights (p. 93) are abstract and do not take account of the normative breadth of contemporary practice.

[14] Robert Brandom, "Freedom and Constraint by Norms," in *Hermeneutics and Praxis*, ed. Robert Hollinger (Notre Dame, IN: University of Notre Dame Press, 1985), 178.

support them, and the weight to be accorded to considerations about human rights when they come into conflict with other values. International human rights institutions lack capacities for authoritative adjudication of disputes and coercive enforcement of the practice's norms. The division of labor between public human rights institutions and nongovernmental organizations that participate in international institutional processes is unstable. Most importantly for our purposes, there is no unambiguous basis for establishing the boundaries of the discursive community within which the practice takes place. I have said that the meaning of the idea of a human right can be inferred from its role in a discursive practice, but if the boundaries of the discursive community are indistinct—for example, if there is no authoritative basis for ruling participants in or out—then there may be unavoidable indeterminacy in our understanding of the idea. All of these features reflect the practice's emergent character and all complicate a practical analysis. Notwithstanding the complications, however, there is no denying the existence or the doctrinal and institutional complexity of the practice of human rights: it organizes much of the normative discourse of contemporary world politics and commands the energy and commitment of large numbers of people and organizations.

As we shall see, the most general consequence of taking a practical approach is to call into question the two familiar conceptions mentioned earlier—the idea of human rights as entitlements that belong to people "by nature" or "simply in virtue of their humanity" and the distinct idea of human rights as objects of agreement among diverse moral and political cultures. Here I should anticipate an objection. A practical approach does more than notice that a practice of human rights exists; it claims for the practice a certain authority in guiding our thinking about the nature of human rights. But someone might wonder why the practice considered as an empirical phenomenon should be allowed any such authority. For example, why should we count it against an otherwise attractive philosophical theory of human rights that its conception of a human right diverges from the conception found in the practice, under its best available interpretation? Why not say, so much the worse for the practice?

In summary, the reply I shall suggest is this. There are many questions that might be asked about human rights. We might ask, for example, which values count as human rights, which agents have responsibilities to act when a right is violated, and what kinds of actions these agents have reason to

discursive practice

carry out. We might also ask—indeed, the question arises prior to the others I have listed—what kind of object a human right is or, as I shall interpret this question, what an ordinarily competent participant in the discourse of human rights would understand herself to be committed to if she were to acknowledge that a human right to such-and-such exists. The approach taken in this book allows the practice to exercise some degree of authority over the prior question but not, or anyway not directly, over the others. The basic idea is to distinguish between the problem of describing human rights from the problems of determining what they may justifiably require and identifying the reasons we might have for acting on them. These questions are related, of course, because any view about the nature of human rights will have implications for their grounds and requirements. Still, the questions are distinct.

Two considerations explain why it seems legitimate to allow the practice even this degree of authority. First, as I have said, the practice exists: it is elaborate both doctrinally and politically, it consumes a considerable amount of human and other resources, and people tend to regard its norms with great seriousness. If the focus of critical interest is the idea of human rights as it arises in public reflection and argument about global political life, then it seems self-evident that we should take instruction from the public practice in conceptualizing its central terms. This does not mean that there is no point in investigating other conceptions of human rights such as those that might be inspired by various ideas found in the history of thought; only that we ought not to assume that this would be an investigation of human rights in the sense in which they occur in contemporary public discourse. The second point is that we have *prima facie* reason to regard the practice of human rights as valuable. On the face of it, its norms seek to protect important human interests against threats of state-sponsored neglect or oppression which we know from historical experience are real and can be devastating when realized. As I shall put the point later, a global practice of human rights offers the hope of constraining one of the two main perils of a global political order composed of independent states. (The other is the propensity to war.)

I do not suggest that these are reasons to accept the contents of existing human rights doctrine as binding on us or to agree that the practice as we find it is the best way to realize the hope one might see in it as a matter of first impression. These are questions to be examined in their own right. But

connection to just
war theory?

neither question can be rendered coherently without a clear grasp of the idea of human rights. To achieve such a grasp we do not suppose that human rights must express or derive from a single basic value or that they constitute a single, fundamental category of moral concern. Instead, we treat international human rights as a normative practice to be grasped *sui generis* and consider how the idea of a human right functions within it.

IHR as 'normative practice'

2

The Practice

THE central idea of international human rights is that states are responsible for satisfying certain conditions in their treatment of their own people and that failures or prospective failures to do so may justify some form of remedial or preventive action by the world community or those acting as its agents. This idea is incorporated in the human rights provisions of the United Nations Charter, which, as a US court put it, "makes it clear that in this modern age a state's treatment of its own citizens is a matter of international concern."[1] Since the end of World War II, the idea has taken form in what I shall call an [emergent practice of human rights.] In this chapter I try to describe the main elements of this practice.

The description seeks to be selective and thematic rather than comprehensive. I begin with a historical precis devoted to the origins of the modern practice of human rights. I then comment about the two main elements of human rights practice—its doctrinal content and the various mechanisms that have evolved for the propagation and enforcement (or "implementation") of human rights. All of this will be elementary for those familiar with the subject, but not all philosophical readers will have this familiarity and it is essential for what follows to see that human rights as we find them in contemporary world politics constitute a public political project with its own distinctive purposes, forms of action, and culture. The aim is to describe the most important features of this practice in a schematic and reasonably charitable way, if possible without prejudging the outcome of some interpretative and normative issues that arise when one thinks critically about it. At the end of the chapter, I try to anticipate these issues.

---

[1] *Filártiga* v. *Peña-Irala*, 630 F.2d 876 (1980), 881. The court held that the Alien Tort Claims Act of 1789 (28 U.S.C. § 1350) authorizes the federal courts to try cases brought by aliens alleging egregious violations of human rights, wherever committed, by agents found within the US.

Inevitably, I shall have to leave aside some subjects that would belong in a more comprehensive account of human rights as a legal and political phenomenon. For example, I shall not discuss, except to mention, the development of regional human rights regimes, principally in Europe, Africa, and the Americas. These regimes are increasingly significant; indeed, it would not be surprising if the legal and institutional capacity to protect human rights were to develop more impressively within regions (as it has begun to do in Europe) than at the global level. I shall also leave aside the development of the law of war, known by convention as "humanitarian law" but perhaps better described as the law of "human rights in armed conflicts."[2] The practical importance of this is obvious, but it raises special problems peculiar to the context of war. I pass over these subjects to concentrate on the phenomenon of human rights in its most encompassing manifestation: as a public normative practice of global scope whose central concern is to protect individuals against the consequences of certain actions and omissions of their governments.

4. Origins

Modern international human rights practice dates from the settlement of World War II and the adoption in 1948 of the Universal Declaration of Human Rights (UDHR). However, its central idea has a long prehistory in the international system of Europe and the Atlantic. A precursor, though hardly the same idea, was present in the Peace of Westphalia (1648) itself, whose main historical significance is to have laid the foundation of the modern European states system, in the provisions limiting the sovereign rights of the German principalities through a collective guarantee of religious toleration.[3] A similar idea was present in the antislavery movement of the late-eighteenth and nineteenth centuries and in the series of great-power interventions in the Ottoman Empire to protect religious minorities in the later-nineteenth century. The Congress of Berlin of 1878 adopted the principle of religious liberty as a condition precedent for the recognition of

---

[2] The phrase is due to Sean MacBride, quoted in Geoffrey Best, "Justice, International Relations and Human Rights," *International Affairs* 71 (1995), 780.

[3] Leo Gross, "The Peace of Westphalia, 1648-1948," *American Journal of International Law* 42 (1948), 21-2. For the treaties see *Consolidated Treaty Series*, ed. Clive Parry (Dobbs Ferry, NY: Oceana Publications, 1969), i.

new states.[4] The Covenant of the League of Nations conspicuously omitted any reference to human rights: a Japanese-sponsored effort to include a guarantee of nondiscrimination on grounds of race and religion notoriously failed, notwithstanding a majority vote of the drafting commission.[5] But the idea can be found in the Constitution of the International Labor Organization, also established at the Paris Peace Conference, which was committed to setting international standards for the elimination of forced labor, development of fair labor practices, reduction of poverty, and protection of freedom of expression and association.[6] It can also be found in the postwar "minorities treaties" which provided international guarantees of various civil, political, and social rights of national minorities in Central and Eastern Europe and the Balkans.[7] All of these were measures by which states limited their sovereign authority and committed their influence to protect certain interests of individuals, effectively placing what had been treated as aspects of the domestic jurisdiction of states under one or another form of international supervision.

A transnational human rights movement developed after the war, stimulated in part by the failure of the League Covenant to include protections of human rights. "Leagues for the rights of man" proliferated across Europe. The Fédération Internationale des Droits de l'Homme was established in Paris in 1922 and began a campaign advocating the framing of an authoritative world declaration or bill of human rights. Also in Paris, the Académie Diplomatique Internationale, founded by an international group of lawyers in 1926, established a commission to draft an international declaration of human rights, whose report became a source of the Declaration of the International Rights of Man published in 1929 by

[4] George A. Finch, "The International Rights of Man [Editorial Comment]," *American Journal of International Law* 35 (1941): 662–5. More generally, Ian Brownlie, *Principles of Public International Law*, 5th edn. (Oxford: Clarendon Press, 1998), 568–73.

[5] The proposal was opposed by the UK and the US. David Hunter Miller, *The Drafting of the Covenant* (New York: G. P. Putnam's Sons, 1928), i. 268–9, 461–5. With the exception of a provision related to traffic in women and children, the drafting commission also declined to include guarantees of the rights of women recommended by representatives of women's groups. (Woodrow Wilson, who chaired the conference, said this "was only because the League could not begin by arranging all the affairs of mankind, not because the Commission did not agree that the demands were excellent.") Ibid., ii. 362.

[6] Jan Herman Burgers, "The Road to San Francisco," *Human Rights Quarterly* 14 (1992), 449; Paul Gordon Lauren, *The Evolution of International Human Rights*, 2nd edn. (Philadelphia: University of Pennsylvania Press, 2003), 97–102, 111 ff.

[7] Burgers, "The Road to San Francisco," 450, and the authoritative contemporary study by Julius Stone, *International Guarantees of Minority Rights* (London: Oxford University Press, 1934).

the Institute of International Law in New York. This declaration had broad influence among jurists in the 1930s and in the composition of the 1948 declaration.[8]

The human rights movement was set back by the Depression, then revitalized by the onset of World War II, in part because it was believed that the war might have been avoided if there had been effective international mechanisms to identify and sanction violations of human rights in Nazi Germany. In the UK, H. G. Wells began an international campaign advocating inclusion of a declaration of the "rights of man" or an "international bill of rights" in the postwar settlement.[9] Organizations of lawyers, educators, and other professionals pressed for incorporation of a declaration of human rights in the peace settlement and for establishment of an international capacity to enforce human rights standards on governments. An example is the American Law Institute's project to draft an international bill of rights, which issued a "Statement of Essential Human Rights" in 1944 that served as another source for the Universal Declaration.[10]

Even before the US entry into the war, Franklin Roosevelt, in his 1941 State of the Union address, had stressed the importance of "four freedoms" (of expression and worship, from want and fear) and associated "the supremacy of human rights everywhere" with a secure peace.[11] Subsequently the statement of war aims agreed by Roosevelt and Churchill in the Atlantic Charter (1941) described a postwar world order in which "all peoples"

[8] Burgers, "The Road to San Francisco," 450-4. An editorialist described the Institute of International Law declaration as "a revolutionary document [that] marks a new era which is more concerned with the interests and rights of sovereign individuals than with the rights of sovereign states." Philip Marshall Brown, "The New York Session of the Institut de Droit International," *American Journal of International Law* 33 (1930), 127. On the influence of this document, see Louis B. Sohn, "How American International Lawyers Prepared for the San Francisco Bill of Rights," *American Journal of International Law* 89 (1995), 540-53.

[9] H. G. Wells, *The Rights of Man: or What are We Fighting for?* (Harmondsworth, Middlesex: Penguin, 1940). On Wells's activities and influence, see Burgers, "The Road to San Francisco," 464-8 and A. W. B. Simpson, *Human Rights and the End of Empire: Britain and the Genesis of the European Convention* (Oxford: Oxford University Press, 2001), 160-7.

[10] Sohn, "How American International Lawyers Prepared for the San Francisco Bill of Rights," 546-53. The "Statement" was widely circulated in pamphlet form. For the text, see *Annals of the American Academy of Political and Social Science,* 243 (January 1946), 18-26. Also influential was the Commission to Study the Organization of Peace, "International Safeguard of Human Rights" [Fourth Report of the Commission, sect. III], repr. in *International Conciliation,* 403 (September 1944), 552-75.

[11] Franklin. D. Roosevelt, Annual Message to Congress, January 6, 1941, *The Public Papers and Addresses of Franklin D. Roosevelt, 1940 Volume: War—And Aid to Democracies* [vol. ix], comp. Samuel I. Rosenman (New York: Macmillan, 1941), 672.

would enjoy an array of rights—for example, to self-government, improved labor standards, social security, and (again) "freedom from want and fear."[12] A similar catalog of rights appears in the "Declaration of the United Nations" of January 1942, issued by the US and UK and subsequently adhered to by all of the wartime allies. Notwithstanding, as planning for the postwar world proceeded, resistance developed among the great powers to the idea of an international bill of rights. As a result, the proposals advanced at the Dumbarton Oaks conference (1944) for establishment of an international organization included only one reference to human rights and contained no provision for their definition or enforcement. Of the four powers represented, only China pressed for more.[13]

The omission prompted a vigorous public reaction from religious, lawyers', and internationalist groups in the US and the UK. The protest was joined by a number of small states, among which Latin American governments were especially active. The Roosevelt administration supported this movement. Several references to human rights were inserted into the United Nations Charter late in the drafting process, committing the organization and its member states to cooperate to promote respect "for human rights and for fundamental freedoms" (arts. 1, 55). But these provisions give no account of the content of human rights or of the steps the UN might take in cases of abuse. Instead, the charter delegates concern for human rights to a permanent commission responsible to the Economic and Social Council (arts. 62, 68).[14] More importantly, the UN's authority to promote human rights is qualified by another provision of the charter denying it authority "to intervene in matters which are essentially within the domestic

[12] Franklin D. Roosevelt and Winston S. Churchill, The Atlantic Charter, August 14, 1941, *The Public Papers and Addresses of Franklin D. Roosevelt, 1941 Volume: The Call to Battle Stations* [vol. x], comp. Samuel I. Rosenman (New York: Harper Brothers, 1942), 314.

[13] For a close study of the Roosevelt administration's approach to human rights during this period, see Rowland M. Brucken, "A Most Uncertain Crusade: The United States, Human Rights and the United Nations, 1941-1954" (Ph.D. dissertation, Ohio State University, 1999), 25-94 and the references cited there. Also Lauren, *The Evolution of International Human Rights*, 154-65, and John P. Humphrey, *Human Rights and the United Nations: A Great Adventure* (Dobbs Ferry, NY: Transnational, 1984), 12-13, 24.

[14] Lauren, *The Evolution of International Human Rights*, 166-93; Brucken, "A Most Uncertain Crusade," 94-116. On the important role of small states in 1944 and later, see Susan Waltz, "Universalizing Human Rights: The Role of Small States in the Construction of the Universal Declaration of Human Rights," *Human Rights Quarterly* 23 (2001): 44-72; and on the role of the Latin American countries in particular, Mary Ann Glendon, "The Forgotten Crucible: The Latin American Influence on the Universal Human Rights Idea," *Harvard Human Rights Journal* 16 (2003): 27-39.

jurisdiction of any state" (art. 2(7)). The recognition of each state's exclusive domestic jurisdiction was a critical element of the political calculus by which many governments, including those of the UK and USSR, were brought to accept the commitment of the UN to advance human rights. It would also be critical in achieving ratification of the charter in the US Senate.[15]

There is no explicit reference in the charter to a bill or declaration of human rights, but with US support the expectation developed at the founding conference in San Francisco that the preparation of a declaration or treaty on human rights would be among the organization's first priorities. In 1946, the newly constituted UN Economic and Social Council established a Human Rights Commission and instructed it to report about an "international bill of rights." This was understood to be an instrument of constitutional stature that would have the force of international law and would be accompanied by establishment of "an international agency of implementation" to oversee compliance with human rights standards by governments.[16] As before, the chief advocates of an enforceable bill of human rights were small states and nongovernmental organizations. They were opposed by both the United States and the Soviet Union. In the face of this, the commission adopted an incremental strategy, beginning with a nonbinding proclamation that could be adopted by the General Assembly but would not require ratification by states. It planned to develop a binding human rights convention and mechanisms for implementation after a declaration had been accomplished. The first task was completed with the adoption of the Universal Declaration in December 1948.[17]

I shall defer commenting about the content of the declaration until the next section, but something should be said about its general character and ambitions. Although the declaration consists of a series of articles most of which formulate more-or-less specific protections, it was plainly intended

[15] Ruth B. Russell and Jeannette E. Muther, *A History of the United Nations Charter: The Role of the United States, 1940-1945* (Washington, DC: Brookings Institution, 1958), 900-10; Stephen C. Schlesinger, *Act of Creation: The Founding of the United Nations* (Boulder, CO: Westview Press, 2003), 263-79; Simpson, *Human Rights and the End of Empire*, 261-8.

[16] Johannes Morsink, *The Universal Declaration of Human Rights: Origins, Drafting and Intent* (Philadelphia: University of Pennsylvania Press, 1999), 12-14. Also UN Economic and Social Council, *Report of the Commission on Human Rights to the Second Session of the Economic and Social Council* (E/38/Rev. 1), May 21, 1946, 5.

[17] The most comprehensive studies of the drafting process are Morsink, *The Universal Declaration of Human Rights*, and Mary Ann Glendon, *A World Made New: Eleanor Roosevelt and the Universal Declaration of Human Rights* (New York: Random House, 2001).

UDHR

to form an integrated whole. It begins with a preamble that refers to the "inherent dignity" of human beings as part of the grounds of human rights; notes that "disregard and contempt for human rights" have resulted in "barbarous acts" that might be avoided in the future if human rights are "protected by law;" suggests that respect for human rights would "promote the development of friendly relations between nations;" describes the declaration as stating "a common standard of achievement for all peoples and all nations;" and calls on individuals and organizations, "by progressive measures, national and international," to take steps to secure human rights. There follows a list of rights organized roughly according to the nature of the interests they are meant to protect. Principally these are interests in personal security and liberty, legal personality, freedom of expression and association, participation in the political process, economic and social security, and participation in cultural life. The declaration calls for "a social and international order" in which human rights "can be fully realized" and concludes with the admonition that "[e]veryone has duties to the community in which alone the free and full development of his personality is possible."[18] The integration of the political conception stated here is conveyed in Mary Ann Glendon's description of the document as a "declaration of interdependence . . . of people, nations, and rights."[19]

Broadly speaking, there are two distinguishable themes in the characterization given in the preamble of the declaration's justifying aims: that international recognition of human rights is necessary to protect the equal dignity of all persons and that respect for human rights is a condition of friendly relations among states. At the end of the war, the latter concern, although seldom registered in the records of the Human Rights Commission or in the accounts of participants, was plainly in the background. The view of the drafters seems to have been that regimes that engage in gross violations of human rights are also likely to be threats to international peace and security. Indeed, the case of Nazi Germany suggested that both kinds of conduct might arise from the same general properties of a regime— in the German case, from an ideology of racial supremacy systematically

[18] For the text, see Ian Brownlie and Guy S. Goodwin-Gill, eds., *Basic Documents on Human Rights*, 5th edn. (Oxford: Oxford University Press, 2006), 23–8. The basic documents are also available at http://www2.ohchr.org/english/law/index.htm#core (consulted March 3, 2008).

[19] Glendon, *A World Made New*, 174. The whole of Glendon's commentary on the text is illuminating; see 174–91. On the aspiration of the framers to produce a document that could be read as an integrated whole, see Morsink, *The Universal Declaration of Human Rights*, 232–8.

propagated and reinforced by a repressive state apparatus.[20] These two themes represent two different types of considerations and there is no reason to believe *ex ante* that either, taken by itself, would yield the same catalog of protections as the other, or for that matter the same kind of normative practice. The tension that has sometimes been noted in human rights practice between the aim of protecting basic individual interests and that of protecting international peace and stability thus has a basis in the declaration itself (though the possibility of conflict does not appear to have concerned the drafters).[21]

Relatedly, it should be observed that the preamble does not seek to locate the universality or significance of the value of equal human dignity in further considerations of human nature or divine gift; it is simply asserted as a fundamental value in its own right. This is in contrast to the parallel passages in the American Declaration of Independence and the French Declaration of the Rights of Man, which hold, respectively, that people are "endowed by their Creator" with certain rights and that human rights are "natural" and "sacred."[22] Under the circumstances, of course, it could not have been otherwise. The drafters represented not only different countries, but also different religious and philosophical traditions and political positions; although there was a shared commitment to the idea of human rights, there was no shared philosophical view about the reasons why it should be thought urgent that these rights be given some form of international recognition and protection. There was, for example, no agreement that human rights should be regarded as the expression in law of a more fundamental order of rights possessed by human beings "by nature" or by

---

[20] As Michael Ignatieff observes, "[i]t was Hitler the warmonger, not Hitler the architect of European extermination, who preoccupied the drafters" of the charter: "Human Rights, Sovereignty, and Intervention," *Human Rights, Human Wrongs: The Oxford Amnesty Lectures 2001*, ed. Nicholas Owen (Oxford: Oxford University Press, 2002), 53. On the significance of the war for the declaration, see Morsink, *The Universal Declaration of Human Rights*, ch. 2.

[21] For example, in an article describing the drafting of the declaration, Eleanor Roosevelt, chair of the drafting committee, observes that "many of us thought that lack of standards for human rights . . . was one of the greatest causes of friction among the nations, and that recognition of human rights might become one of the cornerstones on which peace could eventually be based." Yet her remarks about the basis of various individual rights, and of the declaration as a whole, refer exclusively to the need for "certain protections which the individual must have if he is to acquire a sense of security and dignity in his own person." There is no reflection that these aims might not coincide in doctrine or practice: "The Promise of Human Rights," *Foreign Affairs* 26 (1948), 471, 477.

[22] Michael Ignatieff, *Human Rights as Politics and Idolatry* (Princeton: Princeton University Press, 2001), 77-8.

the gift of a creator. The drafters considered these matters, as did the General Assembly's Third Committee, which reviewed the draft declaration in great detail, and concluded that either idea would import a parochial theological position that would be inappropriate in a declaration aspiring to broad international acceptability.[23]

The problem was to frame a public doctrine that was capable of endorsement from a variety of moral and cultural points of view but did not presuppose any more of a single, commonly accepted justifying theory than what could be extracted from an abstract appeal to the value of human dignity. Jacques Maritain, a member of the UNESCO Committee on the Theoretical Bases of Human Rights, reported a colleague's remark that "we agree about the rights *but on condition that no one asks us why*." He did not intend this only as a humorous aside: he went on to describe international human rights as "practical conclusions which, although justified in different ways by different persons, are principles of action with a common ground of similarity for everyone."[24] This conception of international human rights as a public doctrine open to a variety of justifications is indispensable to a proper appreciation of its historical uniqueness.[25]

As I observed earlier, one reason why governments found it possible to accept the principle of international concern for human rights was the expectation that the UN would respect the domestic jurisdiction of states by refraining from intervention in their internal affairs.[26] The declaration, which lacks provisions for implementation and in any event does not have the legal force of a treaty, was compatible with this expectation: it professes

[23] UN General Assembly, Third Committee, *96th–100th Meetings*, Official Records, October 7-12, 1948 (A/C.3/SR 96-100), 95-125. See also the memoir of John Humphrey, *Human Rights and the United Nations*, 37-49, 63-77. Humphrey was a Canadian civil servant who served as staff to the commission.

[24] Jacques Maritain, "Introduction," in UNESCO, *Human Rights: Comments and Interpretations* (London: Allan Wingate, 1949), 9, 10 (emphasis in original). I believe this describes the perspective of most of the members of the Human Rights Commission as well as that of UNESCO's experts, even though some of the commissioners regarded the UNESCO study as rivalrous. UN Economic and Social Committee Commission on Human Rights, 2nd Session, *Summary Record of the Twenty-Sixth Meeting* (E/CN.4/SR.26), December 3, 1947, 11-17.

[25] The final report of the UNESCO committee observes that "[T]he philosophical problem involved in a declaration of human rights is not to achieve doctrinal consensus but rather to achieve agreement concerning rights, and also concerning action in the realization and defense of rights, which may be justified on highly divergent doctrinal grounds." UNESCO, *Human Rights*, appendix II, 263.

[26] As Geoffrey Best puts it, although each state committed itself to satisfy international standards, the commitment was accompanied by the caveat that "how we do it is our business, not yours." Best, "Justice, International Relations and Human Rights," 787.

to state "a common standard of aspiration," not a set of enforceable commitments. One might therefore think that the declaration represents a compromise between the competing values of global human rights and the sovereign rights of states. We shall return to the question of what should be made of this fact in interpreting the practice of human rights as it has developed subsequently. What might be said as a matter of history is this. The drafting and promulgation of the declaration was part of a larger project that had envisioned from the outset the eventual adoption of a binding international agreement defining the human rights obligations of states more precisely and establishing an international capacity for implementation. Indeed, the drafting of an international covenant had begun even before the declaration was adopted. It should be remembered that the idea of a state's domestic jurisdiction is itself a creature of international law: its scope is constrained by a state's international legal obligations, and a state's immunity from interference operates only within these constraints. If human rights were to come to be recognized in international law, then they would limit the scope of a state's domestic jurisdiction; they would not conflict with it.[27] Although the charter does not call for such a development, it does not foreclose it, either: the matter is simply left for the future. In this perspective, the significance of the declaration at the time of its adoption was not so much to pose a challenge to the principle of domestic jurisdiction as to advance a larger project of redescribing it.

Finally, a comment about the inclusion of economic and social rights. This has sometimes been thought to have been a political accommodation required to secure the support of the Soviet bloc. The inference is that the declaration embodies an unstable combination of incompatible conceptions of social justice.[28] Leaving aside the question of the coherence of the declaration's political vision, what should be observed is that the inference rests on a false historical premise. Economic rights were included in the draft declaration from the beginning because their importance was widely accepted—for example, in the "four freedoms" of which Franklin Roosevelt had spoken in his 1941 State of the Union message ("freedom from want...translated into world terms"), in the Atlantic Charter, and in some of the draft declarations prepared by nongovernmental organizations before and during the war. Advocacy of economic rights by the

---

[27] For a discussion, see Brownlie, *Principles of Public International Law*, 293–7.
[28] E.g. Maurice Cranston, *What Are Human Rights?*, rev. edn. (London: Bodley Head, 1973), 54.

Latin American delegates in the deliberations leading to adoption of the declaration by the General Assembly was especially influential.[29] It is true that the Soviet delegate advocated including economic and social rights and that the US Department of State was initially resistant. But most members of the Human Rights Commission shared the Soviet view, and the US itself eventually proposed a draft declaration that included economic rights (to "a decent living; to work . . . to health, education, and social security").[30] There was never any chance that economic and social rights would not be part of the declaration.[31]

The promulgation of a declaration of human rights was the first of the three tasks the Human Rights Commission set itself. The others were to draft a binding international convention and to work out a mechanism for implementation. I comment on these in reverse order because the discussion of implementation began simultaneously with the drafting of the declaration.

The commission established a working group to devise an international means of propagating and enforcing human rights. The working group assumed that human rights would eventually be incorporated in an international convention that would be binding (only) for its signatories and would include provisions for implementation. It developed what might be described as a "juridical" paradigm best conceptualized as having two tiers. The first tier was domestic: state governments would have the primary responsibility for bringing about adherence to human rights within their borders and were expected to do so primarily by incorporating protections of human rights into their constitutions and laws. The idea was that individuals should be enabled to seek redress for violations of human rights through their domestic legal systems. But of course the basic problem was the absence of any guarantee that domestic governments left to their own devices would provide effective protection of human rights. It was unanimously agreed, and explicit in the charter, that a government's failure to adhere to human rights standards should be a matter of international concern. The question was how international concern should be manifested.

[29] Glendon, "The Forgotten Crucible," 35-6; Waltz, "Universalizing Human Rights," 65.

[30] UN Economic and Social Council, Commission on Human Rights, 2nd Session, *Proposal for a Declaration of Human Rights Submitted by the Representative of the United States* (E/CN.4/36), November 26, 1947, art. 9. However, there is no parallel article in the US proposal for a human rights convention, submitted the same day (E/CN.4/37).

[31] Glendon, *A World Made New*, 42-3, 115-17, 185-90; Morsink, *The Universal Declaration of Human Rights*, 222-30.

The working group considered several possibilities, including mandated reporting, petition and inquiry by special commissions or a special human rights court and, in cases where violations were found, public censure and "extreme action involving reprisals and the use of sanctions."[32] At least one delegate proposed that military intervention should be authorized as a last resort in cases of egregious abuse.[33] The group settled on a scheme of implementation combining elements of periodic reporting, monitoring, negotiation, and adjudication. A committee of independent experts would receive information from states about their observance and enforcement of human rights; accept petitions from individuals, groups (including nongovernmental organizations), and states; investigate and judge whether violations had occurred; in cases of violation, negotiate remedies with the offending state; and report to the Commission on Human Rights about cases in which negotiated solutions could not be reached. The group also recommended the creation of an international court of human rights, which would adjudicate cases that could not be resolved by other means; it would be authorized to reach "final and binding decisions" (rather than merely to furnish advisory opinions). The group could not, however, agree on sanctions for noncompliance by states with judgments of the human rights court other than that instances of noncompliance should be reported to the General Assembly.[34]

The full commission took no action on the recommendations of its working group and the declaration itself acknowledged the need for an enforcement procedure only in the most abstract terms. The working out of provisions for implementation was thus left as a task for the drafters of the covenants. As we shall see, these instruments, together with the conventions, embody in various forms the reporting and monitoring elements of the original working group's implementation scheme. But there are no

---

[32] O. Frederick Nolde, *Freedom's Charter: The Universal Declaration of Human Rights*. Headline Series, 76, July 20, 1949 (New York: Foreign Policy Association, 1949), 24. Nolde attended the meetings of the Human Rights Committee as an observer for a US church-related organization.

[33] M. Glen Johnson, "A Magna Carta for Mankind: Writing the Universal Declaration of Human Rights," in *The Universal Declaration of Human Rights: A History of its Creation and Implementation*, ed. M. Glen Johnson and Janusz Symonides (Paris: UNESCO, 1998), 32.

[34] UN Economic and Social Council, Commission on Human Rights, 2nd Session, *Draft Report of the Working Group on Implementation* (E/CN.4/53), December 10, 1947; for the proposals regarding international "supervision and enforcement," see pp. 9-33. The group imagined that a convention-based implementation regime would operate in parallel with a "system of communications" between governments and the Economic and Social Council established under the authority of the Charter itself. See also Humphrey, *Human Rights and the United Nations*, 48-9.

provisions for independent investigation of complaints, no system of sanctions for noncompliance, and, of course, no human rights court. These mechanisms were opposed by the US, the UK, and the USSR. The failure to agree on effective mechanisms of enforcement for the human rights commitments of states must be counted as the most serious disappointment for the aspirations of the framers of human rights.[35]

The last of the commission's tasks was to prepare a binding international convention or "covenant." The drafting began even before the declaration was completed and continued until 1954. In contrast to the preparation of the declaration, the drafting of the covenant was fraught with ideological conflict and interrupted by changes in the human rights policies of the US, USSR, and UK, all of which at one or another time resisted the development of a comprehensive treaty and sought to avoid the establishment of an effective international implementation regime. The intervention of the General Assembly, which in this case was moved by a majority consisting of socialist and less developed countries, was necessary to secure the inclusion of economic and social rights, which the US and UK opposed (although they had supported them in the declaration).[36] In the midst of the drafting, it was decided to divide the covenant into two documents, which would become the International Covenant on Civil and Political Rights (ICCPR) and the International Covenant on Economic, Social, and Cultural Rights (ICESCR). This came about in response to pressure from the US and its allies and is sometimes interpreted as expressing a hierarchy of importance among rights. This was certainly the US position, but, since the decision was a political compromise, it is difficult to regard it as an expression of any single view.[37] The rationale, which does not seem to presuppose any view about the intrinsic importance of either category of right, was that civil and political rights could be implemented immediately

---

[35] The working group's own assessment was prophetic: "Either a full and effective observance of human rights is sought, or it is not. If it is sought, then the consequences of this principle must be admitted and the idea of compulsory judicial decisions must be accepted." *Draft Report of the Working Group on Implementation*, 28. See also H. Lauterpacht, *International Law and Human Rights* (New York: Praeger, 1950), ch. 17. On the role of the major powers in blocking more effective implementation measures, see Roger Normand and Sarah Zaidi, *Human Rights at the UN: The Political History of Universal Justice* (Bloomington: Indiana University Press, 2008), 235-40.

[36] UN General Assembly, 5th Session, *Resolution 421 [Draft International Covenant on Human Rights and Measures of Implementation: Future Work of the Commission on Human Rights]* (A/1620), December 4, 1950.

[37] For the "hierarchy" interpretation, see Normand and Zaidi, *Human Rights at the UN*, 204-8.

whereas economic and social rights could only be realized "progressively" by each state acting "individually and through international assistance and co-operation, to the maximum of its available resources" (ICESCR, art. 2.1).[38] Both conventions incorporate mechanisms for international monitoring of compliance by states. An optional protocol to the ICCPR provides a means for individuals to submit complaints for review by the treaty committee.[39] There is no similar procedure for the ICESCR (indeed, it did not acquire its own monitoring committee until 1986). Drafts of both covenants were referred to the General Assembly in 1954 but were not finally approved by it until 1966 and did not come into force for ten more years.[40]

The two covenants, together with the declaration, comprise what is conventionally known as the "International Bill of Rights." To these instruments should be added at least four more treaties usually regarded as constituting the "core" documents of international human rights doctrine. These are the Convention on the Elimination of all Forms of Racial Discrimination (CERD, entered into force in 1969), the Convention on the Elimination of all Forms of Discrimination against Women (CEDAW, 1981), the Convention against Torture and other Cruel, Inhuman or Degrading Treatment or Punishment (CAT, 1987), and the Convention on the Rights of the Child (CRC, 1990).

This list of "core" instruments omits several other measures including, importantly, the Convention on the Prevention and Punishment of Genocide (1948), the International Convention against Apartheid (1973), several treaties relating to conditions of work sponsored by the International Labor Organization, the ILO Indigenous and Tribal Peoples Conventions

---

[38] The Committee on Economic, Social and Cultural Rights later held that "the phrase 'to the maximum of its available resources' was intended by the drafters of the Covenant to refer to both the resources existing within a State and those available from the international community through international cooperation and assistance." UN Committee on Economic, Social and Cultural Rights, 5th Session, *Report on the Fifth Session*, suppl. 3, annex III, *General Comment 3 (1990), The Nature of States Parties' Obligations*, Economic and Social Council Official Records, 1991 (E/1991/23), 86.

[39] Neither the US nor the UK has adhered to the protocol. The Russian Federation acceded to it in 1991. UN Office of the High Commissioner for Human Rights, "Ratifications and Reservations" (http://www2.ohchr.org/english/bodies/ratification/index.htm) (consulted November 2, 2008).

[40] Vratislav Pechota, "The Development of the Covenant on Civil and Political Rights," in *The International Bill of Rights: The Covenant on Civil and Political Rights*, ed. Louis Henkin (New York: Columbia University Press, 1981), 39-42; Matthew C. R. Craven, *The International Covenant on Economic, Social, and Cultural Rights: A Perspective on its Development* (Oxford: Clarendon Press, 1995), 16-22, 42 ff.

(no. 107, 1957, and no. 169, 1989), and the regional treaties of Europe, Africa, and the Americas. One should also take note of the Helsinki Final Act (1975), significant both for establishing human rights compliance as a legitimate concern of diplomacy in the Conference for Security and Cooperation in Europe and for its unanticipated but historically important role in stimulating human rights activism in the Soviet Union and Eastern Europe.[41]

5. Doctrine

The rights listed in the declaration and the core treaties consist of protections of an array of human interests, and their requirements bear on many aspects of a society's political, legal, economic, and social structure. There are various ways to sort these protections. One classification of the rights in the declaration, due to René Cassin, distinguishes four categories:[42]

1. Rights to liberty and personal security—such as life, liberty, and security of the person; prohibition of slavery, torture, cruel or degrading punishment; right to recognition as a legal person; equality before the law; no arbitrary arrest; presumption of innocence;

2. Rights in civil society—protection of privacy in family, home, correspondence; freedom of movement and residence within the state; right of emigration; equal rights of men and women to marry, within marriage, and to divorce; right to consent to marriage;

3. Rights in the polity—freedom of thought, conscience, and religion; freedom of assembly and association; rights "to take part in the government of the country" and to "periodic and genuine elections... by universal and equal suffrage"; and

4. Economic, social, and cultural rights—adequate standard of living including adequate food, clothing, housing, and medical care; free, compulsory elementary education; free choice of employment; just and favorable

---

[41] An authoritative inventory and collection of these documents can be found in Brownlie and Goodwin-Gill, eds., *Basic Documents on Human Rights*, 5th edn. For signatories, see UN Office of the High Commissioner for Human Rights, "Ratifications and Reservations." On the significance of the Helsinki Final Act, see Daniel C. Thomas, *The Helsinki Effect* (Princeton, NJ: Princeton University Press, 2001), esp. ch. 5.

[42] Glendon, *A World Made New*, 174.

remuneration; equal pay for equal work; right to join trade unions; reasonable limitation of working hours; social security.

In addition to these rights found in the declaration, both covenants, in common articles, incorporate what is effectively a fifth category of rights:

5. Rights of "peoples" (conceived as collective entities)—most import-antly, self-determination and communal control over "natural wealth and resources."[43]

The covenants are sometimes regarded as expressions of the rights of the declaration put into a form appropriate for an international agreement, but in fact they expand in both scope and detail the doctrine formulated in the declaration. Thus, for example, whereas the declaration speaks of a right to "medical care" which is "adequate for health and well-being," the corre-sponding passage in the Covenant on Economic, Social, and Cultural Rights postulates a right to "the highest attainable standard of physical and mental health."[44] The declaration guarantees everyone the right "to take part in the government of his country" but beyond what might be inferred from this takes no explicit position about colonial rule; both covenants specifically recognize a right of self-determination. The declaration holds that "higher education shall be equally available to all on the basis of merit;" the Covenant on Economic, Social, and Cultural Rights calls for "the progressive introduction of free [higher] education." The only significant reduction in scope concerns the right to own property: vaguely acknow-ledged in the declaration (art. 17), it is missing altogether from both covenants.[45]

The four "core" conventions yield a further enlargement of the scope of international human rights doctrine. So, for example, the Convention on the Elimination of All Forms of Racial Discrimination commits the parties not only to eliminate racial discrimination in law and the practices of public institutions but also to use state power to prohibit and punish the public expression of "ideas based on racial superiority or hatred" (art. 4(a)). More strikingly, the Convention on the Elimination of All Forms of Discrimin-ation against Women commits the parties "to modify the social and cultural patterns of conduct of men and women" so as to eliminate "prejudices

---

[43] ICCPR and ICESCR, arts. 1(1)–1(2).
[44] Compare UDHR, art. 25, with ICESCR, art. 12.
[45] The covenants also omit the right to asylum (UDHR, art. 14(1)).

and customary and all other practices which are based on the idea of the
inferiority or the superiority of either of the sexes." (art. 5). Both conventions
call on parties to eliminate discrimination "without delay:" unlike portions
of the Covenants, neither bears interpretation as establishing long-term
policy goals or "manifesto rights" that do not require immediate action.
The Convention on the Rights of the Child is the most detailed of the
sector-specific conventions. It establishes the principle that "a primary
consideration" in public policies affecting children should be "the best
interests of the child" (art. 3(1)) and enumerates a series of rights that
go well beyond the specific provisions of the declaration and covenants,
including the child's right to preserve his or her identity, the right of
indigenous children to practice their own culture, and the right of the
child "to freedom of expression" including "freedom to seek, receive and
impart information and ideas of all kinds" (arts. 8, 13, 30). Parties are
required to adopt minimum age and hours provisions for child employment
to protect against exploitation and work likely to interfere with their
education (art. 32). The convention also commits parties to adopt some
policies that cannot readily be seen as protecting individual rights at all—for
example, to "encourage the production and dissemination of children's
books" and to take measures to educate parents about "child health and
nutrition, the advantages of breast feeding, hygiene and environmental
sanitation" (arts. 17(c), 24(2)(e)).[46]

I comment here on several general features of human rights doctrine. The
first and most important is its broad normative reach. Human rights are
sometimes conceived as minimal requirements—"minimum conditions for
any kind of life at all" or protections against the most "unambiguous" kinds
of "abuse of power."[47] Perhaps there is a sense in which these phrases
describe earlier declarations of rights, but neither applies in any straightforward way to the human rights of the postwar enactments, which differ
strikingly from their predecessors in the range of their provisions. International human rights seek not only to protect against threats to personal
security and liberty and to guarantee some recourse against the arbitrary use
of state power, but also to protect against various social and economic

[46] The possibility of further enlargement is suggested by efforts to promulgate declarations in
other areas, with the hope that treaties will follow. Consider e.g. Declaration on the Right to
Development (1986) and Draft Declaration on the Rights of Indigenous Peoples (1994).

[47] Ignatieff, *Human Rights as Politics and Idolatry*, 56; Bernard Williams, "In the Beginning Was
the Deed," *In the Beginning Was the Deed* (Princeton, NJ: Princeton University Press, 2006), 19.

dangers and to guarantee some degree of participation in political and cultural life.

A second and related feature is the heterogeneity of these requirements. Different rights are open to different strategies of implementation: some describe structural features of acceptable institutions whereas others are standards for policy and action that can be satisfied in many different types of institutions. Among the latter, some prescribe relatively specific policies whereas others state more general political goals. This means that for some rights, and under some circumstances, human rights may not serve as grounds on which any individual agent who is deprived of the substance of the right is entitled to press claims for the satisfaction of the right against any other identifiable agent.

Third, owing to their range and heterogeneity, not all of the human rights of contemporary doctrine can plausibly be regarded as preemptory. Under the economic and social conditions prevailing in some societies it may not be possible to satisfy all of these rights immediately, and even if it is possible to satisfy a right, it may be so only at the cost of not satisfying another or of sacrificing some other important aim of public policy.[48] In this respect human rights seem to depart from a familiar (if perhaps a naive) paradigm of fundamental rights.

A fourth significant feature is the relativity of human rights to social circumstances of a certain general kind. Human rights are sometimes described as timeless—as protections that might reasonably be demanded in all times and places. But this description is difficult to reconcile with the content of international doctrine. Many of the threats protected against (e.g. unfair pay, lack of educational opportunity and access to medical care, loss of nationality) arise distinctively in modern or modernizing societies; they are not generic in the way that assault, say, was conceived as a threat in traditional "state of nature" theories. Moreover, some human rights are only comprehensible against a background assumption that certain types of institutions either do or can be brought to exist—for example, the rule of law, elections for public office, a public capacity for taxation and welfare provision, at least a rudimentary administrative state. Modern human rights doctrine cannot plausibly be regarded as seeking to articulate protections of

---

[48] These facts are recognized, although incompletely, in the provisions governing derogability in the ICCPR, art. 4.

timeless significance; it speaks to what might be described broadly as the conditions of modern life.[49]

Finally, human rights doctrine is not static. The 1948 declaration is seminal but neither it nor the covenants set limits to the range and content of human rights. The conventions on racial discrimination, discrimination against women, and the rights of the child, in particular, bring about a substantial enlargement of human rights protections. They do not simply present more specific formulations of the provisions of the declaration and covenants. To recall some illustrations, the convention on racial discrimination requires governments to prohibit and punish the public expression of "ideas based on racial superiority or hatred."[50] The women's convention requires governments "to modify the social and cultural patterns of conduct of men and women" so as to eliminate "prejudices and customary and all other practices which are based on the idea of the inferiority or the superiority of either of the sexes."[51] The children's convention holds that "a primary consideration" in public policies affecting children should be "the best interests of the child."[52] These provisions show both the substantive expansion of human rights doctrine and the extension of its reach from a society's constitution and basic laws to its public policies and customs. The evolutionary enlargement of human rights doctrine is sometimes disparaged as subversive of the effectiveness of human rights. Whether and in what sense this might be true are complicated questions. What should be observed here is that another view is possible. The evolution of human rights doctrine might be regarded as integral to the larger normative practice, a feature that could be important in forming an adequate grasp of its point.

6. Implementation

Human rights are of practical interest because a failure or threat of failure by a government to satisfy their requirements supplies a reason for remedial or preventive action, primarily within individual societies and secondarily beyond them. As I put it earlier, human rights are standards for the

---

[49] This is in accord with an observation of H. G. Wells in his influential wartime tract advocating an international declaration of rights: such a declaration "must because of the increasing complexity of the new social structure be more generous, detailed and explicit than any of its predecessors." *The Rights of Man: or What are We Fighting for?*, 19.

[50] CERD, art. 4(a).   [51] CEDAW, art. 5.   [52] CRC, art. 3(1).

governments of states whose breach is a matter of international concern. Stated in these terms, the question of "implementation" is about how "international concern" is to be expressed.

The framers conceived of a juridical paradigm of implementation. They expected that human rights would be embodied in domestic law and enforced in domestic courts or, in the case of rights not easily made justiciable, that they would be accepted as priorities for state policy.[53] The international role was to monitor compliance at the domestic level by auditing the self-reports of states and to act when domestic enforcement was determined to have failed. The most ambitious of the framers hoped for an international judicial capacity, such as a human rights court, that could adjudicate disagreements between states and the international monitors and assign penalties when accommodations could not be reached. But no such capacity was established, and the actions available to the monitoring agencies were confined to consultation, reporting, and public censure. The hope was that, over time, these elements of a system of accountability would establish incentives for domestic-level compliance.

What has actually emerged at the global level is considerably more complex.[54] The juridical paradigm has been realized in some parts of human rights practice—most fully, perhaps, in the regional human rights systems, particularly that of Europe, which includes a human rights court with a capacity to insist (though not always effectively) upon compliance by states with its rulings.[55] It can also be found, though in attenuated form, within the UN human rights system. But as the limitations of this paradigm have become apparent and human rights practice has developed, the forms of action for which justification tends to be sought in considerations about human rights have proliferated well beyond what the framers envisioned.

[53] The ICCPR requires parties "to adopt such laws or other measures as may be necessary to give effect to the rights recognized in the present Covenant" (art. 2). The parallel provision in the ICESCR requires states "to take steps, individually and through international assistance and co-operation . . . with a view to achieving progressively the full realization of the rights recognized in the present Covenant by all appropriate means, including particularly the adoption of legislative measures" (art. 2).

[54] For summary accounts, see Rosemary Foot, *Rights beyond Borders: The Global Community and the Struggle for Human Rights in China* (Oxford: Oxford University Press, 2000), ch. 2; and Jack Donnelly, *Universal Human Rights in Theory and Practice*, 2nd edn. (Ithaca, NY: Cornell University Press, 2003), chs. 8-9, especially the perspicuous schematic account of the evolution of human rights practice at pp. 129-38.

[55] On the development and deficiencies of the European system, including an analysis of problems of compliance, see Steven Greer, *The European Convention on Human Rights: Achievements, Problems, and Prospects* (Cambridge: Cambridge University Press, 2006).

This is particularly true of the global politics of human rights since the Helsinki Final Act of 1975.

One way to grasp this complexity would be to distinguish among the various types of international and transnational agents that participate in human rights practice: for example, the UN human rights agencies devoted to monitoring and reporting, other international organizations with the capacity to influence the conduct of domestic actors, individual states and coalitions of states, and a heterogeneous array of nongovernmental agents (e.g. NGOs, social movement organizations, business firms). But most of these agents face a choice of means of action and I believe it will be more illuminating for our purposes to distinguish these various mechanisms by their functional characteristics. Looked at in this perspective, a rough typology would count at least six paradigms of action through which various agents might seek to prevent or remediate failures by the governments of states to respect and enforce human rights. I shall refer to these as "paradigms of implementation" or "enforcement," even though these conventional terms may come to seem artificially narrow. The typology includes (1) accountability, (2) inducement, (3) assistance, (4) domestic contestation and engagement, (5) compulsion, and (6) external adaptation. I comment briefly about each of these and then offer some more general observations about these paradigms, taken as a whole.

[1. Accountability] The reporting and auditing processes carried out by the UN human rights agencies come closest to the juridical paradigm. These agencies consist primarily of a series of bodies established by the major human rights treaties, each of which provides for its own implementation.[56] Abstracting from some differences, the main work of these "treaty bodies" is the review and audit of periodic reports that states parties to the treaties are required to provide documenting their compliance. Nongovernmental organizations play a quasi-official role in these processes as independent sources of information. In addition, four of the treaties optionally allow an individual right of complaint and two establish an independent procedure of inquiry at the initiative of the treaty body. Each body's principal recourse when it finds evidence of violations is consultation with the violating state

---

[56] In addition, the Charter established a Human Rights Commission, now succeeded by a Human Rights Council. At this writing the Council's monitoring and review procedures are in flux. For a discussion of the deficiencies of the old commission and the prospects for reform, see Philip Alston, "Reconceiving the U.N. Human Rights Regime: Challenges Confronting the New U.N. Human Rights Council," *Melbourne Journal of International Law* 7 (2006): 185-224.

3 conditions of accountability

to identify means of ending the violation. It may also publish its findings. There is no provision for a judicial process to adjudicate disagreements or to determine and apply sanctions for non-cooperating states.[57]

Why describe these processes as affording "accountability?" In general, agent B is accountable to agent A if three conditions obtain: (i) A can require B to give an account of its compliance with a set of expectations or standards; (ii) A is empowered to judge whether B has complied with the standards; and, typically, (iii) A may impose sanctions on B if not.[58] The effectiveness of the relationship as a means of influencing the conduct of the accountable agent depends on all three elements. In the case of the human rights treaty bodies, however, each element is problematic. Reporting by states tends to be late and incomplete, the treaty bodies lack sufficient resources to audit these reports, and the sanctions available in the event of noncompliance are limited, for the most part, to "naming and shaming"— that is, public reporting of the violations and perhaps censure.[59] One might therefore think it deceptive to describe these processes as establishing accountability.

This may be true in the sense that these mechanisms are likely to be relatively ineffective.[60] But it is one thing to judge the effectiveness of the reporting and monitoring mechanisms and another to classify them as

---

[57] The ICCPR is a partial exception to the last point; under an optional protocol, the treaty body has developed a quasi-judicial procedure for hearing and adjudicating complaints. The details of these procedures may be found in Manfred Nowak, *An Introduction to the International Human Rights Regime* (Leiden: Martinus Nijhoff, 2003), ch. 4.3. On the role of NGOs, see Andrew Clapham, "Defining the Role of Non-Governmental Organizations with Regard to the UN Human Rights Treaty Bodies," in *The U.N. Human Rights Treaty System in the 21st Century*, ed. Anne F. Bayefsky (The Hague: Kluwer Law International, 2000), 183–94.

[58] Ruth Grant and Robert O. Keohane, "Accountability and Abuses of Power in World Politics," *American Political Science Review* 99 (2005), 29. I say that accountability relationships "typically" include a threat of sanctions because I do not believe this is an essential part of the idea of accountability. For instructive discussion see Mark Philp, "Delimiting Democratic Accountability," *Political Studies* 57 (2009), 34–6.

[59] Philip Alston, *Final Report on Enhancing the Long-Term Effectiveness of the United Nations Human Rights Treaty System* (E/CN.4/1997/74), March 27, 1996, paras. 10–12 and *passim*. For critical studies of the performance of the treaty monitoring system see Bayefsky, ed., *The U.N. Human Rights Treaty System in the 21st Century* (n. 57 above), and Philip Alston and James Crawford, eds., *The Future of UN Human Rights Treaty Monitoring* (Cambridge: Cambridge University Press, 2000).

[60] There is very little systematic evidence to date about the efficacy of these processes. For a skeptical view that takes note of the uncertainties, see Emilie M. Hafner-Burton and Kiyoteru Tsutsui, "Human Rights in a Globalizing World: The Paradox of Empty Promises," *American Journal of Political Science* 110 (2005): 1373–411.

accountability systems. The mechanisms do, in fact, satisfy the conditions mentioned above. Indeed, this is uniquely true of these mechanisms, viewed in relation to the other paradigms of implementation considered here: only the treaty monitoring systems seek to influence the behavior of states by requiring them to give public accounts of their conduct.

2. Inducement Accountability systems might be understood as incentive structures defined by rule-governed processes that aim to induce respect for human rights requirements by threatening sanctions in the event of non-compliance. But of course there are also less structured ways to induce compliance. The most common of these in human rights practice are various policies available to national governments and international organizations that would create incentives and disincentives for other governments.

Leaving aside coercive threats, to which we shall return, the primary means available to national governments are offers of diplomatic incentives, manipulation of access to economic, social, and cultural resources, preferential treatment in economic relations, and the attachment of conditions to bilateral assistance.[61] The use of incentives to encourage respect for human rights has become more common since the 1970s, when the United States, followed by some European states, Japan, and eventually the European Union, adopted the protection of human rights as a goal of foreign policy. In the US, for example, limited human rights conditions were imposed on foreign assistance and arms sales programs and the State Department was required to publish annual reports on the human rights practices of other governments.[62] The means available to international organizations are analogous although more limited. For example, the international financial institutions might include conditions bearing on human rights compliance in development lending agreements ("conditionality") or attach human rights requirements to structural adjustment assistance.[63] Similarly, the

[61] Evan Luard, *Human Rights and Foreign Policy* (Oxford: Pergamon, 1981), 26-7; compare Peter R. Baehr, *The Role of Human Rights in Foreign Policy*, 2nd edn. (Houndmills, Basingstoke: Macmillan, 1996), 31-47; Foot, *Rights beyond Borders*, 42-51; Donnelly, *Universal Human Rights in Theory and Practice*, ch. 9.

[62] 22 U.S. Code Sec. 2304. See also Glenn Mower, *Human Rights and American Foreign Policy* (New York.: Greenwood Press, 1987), ch. 4.

[63] There is controversy about the legal basis of the human rights obligations of these institutions. See Andrew Clapham, *Human Rights Obligations of Non-State Actors* (Oxford: Oxford University Press, 2006), 137-59. It is worth noting that US law declares as policy that these institutions should channel assistance to governments that do not violate human rights (22 U.S. Code Sec. 262d(a)).

World Trade Organization has a capacity, so far not much used, to deploy incentives (and to remove disincentives) through its procedures for dispute resolution.[64] A more ambitious suggestion is that states and international organizations might use a government's compliance with human rights standards as conditions for recognition and membership.[65]

[3. *Assistance*] Some societies may be deficient in the capacities required to comply with human rights. For example, a society might lack the economic capacity to produce the goods needed to satisfy human rights or the institutional capacity to carry out the measures necessary to deter or compensate for deprivations. In such cases the paradigms discussed so far are not likely to improve compliance.

The idea that certain forms of external assistance might help develop domestic capacities is familiar enough in connection with economic development aid,[66] but it should be stressed that it also applies to the development of institutional capacity. Human rights doctrine lodges the primary responsibilities for compliance with domestic governments. These are not limited to the responsibility to satisfy human rights, when this requires affirmative provision, and to avoid violating them, when this requires abstention from action. They also include responsibilities to protect against various kinds of harmful action by third parties and to provide recourse when protection fails. The successful performance of these latter responsibilities requires institutional capacities that may be beyond the reach of some societies. For example, the courts and the judiciary may be insufficiently developed, law enforcement may be unreliable, and capacities for public administration may be lacking. Outside agents may be in a position to assist in the strengthening of these capacities. International election assistance for societies with relatively undeveloped electoral institutions is another example. Such measures, although not readily classified under the familiar headings of compulsion and inducement, plainly belong in any inventory of the means

[64] On the possibilities see Joost Pauwelyn, "Human Rights in WTO Dispute Settlement," in *Human Rights and International Trade*, ed. Thomas Cottier, Joost Pauwelyn, and Elisabeth Bürgi Bonanomi (Oxford: Oxford University Press, 2005), 205-31. Also Clapham, *Human Rights Obligations of Non-State Actors*, 161-77.

[65] E.g. Allen Buchanan, *Justice, Legitimacy, and Self-Determination* (Oxford: Oxford University Press, 2004), 266-81.

[66] For example, in advocacy of a "human right to development." See e.g. Arjun Sengupta, "The Human Right to Development," *Oxford Development Studies* 32 (2004): 179-203. The General Assembly adopted a "Declaration on the Right to Development" in December 1986. UN General Assembly, 41st Session, *Resolution 41/128* (A/RES/41/128), December 4, 1986.

available to outside agents to improve the domestic protection of human rights.[67]

4. Domestic contestation and engagement Outside agents can seek to influence a government's conduct by engaging in various aspects of a society's domestic political and social life. Usually these efforts have one of two aims: to mobilize and support domestic actors in bringing pressure on governments for changes in law and policy or to bring about changes in belief and practice within the society. Contestation seeks to influence the conduct of domestic actors, not by altering the payoffs these agents face or by offering support in accomplishing aims they already accept, but rather by affecting their normative beliefs and capacities for action. Typically the external actors are agents of international organizations and transnational nongovernmental organizations (though they might also represent other governments). Their roles might include articulating and translating human rights norms, collecting and disseminating information about local conditions, and organizing and facilitating local and transnational political alliances.[68] There are two patterns. The first is political. External actors seek influence by becoming participants in and providing resources for indigenous political activity, for example by forming partnerships with political parties, nongovernmental organizations, and social movement groups. They may also legitimize and enhance the influence of domestic actors by refracting their political claims from the global to the local level.[69] The other pattern of action is social. Here the primary roles played by transnational actors involve education, persuasion, and perhaps local organization. The immediate aim is to induce change in private behavior rather

Political + social engagement

[67] For a survey of views about the ends and means of assisting the development of legal capacity, see *Promoting the Rule of Law Abroad: In Search of Knowledge*, ed. Thomas Carothers (Washington, DC: Carnegie Endowment for International Peace, 2006). On election assistance, see Eric C. Bjornlund, *Beyond Free and Fair: Monitoring Elections and Building Democracy* (Washington, DC: Woodrow Wilson Center Press, 2004).

[68] For a brief discussion see Sidney Tarrow, *The New Transnational Activism* (New York: Cambridge University Press, 2005), 188-200, and the suggestive case study by Hans Peter Schmitz, "When Networks Blind: Human Rights and Politics in Kenya," in *Intervention and Transnationalism in Africa: Global–Local Networks of Power*, ed. Thomas M. Callaghy, Ronald Kassimir, and Robert Latham (Cambridge: Cambridge University Press, 2001), 149-72.

[69] This is the "boomerang pattern" described by Margaret E. Keck and Kathryn Sikkink, *Activists beyond Borders* (Ithaca, NY: Cornell University Press, 1998), 12-13. A variation on this pattern may be found in the "Helsinki effect"—the process by which the human rights provisions of the Helsinki Final Act (1975) stimulated the development of transnational networks that encouraged and legitimated local resistance to the East European Communist regimes. The most detailed study is Thomas, *The Helsinki Effect*.

than to bring about political or legal change, although these may also result.[70]

Of course, human rights can influence domestic contestation even without the direct involvement of outside agents. Local actors themselves may be empowered and their political activity legitimated by a recognition that their grievances have a basis in human rights doctrine, particularly when their government is a party to the pertinent treaties. For example, litigation strategies may bring pressure for changes in legislation and government policy and social protest may bring specific aspects of the government's human rights compliance onto the public political agenda. Although there may be no active external agent that can be said to interfere, there is a clear causal route through which appeals to a norm whose force derives from its place within the public international doctrine influences the domestic political process.[71]

These processes of domestic engagement are of substantial and probably increasing significance as mechanisms for implementing human rights, but they are sometimes overlooked because, like some forms of assistance, they do not fit within the conventional categories of compulsion and inducement. Although these mechanisms may include a significant transnational component, they are not accurately understood as external efforts to intervene or impose in a recalcitrant local culture. As Sally Merry observes, reflecting on a study of human rights activism in Asia, "Instead of viewing human rights as a form of global law that imposes rules, it is better imagined as a cultural practice, as a means of producing new cultural understandings and actions."[72] In this respect the contestation paradigm is the most substantial of all the departures from the conception of implementation entertained by the framers of modern human rights.

---

[70] See the discussion of efforts by NGOs to end footbinding in China and female genital cutting in Africa in William J. Talbott, *Which Rights Should be Universal?* (New York: Oxford University Press, 2005), 107-11. As Talbott points out, because these means of influence operate by providing information rather than by applying pressure, they may avoid the objection that the interference is paternalistic.

[71] Beth Simmons, *Mobilizing for Human Rights: International Law in Domestic Politics* (New York: Cambridge University Press, 2009), ch. 4 ("Theories of Compliance").

[72] Sally Engle Merry, *Human Rights and Gender Violence: Translating International Law into Local Justice* (Chicago: University of Chicago Press, 2006), 228-9. For case studies of the local impact of international human rights norms, see *The Practice of Human Rights: Tracking Law between the Global and the Local*, ed. Mark Goodale and Sally Engle Merry (Cambridge: Cambridge University Press, 2007).

[5. *Compulsion*] The most dramatic form of implementation of human rights by external action is interference using coercive means. These can range from economic sanctions to ("humanitarian") intervention using armed force. The aims may vary from bringing about a change in the behavior of a standing government to forcing a change in the regime itself. In the absence of an established international capacity to act, intervention has been carried out by states or coalitions of states, sometimes acting with international authorization. Thus, for example, the interventions in Bosnia, Haiti, Somalia, Kosovo, and East Timor were all justified as efforts to stop violations of one or another human right. The permissibility of humanitarian intervention in international law is disputed but its acceptability as a means of policy has been increasingly widely acknowledged.[73]

Of course, the effectiveness of coercive intervention as a means of protecting human rights is another matter. The experience of the period since 1990 is mixed and suggests that the prospects for success vary with the particular political aims of an intervention, the circumstances of the society intervened in, and the military capabilities and political will of the intervening agent. The quality of strategic planning by the intervening agent and that agent's ability to mobilize a political commitment sufficient to carry out the strategy are critical.[74] One might be tempted to overestimate these prospects, but there is no doubting the significance of coercive intervention as a potential remedy *in extremis* for gross violations. The important point for present purposes is that it is the limiting case, not the modal case, of international action to protect human rights. Within the practice it is exceptional.

[6. *External adaptation*] The first five paradigms consist of mechanisms that aim to influence the behavior of domestic agents, whether by creating incentives to comply with human rights norms, aiding in the development

---

[73] The question of the status of these interventions in international law is complicated by the pressure to subsume humanitarian action under the heading of "threats to the peace" (cf. UN Charter, art. 7). For a discussion, see Simon Chesterman, *Just War or Just Peace? Humanitarian Intervention and International Law* (Oxford: Oxford University Press, 2001), esp. ch. 4. On the acceptability of humanitarian intervention as a matter of public political morality, the most important source is the report of the International Commission on Intervention and State Sovereignty, *The Responsibility to Protect* (Ottawa: International Development Research Centre, 2001). Its principal conclusions were endorsed by the 60th Session of the UN General Assembly in 2005. See *Resolution 60/1 [2005 World Summit Outcome]* (A/Res/60/1), October 24, 2005.

[74] For a comprehensive study, see Taylor B. Seybolt, *Humanitarian Military Intervention: The Conditions for Success and Failure* (Oxford: Oxford University Press, 2007).

of the capacities and dispositions needed to do so, or compelling changes in policy or governments. But it might be that the obstacles to a government's compliance are to be found in the policies of other states, multinational actors, or regimes rather than in its own lack of resources, capacity, or will. Consider, for example, trade policies that discriminate against agricultural products or intellectual property rules enforced in international law that increase the costs of pharmaceuticals. If it were true that without adaptations in these "external" policies, a government would not be in a position to ensure the satisfaction of its people's human rights, then, although it may seem to be a linguistic stretch, reform of the policies might plausibly be considered a means of "implementation." (It may seem less of a stretch if one recalls the declaration's recognition of the need for "an international order . . . in which human rights can be fully realized.") In any case, it is clear that external adaptations are among the forms of action for which justifications are sometimes sought in considerations about human rights.

I intend this typology as a rough classification of the main forms of transnational political action for which the protection of human rights might be and often is taken to be a reason. In the nature of the subject, there is overlap among the paradigms; and, taken together, they may not present a complete inventory. The point of the survey is to illustrate the complexity of human rights as an ongoing global practice and to underscore how substantially its repertoire of measures of implementation diverges from the juridical paradigm.[75]

The most prominent difference is that most international and transnational efforts to promote and defend human rights are more accurately understood as political rather than legal. Neither the charter-based nor the treaty-based components of the UN human rights system have evolved effective mechanisms for the appellate review of findings or for the judicial application of sanctions. On the other hand, a wide array of political forms of action, lacking any capacity for the appeal and review of decisions to act, have developed both within and outside the UN system. These forms of political action are not well described in terms of the conventional distinction between coercive intervention and consensual assistance. Some activities aimed at promoting human rights are primarily persuasive, others involve the support, coordination, and mobilization of domestic political agents, and others involve the formation of transnational coalitions of

---

[75] Again, I note that the prospects of judicial enforcement are greater within the regional human rights systems.

political > legal

nongovernmental agents for purposes of communication and public advocacy. It would not be inaccurate to describe most of these as forms of "interference" by outside agents in the political life of a society. But it should be repeated that coercive intervention is the limiting, not the modal, case of "interference" and that some of the common forms of action for which agents claim to find justification in considerations about human rights can be counted as "interference" only in a capacious sense of the term.

A second difference concerns the actors involved in these forms of action. In the juridical paradigm, public bodies established and authorized by treaty carry out the international monitoring and oversight role. In principle, these institutions act as agents for and can be held accountable by the states that established them. Within the juridical paradigm, human rights supply reasons for action for these legally constituted agents of the international community. In practice, however, with the development of political rather than juridical paradigms of implementation, human rights violations have come to supply reasons for action to other kinds of agents as well, frequently acting without specific legal authority. The most important of these are states acting individually or in coalitions, international organizations which are not part of the system constituted by the human rights treaties, and local and transnational nongovernmental actors.

Finally, it is worth recalling that the juridical paradigm is 'juridical' in two distinct respects—in its aspiration for juridical human rights institutions at the global level and in its expectation that to the extent possible individual states would carry out their obligations under human rights agreements by incorporating human rights protections in their constitutions and laws on the model of a "bill of rights." Practice has diverged from expectation in the second as well as the first respect. The domestic-level changes for which human rights are taken as reasons are not limited to changes in constitutional law. Human rights may also bear on policies established by statute or executive action and even on the conduct of the institutions of cultural life (for example, in the case of women's rights against discrimination). The enlargement of international doctrine together with the growth of transnational processes of political contestation means that it is not clearly essential to the idea of a human right that all human rights protections be provided for in the constitutions and laws of states.

In emphasizing the role of human rights as sources of reasons for transnational political action, I do not mean to say, as a descriptive matter, that

within the practice, violations—even of the most urgent human rights—
necessarily require outsiders to interfere in the affairs of domestic societies.
There is no settled view in human rights doctrine about the conditions
under which outside agents may be regarded as under an obligation to act.
It is also not the case that violations within a society serve only to justify
action by agents external to that society. Obviously they may also justify
action by domestic agents. But neither point denies the centrality in the
discourse of human rights of the idea that threats or violations within a
society are matters of global, not just local, concern. When sufficiently
serious, they are taken to justify outside agents in acting to stop or prevent
or remedy the violations. I have stressed that the available paradigms
of implementation, their agents, and their domestic objectives are more
diverse than is usually recognized, and that coercive intervention is an
exceptional case. Nevertheless, this transnational action-justifying role is
definitive of the function of human rights in the normative discourse of
global politics.

7. An emergent practice

The global human rights enterprise constitutes a practice in the following
sense: it consists of a set of rules for the regulation of the behavior of a class of
agents, a more-or-less widespread belief that these rules ought to be complied with, and some institutions, quasi-institutions, and informal processes
for their propagation and implementation. It is a general characteristic of
social practices that under appropriate circumstances agents regard the rules
as providing reasons for action and grounds of criticism. They also tend to
believe it would be advantageous to have social processes that encourage
compliance and discourage noncompliance by other agents. These elements
are plainly present in the human rights system.

Normative practices can be more or less well established. There can be
more or less agreement about the purposes of individual norms and about
their application in various circumstances. Although some level of compliance is essential for a practice to be said to exist, practices can vary in the
extent of compliance. Similarly, institutions for the propagation, interpretation, and enforcement of norms can vary in their articulation and effectiveness. Social background conditions can be such that agents face more or
fewer conflicts between adhering to a practice's norms and pursuing other

interests. When I say that human rights is an "emergent" practice I mean that these dimensions are less fully developed than in mature practices.

Why not describe human rights as an "international regime"—a set of "implicit or explicit principles, norms, rules, and decision-making procedures around which actors' expectations tend to converge"?[76] This would not be incorrect, but it could be misleading in at least two respects. The human rights system lacks some features that are present in most familiar international regimes. For example, most of these regimes (e.g. those for trade and finance) contain institutional capacities for the authoritative resolution of disputes about the application of norms to individual cases and for the application of sanctions to agents that do not comply with authoritative interpretations of these norms. By contrast, the human rights system is notable for the weakness and unevenness of its capacities for adjudication and enforcement. Relatedly, most regimes are properly described in a quasi-technical sense as cooperative arrangements: they were organized and their members participate in them for purposes of mutual benefit. Each party regards participation according to the rules as advantageous on the condition that others participate on the same conditions. However, although there may be cases in which a state's participation in the human rights system is advantageous for the state, in general this need not be true. Like the more familiar regimes, human rights constitute a system of collective self-regulation, but the primary beneficiaries—that is, those whose interests are advanced by cooperation—are not the cooperating agents themselves but rather their individual members.[77]

There is also another respect in which it would be misleading to describe human rights as a "regime." The idea of a regime focuses attention on explicit rules and formal procedures for their application. To some extent these elements are present for human rights, but an exclusive focus on them would fail to embrace the ways in which human rights function as standards of aspiration—for example, as bases of political criticism, elements of a

can't describe HR as "regime"

[76] Stephen D. Krasner, "Structural Causes and Regime Consequences: Regimes as Intervening Variables," in *International Regimes*, ed. S. D. Krasner (Ithaca, NY: Cornell University Press, 1983), 2. On the nature of the human rights system, see Jack Donnelly, "International Human Rights: A Regime Analysis," *International Organization* 40 (1986): 599–642; and James W. Nickel, "Is Today's International Human Rights System a Global Governance Regime?" *Journal of Ethics* 6 (2002): 353–71.

[77] It would not be inconsistent to believe that governments may also have reasons to impose restrictions on themselves, as Andrew Moravcsik argues has been the case in Europe. "The Origins of Human Rights Regimes: Democratic Delegation in Postwar Europe," *International Organization* 54 (2000): 217–52.

shared moral language, and ideals that guide efforts at political change by individuals and nongovernmental organizations. To put the point generally, human rights not only function as standards to which the international community may hold each country's institutions accountable. They also operate as goals of political change for nongovernmental actors and as a global analog of the public conception of justice found in well-ordered domestic societies. I do not mean that the normative requirements of human rights describe or constitute a complete conception of justice. Rather, like a society's public conception of justice, human rights aspire to function, and occasionally do function, as a shared moral touchstone or a common reference point in deliberation about political action and social criticism. No analysis of human rights that did not capture this aspirational aspect would be faithful to the hopes of the framers of modern human rights doctrine or to the roles that human rights have come to play in the discourse of global politics today.

8. Problems

I have described human rights as an emergent discursive practice consisting of a set of norms for the regulation of the conduct of governments and a range of actions open to various agents for which a government's failure to abide by these norms supplies reasons. The main features I have emphasized are the practice's normative breadth, the heterogeneity of the institutional requirements of its constitutive norms, the absence of any authoritative view about the grounds of these norms, the dynamic character of the practice's normative content, and the variety of paradigms of political action that might be understood as justified in response to infringements.

These features together emphasize the novelty of the practice of human rights. Reflection about them points towards several problems of interpretation and justification.

The first concerns the nature of human rights. How are these objects best conceptualized? One might take one's model from various sources—for example, from the history of thought about natural rights or "the rights of man" or from some contemporary conception of fundamental moral rights. But it is difficult to reconcile the obvious historical and analytical models with the normative breadth of human rights, their dynamic character, or their distinctive modernity. The available models also do not fit well with the character of human rights as a public political doctrine, specifying conditions for institutions which are open to support from a variety of foundational views. Yet, if human rights doctrine is to avoid the charge of being no more than an ad hoc collection of values, we must have some coherent conception of the type of objects to which it refers.

A second problem involves the basis for establishing the proper normative scope of human rights doctrine. Even among those who consider themselves friends of human rights, the expansion of the scope of international human rights doctrine can appear to debase its currency.[78] The worry is reasonable, but without a conception of the nature and purposes of the enterprise we have no basis for setting limits to its reach. It will be evident that the problem of scope is connected to the problem of the nature of human rights, because one's understanding of their nature may influence one's view about the considerations it is appropriate to take into account in determining which substantive values should count as parts of the public doctrine.

Third: human rights are supposed to be "universal" but it is not clear that this can be true of the human rights of international practice in any non-vacuous way. Sometimes the concern about "universality" is a worry about whether all of the values embodied in human rights doctrine can be seen as important for everyone, regardless of their associational and cultural ties. At the same time, outside agents who act to protect or advance human rights in a society where they are violated will almost certainly bear costs they would not bear otherwise. The concern about "universality" might arise as a worry about whether there is an adequate justification for imposing these costs. So an account of the "universality" of human rights must work from two perspectives—that of the supposed beneficiaries of political action justified by human rights and that of those who are called upon to act. In view of the beneficiary-centeredness of so much popular discourse about human rights, it is particularly important not to lose sight of the second perspective. The broader the normative scope of human rights doctrine becomes, the more puzzling it seems what such an account would be like.

A fourth problem is how human rights can be action-guiding. It is natural to think of international human rights as a type of moral right, and of moral rights as grounds for the assignment of duties to particular other agents.

[78] For an early example, see Philip Alston, "Conjuring up New Human Rights: A Proposal for Quality Control," *American Journal of International Law* 78 (1984): 607-21.

Most important moral rights center on claims against some determinate set of other agents to the effect that they perform or omit certain actions for the performance or omission of which the right serves as the basis. But it can be difficult to construe certain human rights (e.g. those to work, to an adequate standard of living, or to periodic and genuine elections) as grounds of claims assertable by individuals taken seriatim against particular other agents. This might be for any of several reasons: for example, because no agent or group of agents controls sufficient resources to satisfy the claims or because the claims can only be satisfied by some ambitious change in institutions and policies. Human rights like those just mentioned may not seem to be genuine rights at all.[79] It is not much help to say, in response, that human rights (or anyway some of them) are rights in a special sense of "right" that is detachable from the idea of a claim. The initial difficulty arises from the plausible supposition that any genuine right must be capable of guiding action in the typical circumstances in which it is likely to be claimed. If, in such circumstances, the assertion of the right does not yield reasons for action for any other agent, then the right seems pointless. But rights are not supposed to be pointless; they are supposed to yield reasons for action. The question is whether there is a coherent and otherwise-attractive conception of human rights that preserves a capacity to guide action without forcing a radical paring-back in their substantive scope.

Finally, there is the problem of the significance of intercultural moral diversity for an international practice of human rights. The broad normative scope of the contemporary doctrine together with its characteristic modernity means that human rights are not likely to be neutral among the main moral conceptions found in the world's various societies and cultures. As a result, advocacy of human rights can appear to be a form of partisanship, disrespectful of cultures in which widely accepted norms conflict with their requirements. This can seem objectionably intolerant. From another point of view, however, once we have taken account of all the relevant reasons—whatever they turn out to be—and concluded that there is a sound basis for some particular requirement, it is not clear why considerations of toleration in global politics should argue against it. To allow actual disagreement to count against a normative requirement which is otherwise well founded

---

[79] Thus, for example, Onora O'Neill objects that the "rhetoric of rights" is "evasive" because it does not adhere to the rule that every valid right must be associated with an obligation on the part of some identifiable agent. "Women's Rights, Whose Obligations?" in *Bounds of Justice* (Cambridge: Cambridge University Press, 2000), 97-8.

seems to rob normative discourse of its critical force. These perspectives are not easily reconciled. We need more clarity over the basis of concern about toleration and the ways in which this concern should influence thought about the content of a human rights doctrine suited for a culturally plural world.

Although this is not an exhaustive list, I believe it includes the most troubling general problems we face in thinking about the practice of human rights as we find it today. I propose to begin with the first—that of the nature of human rights considered as a category of normative idea. I do not suggest that a satisfactory grasp of this idea will yield solutions to the other problems, but I believe it will help to frame them in a way that makes solutions more readily reached.

3

Naturalistic Theories

PHILOSOPHICAL investigations of human rights often begin by asking, "What are human rights?" but it is not always clear what would count as an answer. The question might be read as asking for an analysis of the kind of object that human rights are—about their nature or ontology, so to speak. Or it might be read as asking for a list of human rights, or of the values protected by them. Or it might be read as asking what follows from designating a value as a human right—about the way in which human rights are or should be action-guiding. Or it might be interpreted as an oblique request for an explanation of the significance of human rights—about the reasons we should care about them, or their normativity. These questions are related: a reply to one may imply or exclude some replies to the others. So, for example, a view about the nature of human rights may have implications for the range of values that may plausibly be considered as human rights, or as protected by human rights. A view about the normativity of human rights is likely to have implications about the respects in which human rights can be action-guiding. Still, the questions are distinct, and in asking "What are human rights?" we should be clear which of them we take ourselves to be asking.

In this chapter and the next, we consider two theoretical positions that present themselves as replies to the first question, about the nature of human rights. I shall call these "naturalistic" and "agreement" views. Both seek to understand international human rights as expressions of one or another more abstract idea already on hand. Each has been thought by many to express the intuitive core of the idea of a human right, but I shall argue that both views distort our perception of the human rights of international doctrine. We do better to approach human rights practically, not as the application of an independent philosophical idea to the international realm, but as a political doctrine constructed to play a certain role in global political life.

9. Naturalism about human rights

Naturalistic views conceive of human rights as objects that inherit their main features from the natural rights found in European political and legal thought in the early modern period. Here is how John Simmons describes such a view:

> *Natural* rights . . . are those rights that can be possessed by persons in a "state of nature" (i.e., independent of any legal or political institution, recognition, or enforcement). . . . Human rights are those natural rights that are innate and that cannot be lost (i.e., that cannot be given away, forfeited, or taken away). Human rights, then, will have the properties of universality, independence (from social or legal recognition), naturalness, inalienability, non-forfeitability, and imprescriptibility. Only so understood will an account of human rights capture the central idea of rights that can always be claimed by any human being.

In summary, human rights "are rights possessed by all human beings (at all times and in all places), simply in virtue of their humanity."[1]

This idea is open to several interpretations. These have at least two elements in common. First, human rights are distinct from positive rights—that is, rights actually recognized in a society, or anyway enacted in law. Human rights are critical moral standards, ones that can be invoked as a basis for criticism of actually existing laws and social practices. The notion of a right existing in a state of nature is one way of conceiving of such a right, although it is not the only way. Second, human rights belong to human beings "as such" or "simply in virtue of their humanity." This means, at a minimum, that all human beings are entitled to claim human rights. It may also mean that the grounds on which a particular human right may be claimed are available to everybody because they inhere somehow in each person's nature or status as a human being. Putting these two points together, naturalistic conceptions regard human rights as having a character

---

[1] A. John Simmons, "Human Rights and World Citizenship: The Universality of Human Rights in Kant and Locke," in *Justification and Legitimacy: Essays on Rights and Obligations* (Cambridge: Cambridge University Press, 2001), 185 (emphasis in original; the order of the passages has been reversed).

and basis that can be fully comprehended without reference to their embodiment and role in any public doctrine or practice. According to such a
view, the "human rights" of international doctrine derive their identity and
authority from this more basic level of values. The task of the theorist is to
describe or discover these values and then to say which of the entitlements
represented as human rights in international doctrine embody or can be
derived from them.

Naturalistic views can yield skeptical conclusions about the scope and
content of international doctrine. For example, Maurice Cranston, who held
such a view, argued that many of the human rights recognized in international doctrine—in particular, economic and social rights—are
improperly considered as human rights because they cannot be construed
as having the attributes of natural rights. They should be seen, instead, as
elements of a political ideal without either the universality or the preemptory
force of genuine human rights.[2] Cranston wrote during the Cold War when
it was sometimes thought (incorrectly, as we have seen) that economic and
social rights had been included in international doctrine in order to secure
the support of the Communist countries. But it would be a mistake to
disregard his skepticism as an artifact of the time; it could be a temptation
for anyone who interprets international doctrine as an attempt to embody in
international law a deeper and independently distinguishable order of values
modeled on the natural rights of the tradition. From this perspective, the
international human rights enterprise might seem to have expanded beyond
the boundaries of its motivating idea. The point of potential disagreement
among naturalistic theorists is where the boundary between genuine human
rights and other values that pretend to this status is properly drawn.[3]

Regarded as a thesis in the history of ideas, human rights are indeed the
legacies of natural rights. But it does not follow from the historical thesis that
we understand human rights best by conceiving them as objects that possess
the essential features of natural rights. This is a philosophical thesis, not a
historical one.[4] I shall offer an argument meant to debunk this thesis: our
understanding of international human rights is distorted rather than helped

    [2] Maurice Cranston, *What Are Human Rights?* (London: Bodley Head, 1973), 65-71.
    [3] The range of variation is wide. Compare, for example, Cranston's abstemious position in
What Are Human Rights? with the more capacious view of human rights taken by James Griffin in
On Human Rights (Oxford: Oxford University Press, 2008).
    [4] There are instructive discussions of the relationship between natural and human rights in
James W. Nickel, *Making Sense of Human Rights*, 2nd edn. (Malden, MA: Blackwell, 2007), 12-14;
and Peter Jones, *Rights* (New York: St Martin's Press, 1994), ch. 4.

by conceiving them on the model of natural rights. Moreover, the distortion is not simply a failure of analysis. Adopting a conception of human rights modeled on natural rights has misleading consequences for all the main questions a theory of human rights should illuminate—about their grounds, their scope, and the manner in which valid claims of human right should guide action.

There is a formidable preliminary difficulty in framing the debunking argument. To speak of a "model of natural rights" might suggest more precision than we can reasonably hope to achieve. The idea of a natural right has a long history. Its beginnings are a matter of controversy, although one whose details do not matter for our purposes.[5] What is clear at all events is that conceptions of natural rights have changed over time, so that no philosophical account of human rights as natural rights would be informative without an indication of which among the family of conceptions of natural rights found in the history of thought human rights are to be compared to. The preliminary difficulty is that the debunking argument seems to lack an unambiguous target.

It is not even clear in what sense natural rights may be said to be "natural."[6] There are at least two historically influential conceptions. A right might be "natural" in the sense that we possess it independently of our social relationships and undertakings, and more generally of any conventionally established rank or status. This sense of "natural"—an interpretation of the idea of a right that belongs "by nature" to all human beings—is familiar in modern thought from Grotius, Pufendorf, and Locke. But there is also another conception of the "natural" as that which would be required or permitted by the ideally best law for one's situation—that is, the law one would discover through the use of natural reason if one were perfectly reasonable and had possession of all the relevant facts, including possibly facts about the fixed ends shared by all human beings. This conception dates to the pre-modern natural law tradition. Although they might coincide in some views,[7] these senses are distinct. In the first sense of "natural," what

---

[5] For three different views, see Richard Tuck, *Natural Rights Theories* (Cambridge: Cambridge University Press, 1978), ch. 1; Brian Tierney, *The Idea of Natural Rights* (Atlanta: Scholars Press, 1997), ch. 1; and Annabel S. Brett, *Liberty, Right and Nature: Individual Rights in Later Scholastic Thought* (Cambridge: Cambridge University Press, 1997), esp. ch. 4.

[6] As Tierney observes, the ambiguity can be discerned in thought about natural rights as early as the glossators. *The Idea of Natural Rights*, 133.

[7] As, perhaps, they did in Locke. A. John Simmons, *The Lockean Theory of Rights* (Princeton, NJ: Princeton University Press, 1992), 95-102.

distinguishes natural rights from other rights is a constraint on the range of considerations that can count in a right's justification: a right is natural if the reasons why we are entitled to claim it make no essential reference to contingent features of our situations, such as our voluntary transactions and social relationships. It is a right we could coherently believe exists in a state of nature where there are no established social conventions or institutionalized patterns of reciprocity. This need not be true of rights that are natural in the second sense. The grounds of the ideally best law for our situation might—if our situation is socialized—take account of salient features of the social environment, such as the extent and characteristics of our relationships with others. It is even possible that some rights that are natural in the second sense would be inconceivable in the first sense—for example, rights constituted by social relationships or institutions (e.g., perhaps, the right to take part in the government of one's country).[8]

For the most part, the views we examine here understand the naturalness of natural rights in the first rather than the second sense. This conception has been more influential in modern political thought and has contributed much of the distortion in philosophical understandings of human rights.[9] But even with this restriction, we still do not have an unambiguous target: in view of the rich history of the idea, ambiguity is unavoidable. I do not think it would be profitable to argue that one conception is more faithful to the history of thought about natural rights than others. Instead I proceed less systematically. I observe four features of what I shall loosely call the conceptual space of natural rights, and then consider each feature separately in relation to human rights, briefly for the first three and at greater length for the fourth. I hope the cumulative effect will be to motivate an exploration of a practical conception of human rights by showing how the model of natural rights produces distortions.

The four features are as follows. First, natural rights are requirements whose force does not depend on the moral conventions and positive laws of their society. They are critical standards for a society's conventional and legal rules. Second, natural rights are pre-institutional in a logical (rather

---

[8] Margaret McDonald, "Natural Rights," *Proceedings of the Aristotelian Society*, NS 47 (1946-7), 228-32. See also Anthony Pagden, "Human Rights, Natural Rights, and Europe's Imperial Legacy," *Political Theory* 31 (2003), 176-81.

[9] I do not mean to say that the second conception is missing entirely. It can be found, for example, in Jacques Maritain, *Man and the State* (Chicago: University of Chicago Press, 1951), ch. 4 ("The Rights of Man"), and John Finnis, *Natural Law and Natural Rights* (Oxford: Clarendon Press, 1980).

than a historical) sense: their content is conceivable independently of any reference to the structural features of institutions. Thus we might say that natural rights are the rights (or a subset of the rights) that exist in a pre-political state of nature. Taken together, the first two elements describe standards that reside at a deep level of our normative beliefs and operate as comprehensive constraints on human conduct in whatever realm this conduct may occur—in interpersonal relations, domestic society, and international life. They are in this sense "fundamental." Third, natural rights are possessed by persons "at all times and in all places," regardless of the stage of development of a society and its productive forces, the details of its political structure, or the content of its religious traditions and political culture. This is one way in which natural rights might be said to be "universal." Finally, human rights belong to persons "as such" or, in the customary phrase used by Simmons, "simply in virtue of their humanity." Human rights are grounded in considerations that apply to all human beings, regardless of their spatial locations or social relationships. This is another (and a distinct) sense in which natural rights might be described as "universal."

I have said that naturalistic conceptions inherit their main features from the idea of a natural right, but I do not mean to say that every naturalistic conception must hold that human rights possess all of the features I have listed. The class of naturalistic conceptions is defined by their provenance, not by a canonical list of features. Some of these conceptions combine all of these features; others take over fewer. Some may fasten on only one—most likely one or another interpretation of the idea that human rights belong to persons "as such." On some views the first three features may be thought to be implied by the fourth (though, as I shall suggest, this is not obviously correct). For our purposes these variations do not matter. As we shall see, whatever the details, typical naturalistic conceptions are more restrictive as to the content and basis of human rights than they might at first appear to be; indeed, on many accounts they would rule out substantial parts of contemporary human rights doctrine. This is the truth in the critiques of writers like Cranston. The real question is why we should conceive of international human rights according to a naturalistic model at all.

The first feature, that natural rights are independent of a society's moral conventions and positive laws, is the least problematic for human rights. This is true, at least, if the idea is stated in its simplest form, for in this form it holds only that the content of natural rights is not determined by the moral and legal rules that actually prevail in any particular existing society. Natural rights have some other basis than conventional belief or enactment in law. This is essential if natural rights are to function as critical standards: it must be possible to say, for example, that a slave-holding society violates the natural rights of those whom its laws classify as slaves, and moreover, that the violation occurs even when the society's laws track the content of its moral conventions. Contemporary human rights plainly share this feature of natural rights.

Within the natural rights tradition, the feature of independence of positive law and convention has sometimes been conflated with another feature of natural rights. This is usually framed as an ontological property, as when it is said, for example, that natural rights "exist" independently of positive law. This latter idea—that natural rights have some sort of permanent existence in a separate normative order—is difficult to render clearly. Perhaps it is an elliptical way of stating a view about the justification of natural rights—for example, that they are based on or derivable from the natural law conceived as God's law, knowable by human beings through the right use of reason.[10] If we take this idea as part of the natural rights model, then we have arrived at one point at which the model diverges from contemporary human rights practice, for it is explicit in the origins of this practice that human rights doctrine does not incorporate any view about the justification of human rights in an independent order of natural rights, in the natural law, or in God's commands. To repeat Maritain's characterization of international human rights, they are "practical conclusions which, although justified in different ways by different persons, are principles of action with a common ground of similarity for everyone."[11] Human rights are like natural rights in being critical standards whose content is not determined by the moral conventions and legal rules of any particular society, but they are unlike natural rights in not presupposing any one view about their basis or justification. In that sense it cannot be said—and in any case, it is not part of international doctrine—that human rights are "out there," existing in some separate normative order.[12]

---

[10] See e.g. Maritain, *Man and the State*, 99-102.

[11] Jacques Maritain, "Introduction," in UNESCO, *Human Rights: Comments and Interpretations* (London: Allan Wingate, 1949), 9, 10 (emphasis in original). See § 4, above.

[12] The point is not simply that the human rights treaties do not incorporate any justificatory apparatus. Few treaties do (though the same cannot be said about the historical rights declarations). Maritain was in this respect speaking for the framers (though he was not himself a member of the drafting committee): they wished to articulate a public doctrine the acceptance of which did not require one also to accept any particular view about its justification.

Now consider the idea that human rights are pre-institutional—that they are rights one would have in a pre-political state of nature. The most influential natural rights theorists for modern thought imagined that political society developed by means of a social contract from a pre-political (although socialized) "natural state" or condition in which people had certain rights which it was everyone's responsibility to respect.[13] Locke, for example, holds that the "fundamental law of nature" recognizes rights to "life, health, liberty, [and] possessions."[14] These rights express moral protections upon which people are entitled to insist regardless of their institutional memberships and which, therefore, no political institutions may infringe. The idea of a state of nature models this fact: it imagines that individuals establish institutions in a pre-institutional situation already constrained by certain moral requirements. Because persons have no power to abrogate these requirements, any institutions they establish must respect them.

If natural rights are pre-institutional then it should be possible to conceptualize them as existing in a condition where there are no institutions. It is not difficult to conceive of the Lockean rights in this way. The same cannot be said of some of the rights found in the contemporary human rights documents. Consider, for example, human rights to political asylum, to take part in the government of the country, or to free elementary education. Because the essence of these rights is to describe features of an acceptable institutional environment, there is no straightforward sense in which they might exist in a state of nature.

Although the natural rights theories of the formative period interpreted these rights as pre-institutional, is not difficult to imagine a position reasonably describable as a natural rights theory that extends this idea in a way that makes room for institutional rights. One might hold, for example, that while first-order natural rights should be conceivable in a state of nature (because we should be able to understand their basis as independent of social and institutional contingencies), there are also second-order rights,

---

[13] As Quentin Skinner points out, the *idea* of a state of nature is—because it must be—present in these theories even if the term is not. *The Foundations of Modern Political Thought* (Cambridge: Cambridge University Press, 1978), ii. 155. Cf. pp. 155-66 for a discussion of the purposes served by the idea of a state of nature in the thought of Thomists like Vitoria, Suarez, and Molina.

[14] John Locke, *Two Treatises of Government* [1690], ed. Peter Laslett (Cambridge: Cambridge University Press, 1988), ii.6. Locke himself rarely uses the phrase "natural right" and, as Simmons points out, when he does it is unclear how he understands it. *The Lockean Theory of Rights*, 90 ff.

conceivable only within an institutional setting, that can be derived from the first-order rights with the addition of premises about the character of the social environment and the potential advantages and disadvantages of various kinds of institution. Such a view would be most persuasive if the first-order rights are conceived relatively abstractly (e.g. as rights to life and liberty). Locke himself, citing Hooker, holds that the legislature is bound by the natural law to establish "known authorized judges" who, by adjudicating disagreement about individual entitlements, can help avoid the dangerous disorder likely to arise when each person is judge of his or her own case.[15] Perhaps at least some human rights can be regarded, by analogy, as mechanisms by which first-order natural rights might be protected (and respect for them promoted?) once the state of nature has given way to political society. Indeed, given a sufficiently rich conception of the contents of the first-order rights and sufficiently ambitious premises about the social and institutional environment, it might even be possible to arrive at an extended catalog of rights more-or-less co-extensive with those found in contemporary international doctrine.

There is no reason to rule out this possibility *ab initio* and perhaps we should welcome it. But saving appearances in this way has its cost. The proponent of such a theory faces a dilemma. To remain plausibly within the class of natural rights views, any such theory must build in, from the outset, some normative content, expressed in the form of first-order rights with a basis that does not depend on social or institutional contingencies. This requirement exerts pressure to restrict the range of the normative content. But the more restricted the core content, the less extensive the catalog of second-order (institutional) rights derivable from it. On the other hand, the desire to arrive at a catalog of second-order rights with a breadth that approximates that of the contemporary doctrine of human rights exerts pressure to broaden the core content. There is no reason to doubt that a valid derivation could be produced by introducing appropriate intermediate premises, but any such strategy threatens to exceed the scope of what the underlying idea of "naturalness" will bear. The attempt to produce a view whose foundations are sufficient to justify a catalog of rights something like contemporary human rights risks giving up the generic pertinence to the human situation "as such" that one might have thought attainable by exploiting the idea of "naturalness."

---

[15] Locke, *Two Treatises*, ii. 136. Locke does not, however, say specifically that people have a *natural right* to an independent judiciary.

Returning to the traditional idea that natural rights are pre-institutional, we must ask why we should conceive of *human* rights in the same way. Natural rights theories, at least in modern variants such as Locke's, were primarily attempts to formulate constraints on the use of a government's coercive power in circumstances of religious and moral diversity. They were theoretical devices by which legitimate and illegitimate uses of political power to limit liberty could be distinguished, and the great importance attributed to the rights identified as "natural" makes sense only against a background assumption that a central problem of political life is the protection of personal security and liberty against predictable threats of tyrannical or oppressive government. But the motivating concern of international human rights is evidently broader (though it certainly includes) the protection of individual liberty against infringement by the state: the human rights of international doctrine, taken as a package, are in their own terms an effort to identify the social conditions necessary for the living of dignified human lives. As Charles Malik, one of the framers, said in reference to some of the economic rights, these are "rights of the individual as a member of society" rather than rights "of the individual as such."[16] They represent a more ambitious assumption of responsibility for the public sphere than was required by the motivating concerns of classical natural rights theories. One is entitled to believe this is a mistake, but such a belief would be a substantive position in political theory, not a deduction from a proper understanding of the concept of a human right.

The third feature of natural rights is that their requirements are invariant across time and space. The natural rights of the tradition were supposed to be timeless in this way, but as I observed earlier (§ 5), it is hard to see how some of the rights of the declaration could qualify: consider, for example, the rights to social security or, again, to free elementary education (arts. 22, 26). It is reasonably clear from examples like these that its framers could not have intended the doctrine of human rights to apply, for example, to the ancient Greeks or to China in the Ch'in dynasty or to European societies in the Middle Ages. International human rights, to judge by the contents of the doctrine, are suited to play a role in a certain range of societies. Roughly speaking, these are societies that have at least some of the defining features of modernization: for example, a minimal legal system (including a capability for enforcement), an economy that includes some form of wage labor for at least some workers, some participation in global cultural and economic life, and a public institutional capacity to raise revenue and provide essential collective goods. It is hard to imagine any interesting sense in which a doctrine of human rights pertaining principally to societies meeting these conditions could be said to be "timeless."[17]

Perhaps in response, one philosopher adopts a more cautious formulation: he says that human rights should "have weight and bearing for future human beings in societies not yet existing."[18] But this does not seem right either. International human rights are not even *prospectively* timeless. They are appropriate to the institutions of modern or modernizing societies organized as political states coexisting in a global political economy in which human beings face a series of predictable threats. The list of human rights is explained by the nature of these threats.[19] As the social, economic, and technological environment evolves, the array of threats may change. So, perhaps, may the list of human rights; in fact, some part of the expansion of human rights doctrine since 1948 might possibly be explained in this way. If one imposes from the outset the constraint that human rights must be timeless, any such expansion would be suspect. But, again, it is hard to see why anyone not for other reasons in the thrall of the natural rights tradition—that is, of the modern interpretation distinguished earlier[20]— would wish to impose such a constraint on the content of international human rights.

In the second and third of these ways, the human rights of international doctrine appear to occupy a different conceptual space than that defined by the natural rights model. They have different aims and bear a different relation to the reasons why we should accept them as sources of reasons for action. It is hardly surprising that the conflation of the two ideas would

---

[17] Some contemporary societies—those with frail or failing legal and political institutions, for example—may bear a closer resemblance to feudal societies than to modern ones. Any account of the normativity of contemporary human rights doctrine must take account of this fact, perhaps as an exceptional case.

[18] Rex Martin, *A System of Rights* (Oxford: Clarendon Press, 1993), 74, 75.

[19] For the idea of "standard threats," see Henry Shue, *Basic Rights*, 2nd edn. (Princeton, NJ: Princeton University Press, 1996), 29 ff. and the sources cited in § 17, below. For the connection with distinctively modern social conditions, see Jack Donnelly, *Universal Human Rights in Theory and Practice*, 2nd edn. (Ithaca, NY: Cornell University Press, 2003), ch. 4.

[20] I introduce the caveat because someone who understands human rights as an expression of the requirements of the natural law is not committed to thinking that a public doctrine of human rights should represent them as "timeless." See Maritain, *Man and the State*, 101-5; and Tierney, *The Idea of Natural Rights*, 133-4.

generate skepticism about human rights—indeed, skepticism would seem deeply tempting. But if I am right that the idea of a human right is distinguishable from that of a natural right, then we need not be tempted. This kind of skepticism is rooted in the thought that the enterprise of human rights involves a kind of misappropriation of the historical idea of a natural right. But this is a thought we need not accept.

10. Persons "as such" (1): the demand side

The most broadly influential contribution of the natural rights tradition to contemporary thought about human rights is the idea that human rights belong to persons "as such" or "simply in virtue of their humanity." This idea is present in both of the branches of natural rights thinking distinguished earlier—that which identifies natural rights as rights possessed in a state of nature and that which identifies them as rights prescribed by the natural law in light of a conception of human good or of the fixed final ends of human persons. The idea arises as one explanation of the "universality" of human rights, understood as the property of belonging to or being claimable by any person in any society. As a matter of first impression the connection seems obvious: if human rights can be claimed by anyone, they must somehow be grounded in features that all persons necessarily share. On reflection, however, it is not clear that there is any nontrivial sense in which this need be true.

There are two perspectives. Frequently the idea that human rights belong to persons "as such" is taken to refer to what we might call the "demand side" of human rights—that is, to the reasons why we should regard human rights as good things for their beneficiaries. Taking this first point of view, to say that a human right belongs to persons "as such" is to say roughly that the right protects an interest that any human being may (or perhaps should) be expected to have. This gives us a type of view we might call "demand-side naturalism." But the force of "as such" might also be taken to apply to the "supply side" of human rights—to the reasons why some class of agents should regard themselves as under an obligation to respect or enforce the human rights of others. Taking this second point of view, it will not usually be enough (in fact it may not even be necessary) that the right protect an interest that anyone might be expected to have; a satisfactory account of the right would have to explain in some general way where the resources to satisfy it should come from and why anyone should regard themselves as having a reason to provide them. Since natural rights are supposed to be claimable by persons "simply in virtue of their humanity," it might be inferred that addressees of the claim should have a "natural" reason to respect the right—that is, one that obtains independently of any contingent features of their relationship to the claimant. These two perspectives need separate consideration.

Let us begin with the "demand side." The idea is that human rights are protections of interests or goods that are valuable for all human beings, regardless of their culture, the stage of development of their society, or their particular social ties. How might this idea be understood?

I shall describe two possibilities and then comment on their adequacy as a basis for grasping the concept of a human right found in international practice. We might take as an example of the first possibility the theory of human rights proposed by James Griffin. Looking back at the history of Western thought about rights, Griffin discerns the emergence in the late Middle Ages of the idea of "human standing." This is the status of a being with the capacity to "form pictures of what a good life would be" and to "try to realize these pictures." The idea is found, he believes, in Pico's remark that it is given to man "to have that which he chooses and be that which he wills." Griffin's suggestion is that human rights—those possessed by human beings "as such"—should "be seen as protections of our human standing or, as I shall put it, our personhood."[21]

"Personhood," as Griffin presents it, is an interpretation of the idea of human dignity. He identifies it with "normative agency," which he describes as having three components. These are "autonomy" (the capacity to "choose one's own path through life—that is, not be dominated or controlled"), "minimum provision" (one must have the education, information, capabilities, and resources to choose and act effectively), and "liberty" (one should not be blocked in acting by the forcible intervention of others). The intuitive idea is that because we regard the exercise of our "personhood" as having especially high value, we "see its domain as privileged and protected." The importance and content of human rights are to be grasped in terms of their strategic role in protecting these values.

[21] Griffin, *On Human Rights*, 31-3. This is the most comprehensive recent effort to generate a theory of human rights from naturalistic foundations. For Pico, see Giovanni Pico della Mirandola [1463-94], *On the Dignity of Man*, trans. Charles Glenn Wallis (Indianapolis: Hackett, 1998), 5.

Demand-side (margin note)

reference to Griffin (handwritten note at bottom)

→ When to protect personhood?

Griffin describes such a view as an "expansive naturalism"—"expansive" in including both basic human interests and "events such as their being met or not met" among the grounds of human rights.[22]

As Griffin observes, human rights are supposed to have a certain kind of social existence. A human right is "an effective, socially manageable, claim on others." We need some way of determining when it is reasonable to protect the values of "personhood" by conferring on individuals the power to make such a claim and what form the claim should take. To resolve these questions Griffin turns to a second category of considerations he calls "practicalities." These include a heterogeneous group of factors of which the most important are general facts about human nature and society (these are "universal" facts, "not tied to particular times and places").[23]

Griffin argues that these two categories of considerations—"personhood" and "practicalities"—are sufficient to single out certain substantive protections to be established as human rights and to explain why we should regard these protections as matters of particular importance. They also allow us to rule out various other protections as representing an improper application of the idea of a human right. This aspect of the view is visible in Griffin's analysis of discrepancies between the list generated by his theory and the actual contents of international human rights doctrine. He argues with respect to some of these discrepancies that they are sufficiently serious to provide a reason why international doctrine should be revised to conform more closely to the personhood account.[24]

I shall comment about the personhood theory after introducing another naturalistic view. This is the theory of human rights as protections of "basic

NATURALISTIC VIEW

[22] Griffin, *On Human Rights*, 32-3, 36. These components are elaborated in chs. 8-10.

[23] Ibid. 37-9. Griffin notes that the required facts must be "universal" in this way in order to justify rights "that one has simply in virtue of being human" (p. 38).

[24] The rights found in international doctrine which are unacceptable according to the personhood theory include the prohibition of war propaganda (ICCPR, art. 20(1)), the right against attacks on one's honor and reputation (UDHR, art. 12), the protection of freedom of movement and residence within national borders, the right to work (UDHR, arts. 12, 13, 23), and the right to the "highest attainable standard of physical and mental health" (ICESCR, art. 12(1)). Ibid., 194-6, 206-8. Griffin is dismissive of the right to "periodic holidays with pay" (perhaps more informatively rendered as a right to "rest and leisure," and under this description not obviously insignificant) (UDHR, art. 24). He also argues that there is no "right to inherit," though it must be said that the status of this right in international doctrine is at best uncertain. The "right to inherit" is mentioned in the Convention on the Elimination of All Forms of Racial Discrimination in a list of "other civil rights" (CERD, art. 5(d)(vi)) in the context of a guarantee against discrimination. This provision does not affirm that there is any such human right. There is no reference to a right to inherit in either covenant, both of which were adopted by the General Assembly of the UN the year after the CERD.

value achieved v. formal opportunity

human capabilities" proposed independently by Martha Nussbaum and Amartya Sen.[25] Both writers employ the idea of a capability, but they do so in different ways that yield different conceptions of the discursive roles and normative contents of human rights. After some preliminaries to clarify ideas, I shall concentrate on Nussbaum's position, which more clearly exemplifies an interpretation of the idea of rights that belong to human beings "as such."[26]

According to the capability view, a person's well-being or advantage can be described as the achievement of various valuable actions and states of being ("doings" and "beings"). These "functionings" are the primitives of theories of capability. A person's "capability set" consists of the alternative combinations of functionings the person is in a position to achieve. Capability is to be distinguished, on the one hand, from value achieved (that is, actual functionings) and, on the other, from merely formal opportunity (the absence of restriction by force or law). Capability is a kind of freedom, not achievement: it refers to "the alternative combinations of functionings over which the person has freedom of effective choice" rather than the functionings themselves.[27] The relevant sense of "freedom of effective choice" involves more than the absence of legal or physical constraint; to count as part of a person's capability set, a functioning should be actually achievable as a result of choices open to the person.[28]

If we think of functionings as "valuable doings and beings," then it is clear that the idea of capability is not normatively neutral. Some "doings and beings" will not count as functionings if they are not valuable, and the capability to achieve these doings and beings will not count as a part of a person's well-being or advantage. But this is a relatively weak constraint on the scope of capability: the bare notion that a functioning is a valuable state

CAPABILITY [margin]

[25] Martha C. Nussbaum, "Human Rights Theory: Capabilities and Human Rights," *Fordham Law Review* 66 (1997): 273-300; *Women and Human Development: The Capabilities Approach* (Cambridge: Cambridge University Press, 2000), 96-101 (summarizing portions of the preceding article); and "Capabilities and Human Rights," in *Global Justice and Transnational Politics*, ed. Pablo De Greiff and Ciaran Cronin (Cambridge, MA: MIT Press, 2002), 117-49. For Sen, see "Elements of a Theory of Human Rights," *Philosophy and Public Affairs* 32 (2004): 315-56.
[26] The absence from Sen's view of anything analogous to Nussbaum's list of central human capabilities means that Sen's view is more pluralistic and pragmatic; perhaps it should not be classified as a naturalistic theory at all.
[27] Sen, "Elements of a Theory of Human Rights," 334.
[28] The idea of an outcome's being "actually achievable as a result of choices open to the person" obviously needs further clarification. Achievability is a counterfactual idea and will be ambiguous until it is specified which features of the world are held constant and which left open to variation when it is asserted that some outcome is achievable.

or action will not help much with the problem of indexing capabilities or establishing an order of priority among them. However, it might be possible to identify a subset of capabilities the possession of which people generally have some reason to value highly. If such an idea could be made out, it would have an affinity with the naturalistic conception of a human right, for the rights that protect these capabilities could be seen as belonging to human beings "as such."

Nussbaum has proposed such a list of "central human capabilities" which she argues are "of central importance in any human life, whatever else the person pursues or chooses." She holds that these capabilities are the basis of human rights.[29] This follows a suggestion of Bernard Williams: "The notion of a basic human right seems to me obscure enough, and I would rather come at it from the perspective of basic human capabilities. I would prefer capabilities to do the work, and if we are going to have a language or rhetoric of rights, to have it delivered from them, rather than the other way round."[30]

In Nussbaum's account, human rights might be said to be "delivered from" capabilities in at least three distinct ways. Capability is used as an analytical device to specify the goods and opportunities protected by human rights, as a basis for defining the proper scope of human rights, and as an explanation of the reasons for action to which valid claims of human rights give rise.[31] For our purposes the second and third kinds of dependency are particularly noteworthy. Nussbaum describes a human right as "an especially urgent and morally justified claim that a person has, simply by virtue of being a human adult, and independently of membership in a particular nation, or class, or sex, or ethnic or religious or sexual group."[32] The list of "central human capabilities" serves to identify the types of claim that satisfy this condition. The centrality of these capabilities as constituents of a wide range of ways of life, together with (what Nussbaum holds is) their

[29] Nussbaum, "Human Rights Theory: Capabilities and Human Rights," 286. For a more recent version of the list, see Martha Nussbaum, "Capabilities as Fundamental Entitlements: Sen and Social Justice," *Feminist Economics* 9 (2003), 41-2; compare *Women and Human Development*, 78-80.
[30] Bernard Williams, "The Standard of Living: Interests and Capabilities," in *The Standard of Living*, ed. Amartya K. Sen (Cambridge: Cambridge University Press, 1987), 100.
[31] Nussbaum writes that the justification for claiming that people have certain human rights "usually proceeds by pointing to some capability-like feature of persons.... [W]ithout such a justification the appeal to rights is quite mysterious." "Human Rights Theory: Capabilities and Human Rights," 295.
[32] Ibid. 292.

intrinsic value, also explain why it should matter to us that people enjoy the human rights that protect them.

It is therefore important to ask how the composition of the list is to be justified. Nussbaum describes the capability view as a "form of Aristotelianism" which has at its heart a particular ideal of the citizen "as a free and dignified human being, a maker of choices."[33] She also describes the view as a form of "political liberalism" that can be cross-culturally validated and draws a contrast with the "comprehensive liberalism" of John Stuart Mill and Joseph Raz.[34] These writers adopt ideals of the person very similar to the ideal of the citizen at the heart of her own position, so the significance of this is not clear. In any case, the considerations that determine the content of Nussbaum's conception of human rights are plainly normative. Whether a value should be counted as a human right depends on whether it belongs on the list of "central human capabilities" and this, in turn, depends on a judgment about the centrality of the value in "any human life."

The "personhood" and "basic capabilities" views are similar in two important respects. Both are grounded on one or a few values we might call "basic human interests." In the case of Griffin's theory, these are interests in autonomy, minimum provision, and liberty (the components of "personhood"). The claim is that these interests should matter to any being with the capacity for normative agency. This capacity is universally shared, and once we understand it, we see why it would be reasonable for anyone who had this capacity to care that these interests be satisfied. Nussbaum's position might at first seem similar: she writes that basic capabilities are important for the realization of an ideal of the citizen "as a free and dignified human being, a maker of choices." However, she also identifies these capabilities as ones that are important for a wide range of normal lives and describes them as objects of an "overlapping consensus."[35] So while both views hold that human rights are protections of interests that belong to human beings "as such," their accounts of the derivation of these interests diverge.

The other feature common to these views is the belief that the nature and content of human rights at the most fundamental level can be apprehended

[33] Ibid. 296.

[34] Ibid. 286; Nussbaum, "Capabilities as Fundamental Entitlements," 49.

[35] Nussbaum, *Women and Human Development*, 76. Although John Rawls is the source of the idea of an "overlapping consensus," he does not use it to explicate the idea of human rights (§ 12).

without any reference to the role of human rights in global political life. Human rights express comprehensive requirements for political conduct that can be identified by reflecting on characteristics that human beings unavoidably have in common together with the most general features of social life. Once identified, these rights can be appealed to in the critical appraisal of international doctrine (for example, by looking for discrepancies of content). The fact that human rights must function as public, international standards is, from the perspective of such a theory, simply a historical contingency; it plays no role in conceiving of human rights or in determining which protections a doctrine of human rights should embody.

Theories sharing these features face several challenges when they are relied upon as accounts of the nature of the international human rights. First, as I have just noted, these theories do not incorporate or make use of considerations about the discursive functions of human rights within the existing practice. Griffin remarks that a human right is supposed to be "an effective, socially manageable, claim on others." This is true but only part of the story. International human rights are primarily claims on institutions and other social agents—one's own government, in the first instance, and other states and international actors, when one's own government defaults. International human rights are potential triggers of transnational protective and remedial action and should be suitable to function as justifications of it. This is part of the nature of human rights as they operate in global political discourse, and it seems almost certain to influence one's views about the basis and contents of international doctrine.

Second, these naturalistic views are not sufficiently robust to illuminate what we might call the problem of contribution. These theories put into philosophical form the beneficiary-centeredness of much popular thought about human rights. By framing the central problem as one about which interests of beneficiaries human rights should protect, these theories deflect attention from what are frequently the more difficult questions. These questions would be obvious if the discursive function of human rights as triggers of international concern were taken seriously. The most important of these concern the extent of failure or default at the domestic level required to trigger protective or remedial action by outside agents, the selection of agents from among those in a position to act which have responsibilities to do so, and, most fundamentally, the nature and demandingness of the reasons for action that pertain to these agents.

It is not that naturalistic views lack resources to respond to these questions. But the beneficiary-centeredness of the view limits what can be said. Thus Griffin, who confronts issues of contribution more directly than Nussbaum, holds that the obligation to help satisfy welfare rights rests on a general obligation (perhaps a natural duty) to help those in distress, combined with pragmatic considerations such as proximity and capacity. He also observes that this obligation must be balanced against various competing considerations (e.g. "deep commitments to particular persons, causes, careers, and institutions").[36] From some perspectives this might seem to be a precarious basis for obligations to respect and promote human rights, and conceivably a naturalistic theory could say more; however, as I shall suggest in the next section, the price might be an abandonment of the "supply side" of the idea that human rights belong to persons "as such."[37] In any case, the immediate point is that concentration on the notion that human rights are grounded on "natural" features of persons inclines towards a view of the problem of contribution as subsidiary to the more basic problem of identifying these features, whereas in fact it is both theoretically and practically distinct and typically more difficult.

A third problem is that the normative content of naturalistic theories is likely to fall short of the list of protections actually found in international human rights doctrine. As I observed earlier, in order to conform to the idea that human rights pertain to human beings "as such," naturalistic theories must proceed from more-or-less narrow foundations. In Griffin's view, for example, only protections that can be seen as conditions of normative agency count as human rights. This fact helps to explain some of the discrepancies with international doctrine that he identifies. But these discrepancies may understate the extent of the deviation of a plausible naturalistic account from international doctrine. Griffin's interpretation of the process by which human rights are derived from considerations about personhood and practicalities is generous in the number and range of human rights allowed. But it is not always clear that these rights can be justified by personhood and practicalities alone. Consider, for example, the

---

[36] Griffin, *On Human Rights*, 102–3.

[37] It does not appear that Griffin would do so; he describes a human right as "a claim of all human agents against all other human agents." Ibid. 187. It is not clear to me whether Nussbaum is committed to a similar position; she characterizes human rights as standards for institutions rather than for individual agents but she is ambiguous about the reasons why agents in a position to act when institutions fail to satisfy these standards should do so.

right to an adequate standard of living. On the personhood view, the basis of this right has to do with the material conditions necessary for effective agency.[38] But an "adequate" standard of living may require more than this. International doctrine holds that the satisfaction of economic rights is essential for "dignity." Dignity has a social dimension: it involves one's standing with others and its achievement may require a higher level of material well-being than considerations of agency alone would justify.[39] The general point applies to Nussbaum's construction of the capability view as well: if the idea of an interest's being important in all or most human lives is taken seriously, then the list of capabilities that qualify is likely to be more restricted than the account allows.[40]

This latter possibility points towards a fourth difficulty. When there are discrepancies between international doctrine and the most persuasive naturalistic theory, then the theorist must hold that there is at least *prima facie* reason to reform international doctrine. For example, Griffin holds that when a value recognized as a human right in international doctrine cannot be justified by considerations of personhood and practicalities, the value should be disqualified. Proposals for new rights should satisfy the same philosophical standard.[41] Nussbaum takes a similar view about the conclusions of the capabilities approach.[42] As any naturalistic theorist must, these writers treat the philosophical theory as authoritative for judgments about the proper content of international doctrine. The difficulty is to explain why this should be.

We have seen that, in the development of contemporary human rights doctrine, there was an explicit effort to distinguish the human rights enterprise from the enterprise of natural rights. This was necessary to preserve the international doctrine from a philosophical parochialism that would have limited its appeal and narrowed its normative scope. The same concerns should caution against the superimposition of a philosophical

---

[38] For example, discussing fair pay, Griffin writes that what human rights require is "enough material resources (e.g. pay) to satisfy the necessary conditions for normative agency." Ibid. 307 n. 28.

[39] For an argument that a theory based exclusively on personhood cannot, without more, justify the range of human rights that Griffin himself claims to defend, see John Tasioulas, "Human Rights, Universality and the Values of Personhood: Retracing Griffin's Steps," *European Journal of Philosophy* 10 (2002): 79-100.

[40] This point is stressed by Susan Moller Okin, "Poverty, Well-Being, and Gender: What Counts, Who's Heard?" *Philosophy and Public Affairs* 31 (2003), 296.

[41] Griffin, *On Human Rights*, ch. 11.

[42] See e.g. Nussbaum, "Capabilities as Fundamental Entitlements," 37.

theory that locates the authority of human rights in a received conception of human status or human functioning. It is essential to take seriously the aspiration for a normative doctrine suitable for contemporary international life and open to endorsement from a variety of reasonable points of view. It would be consonant with this aspiration to think of an idea of human status or human functioning as providing a basis for at least some of the protections embodied in international doctrine. But to rely on these conceptions to interpret the idea of a human right at the center of international doctrine in a way that constrains the doctrine's normative scope is to do more. It is this additional critical force—the use of a philosophical conception of human rights to argue for limitations of content and reform of international doctrine—that requires a justification. Why should we insist that international human rights conform to a received philosophical conception rather than interpret them, as they present themselves, as a distinct normative system constructed to play a certain special role in global political life?

11. Persons "as such" (2): the supply side

I observed earlier that the idea that human rights belong to persons "as such" can be understood from two perspectives. We have just considered the perspective of the beneficiary. I turn now, more briefly, to the perspective of the agent(s) for whom human rights are supposed to provide reasons for action—that is, the contributors or suppliers of human rights.

This is the perspective that informs H. L. A. Hart's influential distinction between "general" and "special" rights. According to Hart, special rights are those associated with promises and contracts or memberships in political societies: they arise out of "special transactions [or] some special relationship." General rights, on the other hand,

> do not arise out of any special relationship or transaction between men . . .
> [t]hey are not rights which are peculiar to those who have them but are rights
> which all men capable of choice have in the absence of those special
> conditions which give rise to special rights . . . [and they] have as correlatives
> obligations not to interfere to which everyone else is subject and not merely
> the parties to some special relationship or transaction.[43]

---

[43] H. L. A. Hart, "Are There Any Natural Rights?" *Philosophical Review* 64 (1955), 183, 188. Hart later repudiated much of the argument of this paper. Hart, *Essays in Jurisprudence and Philosophy* (Oxford: Clarendon Press, 1983), 17.

Hart suggests that the rights described by the classical natural rights theorists had these properties, but he himself identifies only one general right— "the equal right of all men to be free." His claim, to be precise, is that "there is at least" this one natural right. He does not mention human rights at all, but many theorists have thought it obvious that human rights must also be general rights.[44] If human rights apply to everybody, what else could they be?

We come to the identification of human rights and general rights in a moment. First, it is instructive to notice the connection between Hart's distinction of general and special rights and the theory of rights developed in subsequent writings. Hart describes this conception of rights as the "choice" theory and juxtaposes it to the "interest" theory found in Bentham and his successors.[45] According to the "choice" theory, what is significant about rights is that they give a person control over another person's choices. If A has a right against B, then A has authority to limit some aspect of B's freedom to choose how to act. In Hart's view, it is this freedom-limiting feature of rights that poses the problem of justification. It poses this problem because there is a background belief that everyone has a general right to be free. The "choice" theory directs attention to the situation of those against whom rights apply and asks whether there is sufficient reason to allow their freedom to be restricted. The force of the claim that the only general right is the equal right of all to be free is that, in the absence of special transactions or relationships, the only ground on which A can make a claim of right against B is that B owes A a general duty to respect A's freedom.

The significance of Hart's distinction between general and special rights is usually thought to lie in its affirmative defense of the general right to be free. But when the analysis is applied to the idea of a human right, its effect is deflationary. If human rights may be said to belong to people "as such" or "simply in virtue of their humanity" only if they are general in Hart's sense, then many of the rights recognized in international doctrine may come to seem dubious—in particular, economic and social rights. This might not be obvious if one fails to appreciate the ambiguity of the quoted phrases. The declaration holds that all persons are "born free and equal in dignity and rights" (art. 1) and that "everyone is entitled to all the rights" subsequently

[44] E.g. Jones, *Rights*, 81; Brian Orend, *Human Rights: Concept and Context* (Peterborough, Ontario: Broadview Press, 2002), 91.
[45] See e.g. H. L. A. Hart, "Legal Rights," in *Essays on Bentham* (Oxford: Clarendon Press, 1982), 162–93.

enumerated (art. 2). These passages say that everyone may claim human rights, regardless of such factors as their place in society or their society's local moral code; human rights are universal in application. However, rights that are universal in application need not be "general" in Hart's sense. The idea of a general right involves a further thesis bearing on the justification of human rights. It holds that human rights must give rise to reasons for action whose force does not depend on aspects of people's contingent transactions and relationships.

Looked at this way, in arguing that a right belongs to persons "as such" it will not be enough to observe that the right protects an interest that any reasonable person might be expected to care about; the cost of respecting the interest might be too great or there might be something else a prospective agent would rather do. So there is the further question why an agent who is in a position to respect or protect the right should do so. Here the force of "as such," interpreted in light of Hart's distinction, is more limiting. For if an agent stands in no special relationship to a claimant and is not party to any transaction that could serve as the ground of the right, there may not be sufficient reason to respect it. This might be true even when the interest protected by the right is important, because the opportunity cost of respecting the right might also be great. Consider, for example, the right to an adequate standard of living. It is not hard to say why the satisfaction of this right should matter to its beneficiary, but an informative account of the right would also have to say where the resources to satisfy it should come from and why anyone should regard themselves as having a reason to provide them. The most plausible answers to these questions may implicate considerations about people's actual or potential social relations. That is why, in the domestic case, analogous questions find their home in discourse about social justice. If we interpret the idea of a right's belonging to persons "as such" as implying that the right is a "general right," then these considerations are excluded from the outset.

Someone might wonder why we should not think that a general right to freedom would be compatible with an international counterpart to a discourse about social justice. Perhaps the structure of global relations, including the various institutions for promoting trade and development, constitutes the type of structure to which requirements analogous to those of social justice properly apply. This line of thought points towards one form of cosmopolitanism. But this is no help to the conception of human rights we are considering. This conception interprets human rights as "general" in Hart's sense, whereas whatever rights turn out to be justifiable according to the cosmopolitan theory would be "special." It is a contingent matter whether the obligations corresponding to these rights have global scope. The rights could not be said to belong to persons "as such" and so could not count as human rights.

The deflationary effect of identifying human rights with general rights should move us to ask whether we must make the identification. I shall suggest two reasons to resist it, although, strictly speaking, only the second is a reason to give it up altogether. First, the underlying view about the grounds of general rights might seem to rule out without argument the possibility that we can have general rights based on other considerations than the value of freedom. But that seems implausible. Consider, for example, Locke's claim that those with "pressing wants" and no other means to satisfy them have a "right to the surplussage" of the goods of others. Although he might have done so, Locke does not hold that such a right is grounded in considerations about the freedom of the claimant. Instead, he appeals directly to the urgency of subsistence needs to explain the basis of the impoverished person's "title to so much of another's plenty" as would satisfy them.[46] Perhaps there are reasons to resist Locke's conclusion, but the appeal to considerations of need to justify a general right does not seem inappropriate on its face. If this is correct, then Hart was wise to hold that there is "at least" one general right, for there may be more. But those who identify human rights with general rights do not often consider this possibility.

The second reason for doubt is this. Those whose conception of human rights has been influenced by Hart's distinction have assumed, almost always without argument, that any right that can properly be said to belong to human beings "as such" must be "natural" in Hart's sense. The reasons to contribute to its satisfaction derive from considerations of humanity independently of people's social relations. But it is not at all obvious that we are compelled to make such an assumption. What is clear is that human rights are supposed to be "universal" in the sense of being assertable by more-or-less anyone in the world. A right could be universal in this sense and yet the obligation to contribute to its satisfaction might not be grounded on considerations of humanity independently of people's social relations. As I

---

[46] Locke, *Two Treatises of Government*, i.42. The idea that those in extreme need have claims to the surplus of others' goods is familiar in the natural law tradition and dates at least to the glossators. See Tierney, *The Idea of Natural Rights*, 69-76.

have suggested, some human rights (in particular, some "economic" rights) might, instead, be conceived as a category of "special rights"—for example, rights that arise out of people's membership in a domestic society or their relationships as participants in a global political economy. Or they might be interpreted as political conclusions arising at an intermediate level of practical reasoning that derive from an array of ethical considerations, including those of humanity, reciprocity, and perhaps compensation. Such rights might still be claimable by more-or-less anyone in the world. Indeed, they might belong to human beings "as such" in the stronger sense that they derive from a more abstract right to be a member of a society, membership in which grounds human rights, or to participate in a global political economy whose participants have claims of justice against each other. For the moment we may regard these possibilities as speculative (I return to some of them in § 25). The immediate point is that the identification of human rights with general rights excludes these possibilities without argument and, as it appears, arbitrarily. If some international human rights cannot be accounted for as general rights in the restrictive sense proposed by Hart, why take this as a reason to prune the list of international rights? Why not say that the conception of human rights as general rights is in this respect simply inapposite?

To conclude: these reflections do not add up to a refutation of naturalistic theories. The aim is to accomplish two more modest tasks. The first is to show that the inferences drawn from naturalistic conceptions about the contents and basis of international human rights are normative positions requiring a defense; it is a mistake to regard them as analytic. The second is to raise doubt about the relevance of such an exercise to the main dilemmas about international human rights. These issues pertain to a developing political and social practice which is in important respects historically novel. It was intended from the outset to afford common grounds for political action to persons situated in cultures with differing moral traditions and political values. It was explicitly agreed by the framers, as a general matter, that international doctrine should not embrace its own justification, and in particular that it should not presuppose that human rights are "natural." It is a mistake to identify the objects of interest with objects that originate in one or another theoretical project whose conception and motivation differ from those of the contemporary practice.

4

Agreement Theories

WHEREAS naturalistic theories typically arise from reflection about what is common in the nature and circumstances of human life, the theories to which we turn now arise more often from reflection about legal and social diversity. These theories conceptualize human rights as standards that are or might be objects of agreement among members of cultures whose moral and political values are in various respects dissimilar. In one formulation, they are "the expression of a set of important overlapping moral expectations to which different cultures hold themselves and others accountable."[1] In another, they are "commonalities [among] the ideals of all cultures."[2] "Agreement conceptions" tend to be found more often in social scientific than in philosophical discussions of human rights (though the basic idea is familiar in political philosophy). Their influence is broader, however, because they represent a natural interpretation of the thought that human rights are matters of common concern.

Like the traditional ideas of the *jus gentium* and the *jus naturale*, the idea of human rights as objects of an intercultural agreement may seem to be a close cousin of naturalistic conceptions. If, for example, we are to think of human rights as protections of interests shared by all human beings in virtue of common aspects of their natures, then we should hardly be surprised if the importance of these values were recognized and affirmed in all social moral codes, or at least in all that gain substantial numbers of adherents. But the conflation of naturalistic and agreement conceptions is to be resisted: they express fundamentally different views about the normative authority of

[1] Sumner B. Twiss, "A Constructive Framework for Discussing Confucianism and Human Rights," in *Confucianism and Human Rights*, ed. W. Theodore de Bary and Tu Weiming (New York: Columbia University Press, 1998), 31.

[2] Alison Dundes Renteln, *International Human Rights: Universalism Versus Relativism* (Newbury Park, CA: Sage, 1990), 139. Earlier, Renteln describes human rights as "cross-cultural universals" that can be shown to be "shared by all cultures in the world" (p. 71).

human rights. Naturalistic theories appeal to what is taken to be an order of moral values whose claim on us does not depend on their acceptance in any particular culture or society, or *a fortiori* in international society. The human rights of international doctrine are interpreted as an attempt to embody in international legal and political practice the values of this independent normative order, which is the source of their (moral) authority. By contrast, according to agreement conceptions, the fact that human rights are in some way common to the moral codes of the world's societies is itself the source of their authority. It is possible, of course, that the normative requirements of the best-justified naturalistic theory and the best-justified agreement theory might coincide. But any such coincidence would be a contingent matter requiring an explanation.

Like naturalistic views, agreement conceptions can lead to skepticism about international human rights. Nobody who takes seriously the contents of the main international human rights instruments could regard them as stating a doctrine that is compatible with all of the world's major moral codes as these are understood and practiced by many of their adherents. This is often observed in connection with the human rights of women and the rights of the child, but the point is not limited to these protections. Still less can we regard international doctrine as somehow actually embodied in existing social moralities. Human rights doctrine as formulated in the leading international instruments does not set forth a culturally or politically ecumenical or syncretistic position. For this reason, adherents of agreement views will feel pressure to distinguish between genuine human rights which fall within the area of actual or potential overlap and the values that fall outside. Here, as before, the question is why we should adopt the under-lying idea as a basis for conceiving of human rights.

12. "Common core" and "overlapping consensus"

The notion that human rights express an intercultural agreement might be understood in several ways. I shall distinguish two of these here, which I refer to as the "common core" and "overlapping consensus" ideas. Later I come to a third idea, which I refer to as "progressive convergence." My aim is to describe these ideas and to inspect the reasons why people have been attracted to them as a basis for conceiving of human rights.

One possibility is suggested by Michael Walzer's distinction between "thin" and "thick" moralities. He speculates that a comparison of social-moral codes might produce "a set of standards to which all societies can be held—negative injunctions, most likely, rules against murder, deceit, torture, oppression, and tyranny." These standards would constitute "the moral minimum."[3] Although Walzer does not make the connection, this idea lends itself to a conception of human rights. As R. J. Vincent writes, on such a view human rights would constitute a "core of basic rights that is common to all cultures despite their apparently divergent theories." They would be a "lowest common denominator."[4]

The metaphor of a "common core" is usually presented as an account of the nature of human rights, but it has obvious implications for the normative questions of their content and scope. For example, rights requiring democratic political forms, religious toleration, legal equality for women, and free choice of a marriage partner would be excluded because, as an empirical matter, these protections are not found in all of the world's main moral systems.[5] Other rights might be excluded if they were understood to generate certain kinds of duties; if, for example, the right to a high standard of physical and mental health were thought to imply that every society has an obligation to ensure the accessibility of health care for all, then the existence of disagreement about the extent of distributive responsibilities outside of families or local communities might exclude this right as well.[6] Adopting a common-core idea of human rights would have the normative consequence of excluding a substantial part of the content of contemporary human rights doctrine.

One might therefore be encouraged to think that this interpretation of agreement relies excessively on the metaphor of a "core" of rights which are common to the world's main conventional moralities. Perhaps this is too restrictive—after all, the idea of a right is itself culturally specific. So one

---

[3] Michael Walzer, *Thick and Thin: Moral Argument at Home and Abroad* (Notre Dame, IN: University of Notre Dame Press, 1994), 9-10.

[4] R. J. Vincent, *Human Rights and International Relations* (Cambridge: Cambridge University Press, 1986), 48-9. This is Vincent's description of a position that he does not himself endorse.

[5] For example, writing about female genital cutting, Renteln observes that "The fact that many women in the society perpetuate the custom is one which must be squarely faced. The presumption of universality cannot alter the reality that the practice is accepted as moral by members of the culture." *International Human Rights*, 58.

[6] For this example, see Walzer, *Thick and Thin*, 28-9.

might shift to a more elaborate conception which sees human rights as
falling within an "overlapping consensus" of political moralities. Such a
view would have two essential elements. The first is a distinction between
human rights, conceived as a set of common global norms adopted for
certain political purposes, and the diverse array of moral, philosophical, and
religious doctrines or outlooks found among the world's cultures. The
second is the hypothesis that, given an understanding of the purposes of
the global norms, it would be reasonable for adherents of any culture to
accept these norms on the basis of their own moral, philosophical, and
religious doctrines. On such a view, we need not conceive of "universal"
human rights as part of a common core in the sense of being actually
recognized by or contained in all conventional moralities; we think of
them, instead, as norms for global political life reachable from a variety of
possibly incompatible foundational positions.[7]

To avoid misunderstanding, we should note that, although John Rawls is
the source of the idea of an overlapping consensus, he does not use this idea
to describe human rights; the thought that human rights exist within an
"overlapping consensus" is the contribution of other writers.[8] (We turn to
Rawls's own view about the nature of human rights in the next chapter.)
Moreover, as it is often set forth, this thought employs the idea of an
"overlapping consensus" in a way that differs from that found in Rawls's
account of justice in domestic societies. There are at least two important
differences. First, Rawls describes a political conception of justice as attract-
ing the support of *reasonable* "comprehensive doctrines," not necessarily of
all such doctrines that occur in a society. The thought about human rights
with which we are concerned here, however, is not similarly qualified; the
idea is that human rights should be seen as supported by an overlapping
consensus of all actually existing "comprehensive doctrines," or anyway of
all that gain substantial numbers of adherents and persist over time. A second
and more fundamental difference is that, in Rawls's account, overlapping
consensus does not play a straightforward justificatory role. The fact that

---

[7] For example, Rex Martin describes human rights as principles that "would be regarded as
reasonable by persons at different times or in different cultures. And such principles, again cross-
culturally, would be thought to have connection . . . with a fairly wide range of differing conventional moralities." *A System of Rights* (Oxford: Clarendon Press, 1993), 75.

[8] E.g. Martha C. Nussbaum, "Human Rights Theory: Capabilities and Human Rights,"
Fordham Law Review 66 (1997), 286; and Charles Taylor, "Conditions of an Unforced Consensus
on Human Rights," in *The East Asian Challenge for Human Rights*, ed. Joanne R. Bauer and Daniel
A. Bell (Cambridge: Cambridge University Press, 1999), 124.

principles of justice lie within an overlapping consensus is not, in itself, a reason to accept them. Relatedly, the contours of a possible overlapping consensus do not determine the content of acceptable principles. In Rawls's account, overlapping consensus is meant to solve a different problem—that of the stability of a political conception of justice in a well-ordered, liberal-democratic state.[9] By contrast, we are interested here in the idea that the content of a possible overlapping consensus among religious and moral doctrines both determines and lends authority to a doctrine of human rights. This idea has evidently been widely entertained and it is worthy of consideration, but it should be remembered that it is not Rawls's idea.

What might we anticipate about the scope of human rights, under this conception? Probably it would be more permissive than the "common-core" idea, but it would still be more restrictive than present international doctrine. To be certain of this, of course, we would need a detailed account of the way in which agreement is constrained by commitment to various cultures' moral codes. We will consider some difficulties below. For the moment, let us take it as a necessary component of any such account that it would not be reasonable to expect a member of a culture to agree to a global norm if compliance with it was incompatible with widely accepted principles of conduct within the culture. If this is right, then, to return to our earlier examples, it seems unlikely that an "overlapping consensus" view would be more successful than a common-core view in accommodating such evidently controversial rights as those to freedom of religious practice, democratic political institutions, or the legal equality of women. This, of course, would not necessarily be an objection to agreement theories, if we had independent reasons for accepting such a theory as an authoritative account of international human rights. But it is not clear that we do.

13. The appeal of agreement conceptions

Notwithstanding the normative shortfall, many people have been attracted to an agreement conception of human rights. Others, while not adopting such a view of the nature of human rights, have held as a normative matter that values that cannot be brought within the scope of a possible intercultural

---

[9] John Rawls, *Political Liberalism* (New York: Columbia University Press, 1996), lecture IV.

agreement should be excluded from the catalog of internationally recognized human rights.[10] The question I wish to raise concerns the appeal of agreement conceptions whether held as views about the nature of human rights or as elements of a view about the determinants of their normative content. Why would anybody find such a conception attractive?

I ask this question because there is an obvious *prima facie* reason to reject views of this kind. Human rights are supposed to be critical standards: they are supposed to provide a basis for criticizing existing institutions and conventional beliefs and justifying efforts to change or revise them. Confining the content of human rights doctrine to norms that either are or could be agreed to among the world's moral cultures threatens to deprive human rights of their critical edge. It is true, of course, that governments may not always conform to the political values of their own cultures, so there is likely to be room for criticism even if human rights are limited to those to which all cultures can agree. But this only pushes the problem back a step. Consider an extreme but not a novel example. Suppose there was a society with a racist political culture in which the prevalent moral code approved of the forced sterilization of members of a racial minority as a means of population control. If we accepted an agreement conception, we would have to delete the right against genocide from the catalog of genuine human rights because it would be neither part of nor consistent with the racist conception and would therefore fall outside of a possible intercultural agreement. But surely we would resist doing so; we would say that the racist society's moral code is deficient in its failure to recognize the evil of genocide and that this failure is irrelevant to the question whether there is a human right against it. Indeed, it seems that a central purpose of human rights is to frame and enable just such a criticism. A theory that cannot make sense of this, the objection holds, cannot be correct. The ground of our belief that there is a human right against genocide has to do, not with the fact that people agree that it is so, but rather with the nature and consequences of genocide itself. Agreement theories seem to get the relationship between agreement and justification backwards.

Why, then, would anybody be attracted to the thought that human rights should be conceived of as objects of intercultural agreement? Here is one

---

[10] E.g. Michael Ignatieff, *Human Rights as Politics and Idolatry* (Princeton, NJ: Princeton University Press, 2001), 56.

reason, which I elaborate from some remarks of Bernard Williams.[11] Let us say that a regime is legitimate if most of its people obey the law from a belief that they are obligated to do so rather than (only) from fear of punishment. In this minimal way, a legitimate regime might be said to be a scheme of social cooperation rather than merely a system of coordinated behavior maintained by force.[12] We know from historical experience that many different kinds of regime can be legitimate in this way. Still, there may be certain conditions that any regime must satisfy in order to be considered sufficiently legitimate by its own people to motivate their willing compliance with its laws. Williams gives several examples: the regime must not torture or execute its people, it must refrain from widespread surveillance, it must respect religious freedom. Now let us say that public norms that require regimes to abstain from these forms of conduct are human rights: they state minimum conditions for the legitimation of a political regime, which is to say that they distinguish schemes of social cooperation from coercively maintained systems of coordination. Agreement across a range of relatively stable societies serves to confirm that the rights we identify as "human" are, in fact, conditions for legitimation, and that our confidence that they have this status is not distorted by our experience living in one rather than another kind of society with one rather than other kinds of institutions.[13]

As a matter of first impression, views of this general kind have some attractive features. They are tolerant of variations in beliefs about political legitimacy related to cultural and perhaps religious differences, and they embody an appealing modesty about the capacity of outsiders to grasp and understand the normative beliefs of members of cultures with which they are unfamiliar. Still, this kind of view does not provide much support for an agreement theory of human rights. Recall that agreement theories treat the fact or prospect of intercultural agreement as both a criterion for identifying authentic human rights and as the basis of an account of their normativity.

---

[11] Bernard Williams, "Human Rights and Relativism," in *In the Beginning Was the Deed* (Princeton, NJ: Princeton University Press, 2006), 62-4. I am grateful to Mathias Risse for emphasizing the appeal of this kind of view.

[12] For the contrast of coordination and social cooperation, see John Rawls, *Justice as Fairness: A Restatement* (Cambridge, MA: Harvard University Press, 2001), 6.

[13] With respect to the "most basic human rights," Williams quotes with approval the Vincentian Canon, "*quod ubique, quod semper, quod ab omnibus creditum est*" (that which has been believed everywhere, always, by all people). "Human Rights and Relativism," 63 (he reverses the first and second phrases). In the application of this principle in Roman Catholic Church doctrine, the extension of "*ab omnibus*" has been problematic. It is no less so in connection with human rights.

Now, according to the conditions-for-legitimation view, there is a fact of the matter about the nature of these conditions. The significance of agreement is to help identify the conditions or confirm hypotheses about them otherwise derived. It does not, by itself, explain either the authority of human rights or their proper content: questions about these matters must be referred back to the premise of the view, which identifies human rights with conditions of legitimation.

Perhaps, however, the significance of agreement is to be found, not at the level of identifying particular human rights, but, instead, at the more basic level of describing their general character. Williams writes that "We have a good idea of what human rights are."[14] Is there agreement that human rights are minimum conditions for legitimation? An answer depends on how we understand the scope of such an agreement. Who are the "we" who agree about the nature of human rights? The reference might be to philosophers interested in human rights, participants in the international human rights enterprise or, perhaps, those who subscribe to some widely held folk view of human rights. But it seems clear that none of these interpretations of the scope of agreement ratifies the conditions-for-legitimation view. The view is incompatible with various other philosophical views on offer (consider, for example, the positions described in the last chapter); it would rule out much of contemporary international doctrine as overreaching (as Williams's criticism of "so-called positive rights" illustrates); and if, indeed, the view resembles a folk conception of human rights, it is only one among several conflicting conceptions. It does not appear that the premise of the view can plausibly be said to be the object of a sufficiently wide agreement to have normative standing. This, of course, does not exclude the possibility that there are substantive moral considerations that argue for the conditions-for-legitimation view. All I mean to say here is that, whatever these considerations might be, they do not consist in an appeal to the fact or prospect of agreement, either about the contents of human rights or about their general character and aims.[15]

A different explanation of the appeal of an agreement conception is rooted in pragmatic considerations. As Abdullahi An-Na'im argues, international human rights doctrine must be widely regarded as acceptable if it is to elicit the willing support of governments and other agents. "[U]nless

---

[14] Ibid. 62.

[15] I leave aside the question whether Williams's examples state conditions that can plausibly be held to have the universality that this account of legitimation requires.

people accept these rights as binding upon themselves from their own cultural, religious and/or philosophical point of view, they will neither voluntarily comply in practice, nor require their government to respect and promote human rights in the official functioning of the State."[16] If human rights are objects of intercultural agreement, then probably most people will, in fact, accept them as binding "from their own . . . point of view." This fact makes for stability of the practice. On the other hand, if human rights cannot be regarded as protecting values within the scope of a possible agreement, then the practice is unlikely to gain the commitment and support it needs to be practically effective.[17]

This reasoning asserts a relationship between broad acceptance and political effectiveness. On reflection, however, it is hardly clear that the relationship is straightforward. Let us accept for the sake of argument that there is a core of human rights that can properly be regarded as objects of intercultural agreement. Now imagine two alternative human rights regimes, one in which the public human rights doctrine is limited to this core of rights and the other in which the public doctrine is more extensive (perhaps it resembles human rights doctrine as we find it today). The effectiveness of a human rights regime is a matter of its success in improving respect for human rights. Confining ourselves for purposes of comparison to rights in the core, why should we expect that respect for *these* rights would be greater in the first imagined regime than in the second? Perhaps one conjectures that the widespread public perception that human rights are matters of intercultural agreement would provide a motivation to defend human rights. But this seems implausible; why should the perception of agreement, rather than a recognition of the importance of the interests protected by human rights, motivate commitment? It is worth observing that the main reasons for the ineffectiveness of the core elements of the human rights system today do not seem to be related to a lack of agreement about the contents of human rights. For example, the international community has been notably reluctant to act decisively where genocide has been an imminent threat, but this failure does not appear to be a consequence of any more-or-less general suspicion that human rights

[16] Abdullahi A. An-Na'im, "Universality of Human Rights: An Islamic Perspective," in *Japan and International Law: Past, Present and Future,* ed. Nisuke Ando (The Hague: Kluwer Law International, 1999), 315.

[17] For similar views, see Michael Ignatieff, *Human Rights as Politics and Idolatry,* 55–6; and Peter Jones, "Human Rights and Diverse Cultures," in *Human Rights and Global Diversity,* ed. Simon Caney and Peter Jones (London: Frank Cass, 2001), 30.

doctrine exceeds what can reasonably be regarded as falling within an intercultural agreement. The absence of political will needs a different explanation. What is clear is that wide acceptance is not a sufficient condition for effectiveness.

Of course, it might at least be necessary. But this does not seem to be true either. Consider the case of the Helsinki Declaration (1975), by which the Soviet Union exchanged international recognition of the postwar boundaries in Eastern Europe for a commitment to respect human rights. At the time the declaration was agreed, it could not have been said that there was broad intercultural agreement (particularly not in the Soviet Union) about the content and importance of such human rights as those to freedom of religion, freedom of association, and the political liberties. Yet (to the surprise of its drafters) the human rights provisions of the declaration energized and legitimized political dissent in the Eastern bloc and contributed to the eventual dissolution of Soviet authority.[18] It may be precisely when the importance of particular rights is a matter of controversy within a culture that their embodiment in the practice's public doctrine can be politically consequential.

Even if it were true that a lack of agreement about the content of human rights is a threat to the effectiveness of the regime, confining the content of human rights doctrine to the objects of a possible intercultural agreement, taking cultures as they are, is not the only conceivable remedy. Social moral codes are capable of change in response to their own internal critical dynamics and to forces in the surrounding social, economic, and cultural environment. An-Na'im recognizes this when he describes human rights "as a *project* to be pursued everywhere."[19] In his view, an "overlapping consensus" about human rights might be achieved, not only through a modification of the content of human rights doctrine, but also as a result of progressive change within the world's moral cultures—through "the socialization of children and development of the social and political institutions in accordance with the human rights ethos."[20] If change of this kind is a genuine historical possibility, then one can acknowledge that intercultural agreement about human rights is desirable because it improves compliance without also accepting that the content of a doctrine of human rights

---

[18] Daniel C. Thomas, *The Helsinki Effect* (Princeton, NJ: Princeton University Press, 2001), ch. 5.

[19] An-Na'im, "Universality of Human Rights: An Islamic Perspective," 318 (emphasis in original).

[20] Ibid. 314-15.

should be confined to what can be agreed to among the world's moral cultures as we find them. This fact points toward a revision of the agreement idea to which I turn in the following section. For the moment, the conclusion is that pragmatic concerns do not offer strong reasons for adopting an agreement conception in either of the forms discussed thus far.

A third and more substantial reason for the attractiveness of agreement conceptions is best framed as a reaction to naturalistic theories. Because these theories typically proceed from a normative conception of human need or human good they can give rise to the anxiety that human rights are in one or another way parochial—an attempt to universalize values originating in some cultures but not shared by others. The canonical statement of this anxiety is found in the American Anthropological Association's Executive Board Statement on Human Rights of 1947. The statement asked how the Universal Declaration of Human Rights, which was then still a proposal, could "be applicable to all human beings, and not be a statement of rights conceived only in terms of the values prevalent in the countries of Western Europe and America."[21] This question was taken to present a problem because the "standards and values" that apply to a culture "are relative to the culture from which they derive." A justifiable conception of "worldwide standards of freedom and justice" should (therefore?) be based on "the right of men to live in terms of their own traditions."[22]

The statement does not actually propose an agreement conception of human rights, but its endorsement of the idea that respect for human freedom requires deference to culturally specific forms of value suggests the following line of thought. We begin by recognizing the interference-justifying role of human rights. Interference to protect people within a

[21] American Anthropological Association, Executive Board, "Statement on Human Rights," *American Anthropologist*, NS 49 (1947), 539. Mark Goodale writes that, with this statement, "anthropology got off on the wrong foot with human rights" ("Ethical Theory as Social Practice," *American Anthropologist* 108 (2006), 25). Anthropologists have since embraced human rights as both subject and cause, although not without ambiguity. According to the association's recent "Declaration on Anthropology and Human Rights," the association "founds its approach [to human rights] on anthropological principles of respect for concrete human differences, both collective and individual, rather than the abstract legal uniformity of Western tradition. In practical terms, however, its working definition builds on the Universal Declaration of Human Rights (UDHR)" and the main human rights covenants and conventions. See American Anthropological Association, Committee on Human Rights, "Declaration on Anthropology and Human Rights" [1999], http://www.aaanet.org/stmts/humanrts.htm (consulted September 2, 2008).
[22] American Anthropological Association, Executive Board, "Statement on Human Rights," 542, 543.

society against that society's own government might seem to be paternalistic
in the sense that it would limit the liberty of those whose society was
interfered in, for their own ostensible good. Ordinarily we regard paternalistic interferences with people's liberties as objectionable: perhaps as an
insult to their capacity for autonomous choice. Paternalistic interference is
justifiable only under special circumstances; for example, when the subjects
of the interference are unable to choose for themselves and when there is
good reason to believe that they would authorize the interference if they
were in a position to do so.[23] If the human rights at stake in an interference
were the actual or possible objects of an agreement that embraces the society
in question, then the aims of the interference could be seen as ones that
those affected, themselves, would accept if they were in a position to bring
their own moral beliefs to bear on the matter at hand. Confining human
rights to the contents of a possible intercultural agreement seems to offer the
best defense against the objection that interference to defend human rights is
unacceptably paternalistic.

I suspect that something like this is the most common reason for adopting
an agreement conception of human rights. But there are two difficulties.
First, the paradigmatic case of paternalistic interference is one in which an
individual's liberty is limited on the grounds that the limitation is good for
that person. The person whose liberty is limited is the person whose good
the interference is supposed to advance. However, in most cases of interest,
human rights-based interferences are different: they involve limiting some
people's liberty for the sake of others. These interferences are more accurately seen as attempts to prevent harm or secure a benefit for some agents
who are threatened by the actions or omissions of others—they are protective, not paternalistic.[24] If most cases of human rights-based interference
are not cases of paternalism, they are, *a fortiori*, not cases of unjustified
paternalism.

It might be thought that, notwithstanding the divergence from paradigmatic cases of paternalism, human rights-based interferences which are not

---

[23] J. S. Mill took such a view in *On Liberty* [1859], in *Essays on Politics and Society I [Collected
Works of John Stuart Mill*, xviii], ed. J. M. Robson (Toronto: University of Toronto Press, 1977),
esp. ch. 3. For a discussion, see Gerald Dworkin, "Paternalism," *Monist* 56 (1972), 64-84.

[24] This is true of most such interferences, but not all. For example, under some circumstances
interference to prevent a young girl from consenting to some form of genital cutting might be
genuinely paternalistic. But reflection about the circumstances under which this would be true
only illustrates how unusual it is, considered as a case of interference to protect human rights.

justifiable in terms of values accepted or acceptable within the culture where the interference takes place would be open to an analogous objection. A paternalistic interference may be objectionable if there is insufficient reason to believe its beneficiary would choose to avoid the harm or enjoy the benefit the interference is aimed to prevent or secure. This might be the case if the beneficiary does not regard the harm as harm or the benefit as benefit, or if the beneficiary does not regard avoiding the harm or securing the benefit as very important. So, the thought continues, we avoid an analogous objection to protective interferences by restricting human rights to values accepted or acceptable within every culture.

This brings us to a second difficulty. The idea of an intercultural agreement relies on the possibility of identifying a reasonably stable and integrated structure of moral beliefs shared among the members of each society which is a party to the agreement.[25] (The belief structures differ, of course, across societies.) Whether one adopts a "common core" or an "overlapping consensus" conception of intercultural agreement, it is these structures of beliefs that explain the content of the agreement, and it is the fact that they are widely shared in their respective societies that explains the agreement's authority. It is critical to any such view that these systems of belief form reasonably stable and integrated structures. If a structure is internally unintegrated—for example, if it contains inconsistent or incompatible principles, or includes abstract principles that do not cohere with more concrete precepts—then any agreement derived from it risks instability. This is because the content of the agreement must attach to the belief structure of the society at some point, and if the belief structure is unintegrated, it is possible that attachment at one point would generate a different agreement than attachment at another. There may be no unique "common core," no single "overlapping consensus" of the world's social moralities. This is a problem because, as an empirical matter, it seems clear that the picture of the world as composed of integrated moral cultures is highly idealized; whatever integration is discovered in social moralities is more likely to have been imposed by a philosophical or social scientific onlooker than actually manifested in the beliefs of individual members of the culture. This picture also idealizes by imagining that cultures are morally univocal. But it seems obvious that·individuals are likely to disagree, either in detail or in principle,

---

[25] For simplicity I assume that "culture" and "society" are coextensive. This, of course, is often not true.

about various elements of the moral systems they share—for example, about the kinds of actions that are allowed or prohibited, about the importance of various types of value that might be sought in action, or about the types and weights of considerations that count as excuses.[26] (Perhaps it would be more realistic to disaggregate the idea of a "moral culture" into the philosophical, moral, or spiritual worldviews of a society's constituent groups. But this will not avoid the problem, because these worldviews are likely to exhibit analogous forms of internal disagreement.)

These observations show that the idea of an intercultural agreement is more complex than is often recognized. Under some empirical assumptions it may be indeterminate. In practice, assertions about the content of such an agreement are likely to refer to something like the predominant understanding within each culture of its conventional morality, or perhaps the understanding accepted by the majority of its conscientious, well-informed members. It is possible that some such construction can rescue the idea of an intercultural agreement on human rights from the threat of indeterminacy, but there is a price. Once it is recognized that the same structure of beliefs may not be shared throughout a culture and that the (idealized) structure attributed to the majority may exhibit greater integration than actually exists, it is no longer clear that the supposed agreement can bear the weight. What made the idea attractive in the first place was the thought that if the aims of interference in defense of human rights were restricted to those that advance or protect values that everybody shares, then the danger that those interfered with would be unjustifiably constrained by the interference would be minimized: it would be reasonable to expect that the intended beneficiaries would approve of the interference if they were in a position to choose. But if individual cultures are unlikely to be univocal about their own systems of moral belief then this expectation would no longer be reasonable.

This is important because, in fact, when we are concerned about a violation of human rights in another society we are typically confronted by disagreement about the justification of the behavior that concerns us.[27] The victims of what we perceive as a violation may interpret the local

---

[26] For a discussion, see Michele M. Moody-Adams, *Fieldwork in Familiar Places: Morality, Culture, and Philosophy* (Cambridge, MA: Harvard University Press, 1997), 43–56.

[27] The point has often been noted, e.g. by T. M. Scanlon, "Human Rights as a Neutral Concern," in *The Difficulty of Tolerance: Essays in Political Philosophy* (Cambridge: Cambridge University Press, 2003), 119.

morality differently from their oppressors or they may adhere to a different set of moral beliefs altogether. Either way, the question whether the putative violation is harmful to its victims by their own lights cannot be settled by considering whether it would be regarded as harmful under the moral beliefs that prevail in the culture. We cannot assume that by restricting human rights to those values falling within an intercultural agreement, where each culture's position is defined by the predominant understanding within the culture, we will have protected against the danger of imposing conceptions of harm and benefit on individuals which they do not themselves accept.

To say this is to reassert the *prima facie* reservation about agreement conceptions. As our example of the genocidal society illustrates, whether a standard should be accepted as a ground of action is not determined by asking whether the standard is actually a part of, or implied by, existing conventional moralities. Actual agreement is, in general, too strong a condition to impose on critical standards, and therefore on human rights. It will not do to reply that agreement is still required, not as a condition of the normative soundness of human rights doctrine but rather as a condition of the empirical stability of the human rights regime. For, as we have seen, this argument depends on speculative empirical premises and its conclusion is most likely overstated. Moreover, if the significance of agreement were taken to be strategic rather than, as we might say, constitutive, then the distinctive reply of agreement theories to the problem of the normative authority of human rights will have been lost. The extent of agreement would become one among several factors to be taken into account in fashioning an effective human rights system rather than the reason, or part of the reason, for compliance with it. Insofar as our interest is in the nature of human rights, the retreat to a strategic view of the significance of agreement does not help.

There is one further virtue that might be claimed for a doctrine of human rights that can be seen as falling within an intercultural agreement. This is that such a doctrine expresses a reasonable toleration of the moral diversity found among the world's cultures. This thought is tempting for reasons associated with the analogy of persons and societies. I do not believe, in the end, that it generates a plausible view of the nature of human rights or a coherent reason to restrict the contents of the doctrine to values on which there is intercultural agreement. But the subject of international toleration is vexed and requires a separate discussion. We come to it later (§ 23).

14. Progressive convergence

Those attracted to agreement theories face a dilemma. On the one hand, human rights are supposed to provide reasons for action to members of every culture to which human rights apply. The idea of an agreement is a natural interpretation of this aspiration. On the other hand, taken as a whole, international human rights doctrine cannot be seen as actually shared among the world's main political-moral cultures nor, therefore, as the object of an agreement. Moreover, the parts of human rights doctrine that fall outside such an agreement include some elements (e.g. freedom of religious practice, the right against discrimination on grounds of sex) one might regard as too important to be abandoned. So it seems that one must either give up the conception of human rights as objects of intercultural agreement or adopt as genuine human rights a subset of those recognized in international doctrine that will seem objectionably limited.

One response to this dilemma is to envision an intercultural agreement as arising, not from the actual contents of existing moral cultures, but instead from the contents of these cultures as they might develop or evolve under pressures for adaptive reinterpretation. It is difficult to state this idea clearly. Human rights would still be conceived as falling within an "overlapping consensus" but the boundaries of the consensus would not be set by the philosophical and moral beliefs that actually prevail in the world's major cultures—presuming this idea has a determinate content—but rather by the best available elaboration of the basic normative materials of these cultures for the circumstances of modern life. To distinguish this idea from that of an overlapping consensus reached from cultural moral codes as they actually exist, I shall refer to it as "progressive convergence."

Several writers have described something like this form of the agreement idea. For example, Charles Taylor imagines an "unforced consensus" (or "convergence") on human rights norms. He does not say that such a consensus exists at present, even implicitly—it is not, so to speak, "there" to be discovered. But there are various ways a consensus might develop. These include a process of evolution or reform within moral cultures that would replace the elements that function as obstacles to agreement to human rights norms with revised understandings of these elements which are supportive. Taylor gives the example of reform Theravada Buddhism in Thailand with its commitment to norms of *ahimsa* (nonviolence) and local control.[28] Similarly, in an analysis of areas of conflict between trad-itional Islamic law and human rights, An-Na'im describes a method of "evolutionary interpretation" of the religious sources which, he argues, could produce political principles compatible with most of international human rights doctrine. A distinctive feature of this method is the role it assigns to historical exigencies in explaining why religious texts that were once interpreted as expressing certain requirements and prohibitions might now be interpreted differently.[29] Finally, in an account of what he calls "justificatory minimalism," Joshua Cohen holds that it would be desirable for human rights norms to be justifiable from within all of the world's main ethical traditions, but notes that for this to be true, these traditions might "require fresh elaboration . . . by their proponents—where it is understood that the point of a fresh elaboration is not simply to fit the tradition to the demands of the world, but to provide that tradition with its most compel-ling statement."[30] He mentions as an illustration the reinterpretation of Roman Catholic Church doctrine at the time of the Second Vatican Council (1962-5) that produced an acceptance of religious toleration as a way of respecting human dignity. As Cohen observes, this reinterpretation was not seen as an accommodation to the practical needs of the Church; instead, it was presented as necessary to bring the Church's moral teaching into conformity with "fundamental truths about the human person that modern 'cultural and political experience' had made manifest."[31]

With these views in mind, although without claiming fidelity to their details, we might say that human rights lie within a "progressive convergence"

---

[28] Taylor, "Conditions of an Unforced Consensus on Human Rights," 124, 133-7. On Theravada Buddhism and human rights, compare Simon Caney, "Human Rights, Compatibility and Diverse Cultures," in *Human Rights and Global Diversity*, ed. Simon Caney and Peter Jones (London: Frank Cass, 2001), 64-70.

[29] Abdullahi A. An-Na'im, *Toward an Islamic Reformation: Civil Liberties, Human Rights, and International Law* (Syracuse, NY: Syracuse University Press, 1990), 179. See also the discussion of Islam and human rights in An-Na'im, *Islam and the Secular State: Negotiating the Future of Shari'a* (Cambridge, MA: Harvard University Press, 2008), 110-25.

[30] Joshua Cohen, "Minimalism about Human Rights," *Journal of Political Philosophy* 12 (2004), 201, 202. Cohen holds that human rights should be justifiable from within various moral traditions, but he does not say that the content of human rights is settled by considering the content of these traditions. In his view the formulation of a doctrine of human rights is "an independent normative enterprise" (p. 200). The requirement that the content of the doctrine be reachable from the best elaboration of each tradition should be understood as internal to this enterprise.

[31] Ibid. 202. Cohen also discusses what a "fresh elaboration" of some Confucian and Islamic ideas might be like, if these ideas were to lend support to certain aspects of a doctrine of human rights (203-10).

of some range of culturally embodied moral and spiritual worldviews if they can be justified from within each worldview by means of an "evolutionary interpretation" or "fresh elaboration" of that worldview. I comment on two related aspects of this idea: its meaning and its significance for a theory human rights.

How should we understand the idea of "progressive convergence?" The aspiration is to demonstrate how elements of the doctrine of human rights could bear what I shall call a "justificatory relationship" to an array of philosophical, moral, and spiritual worldviews actually found in the world. This relationship, however, is distinct from the relationships of containment-within and inferability-from that characterize the common-core and overlapping-consensus conceptions of agreement. Perhaps the most accurate metaphor is "reachability from:" human rights should be "reachable from" each worldview even if, as these are presently understood by (at least some of) their adherents, it could not be said that human rights are "contained within" or "inferable from" them.

An initial question is whether it can make any sense to hold that human rights might be "reachable from" a worldview if they are not either explicit in it or consequences of it as the worldview is presently understood by those whose worldview it is. To make clear why the question is difficult, we must say more about how the idea of "reachability from" differs from that of an overlapping consensus. We should recall that those who hold that human rights fall within an "overlapping consensus" of some set of worldviews need not be understood to assert that all the worldviews in the set actually contain human rights. They need not even hold that these worldviews all contain the *idea* of a human right. All they need to claim is that reasonable persons who adhere to these various worldviews would each have reasons, rooted in their own worldview as they understand it, to accept the same doctrine of human rights. Now of course this is not to say that reasonable persons who adhere to various worldviews do, in fact, accept the same doctrine of human rights, or even that they are committed to do so, on pain of logical error, given all their other beliefs. Someone who, as a result of accepting a false empirical belief, declines to accept a doctrine of human rights that they would have reason to accept if they had only true empirical beliefs, still has a reason to accept it. An analogy from the realm of practical reasoning is Bernard Williams's thought that one has a bona fide reason to act only if the reason can be reached by a "sound deliberative route" from one's actual motivational set.[32] We might say that the doctrine of human rights falls within an overlapping consensus of some set of worldviews if a reasonable person who accepted any of these worldviews could arrive at reasons to accept the doctrine by a "sound deliberative route" from the authoritative normative propositions of that worldview.

In his discussion of the idea of a "sound deliberative route," Williams distinguishes between reasonings and beliefs of fact, on the one hand, and prudential and moral considerations, on the other. Roughly speaking, a person's deliberative route to a practical conclusion can be said to be unsound if acceptance of the conclusion depends on fallacious reasonings or false beliefs of fact. It cannot be said to be unsound if it depends on accepting prudential or moral beliefs that an observer believes to be defective unless these, in turn, depend on fallacious reasonings or false beliefs.[33] Otherwise the internalism of the view would be lost. The distinction illuminates the difference between the ideas of "reachability from" and overlapping consensus. The advocate of an overlapping consensus view holds that the doctrine of human rights can be reached by a "sound deliberative route" from the authoritative normative propositions of each of some set of worldviews. The advocate of a progressive convergence view holds that the doctrine of human rights may be "reachable from" (that is, have a justificatory relationship to) each of some set of worldviews even if it is not reachable by a "sound deliberative route" from the authoritative normative propositions of these worldviews as these are now understood by well-informed and reasonable persons who accept them. The problem is to say how this can be true.

The idea seems to be that human rights are "reachable from" a worldview if there is some revisionist understanding of the worldview, not now accepted by some of its adherents, that provides reasons to support an international regime of human rights. Not just any revisionist understanding will do; the understanding must bear a relationship to the understanding presently accepted under which the normative authority of the worldview is preserved. There does not appear to be any generally applicable analysis of this relationship; what counts will vary from one worldview to another. This is because worldviews of the kind we are concerned with usually contain their own canons of interpretation, and these are likely to vary

---

[32] Bernard Williams, "Internal Reasons and the Obscurity of Blame," in *Making Sense of Humanity* (Cambridge: Cambridge University Press, 1995), 35.

[33] Ibid. 36-7.

from one view to another. Thus, for example, An-Na'im's program for the progressive reform of portions of Islamic doctrine depends on accepting a particular method of scriptural interpretation as valid within Islamic practice.[34] Perhaps the most we can say at a general level is that a revisionist understanding is "reachable from" another understanding of a worldview if someone who accepted the elements of the worldview reasonably regarded as basic by most people who share the worldview could reach the revisionist understanding by means of a sequence of interpretative steps which are consistent with these elements (including any that define acceptable canons of interpretation). Of course, even this may be too simple: it presumes a distinction between basic and nonbasic elements that may itself be controversial among the worldview's adherents. In any case it may seem intolerably vague. Yet some such idea must be presupposed by those who hold that adherents of one or another of the world's moral cultures could come to support human rights that seem to conflict with principles of these cultures as they are now widely understood by a process of "fresh" or "evolutionary" interpretation.

Supposing for the moment that we can make sense of it, why should we take any interest in the possibility that human rights may be "reachable from" some array of worldviews? One reply might be that the iterated application of a process of progressive interpretation to a series of worldviews could help to clarify the *content* of international human rights. This would, in effect, give us a progressive variant of the overlapping consensus idea. But this cannot be right. The reply depends on the thought that there is one "best interpretation" of each worldview that could stand as the basis for an inference to human rights. This is implausible unless it is assumed that interpretation proceeds with the intention of justifying a doctrine of human rights, so that the "best interpretation" could be uniquely identified as that which lends the most support to human rights. But of course this simply assumes the truth of the conclusion for which the method is supposed to provide an argument.

Another reply to our question might invoke the view about the justifiability of paternalistic interference that we considered earlier. It holds that, if human rights are "reachable from" a worldview, then action to enforce human rights in a society where this worldview is widely accepted would

---

[34] This is the method proposed by Ustadh Mahmoud Mohamed Taha and described in An-Na'im, *Toward an Islamic Reformation*, ch. 3.

not be objectionable as a form of unjustifiable paternalism. Members of the society could not complain that the interference imposes values that they have no reason to accept because, by hypothesis, those values would be potentially available to them as adherents of their own society's worldview: members of the society do, in fact, have reason to accept the values imposed, even if the reason is not apparent to them. The problem is that the values relied on to justify interference would not, in fact, be widely established in the society. If the "progressive convergence" hypothesis were accepted, it could be said that these values are potentially available to its members, but it would not follow that the values would actually be accepted by reasonable members of the culture at the time of the interference. The antipaternalism objection is essentially a complaint about an affront to autonomy, to the substitution of someone else's judgment for a person's own about what is good for that person. A doctrine of human rights that is "reachable from" a person's worldview, but incompatible with the worldview as it is actually accepted by the person, provides no shelter from this objection.

There is a third reason to take an interest in the idea of human rights as objects of a progressive convergence. As I observed earlier, one might believe that a public doctrine of human rights should express a form of toleration appropriate to the realm of relations among societies. According to one interpretation of this condition, the doctrine of human rights should be acceptable to persons who adhere to a wide range of the moral and religious worldviews found in the world without requiring them to give up or prescind from essential elements of these worldviews. This is not the same as the idea, just discussed, that human rights should be conceived so that political action in response to violations would escape antipaternalist objections. It is, instead, a consequence of the aspiration of human rights to constitute a widely sharable public doctrine—perhaps as an element of a global "public reason."[35]

I consider the meaning of international toleration and the sense in which it might be a virtue below (§§ 23–24). For now, I simply record my doubt that the idea of "reachability from" a range of worldviews is responsive to the reasons why one might believe that toleration of moral and religious diversity is a virtue. It would be a strange form of toleration that accepts an interference with a person's liberty as justified when a third

---

[35] As Cohen puts it, "No unnecessary hurdles should be placed in the way of adherents of different traditions who wish to embrace the ideas [of human rights]." "Minimalism about Human Rights," 199.

party concludes that the person entertains an inadequate or insufficiently developed interpretation of his or her own religious and cultural norms.[36] But let us assume for the moment that this doubt is misplaced. Even so, it remains the case that a doctrine of human rights which is the object of a progressive convergence may contain values that do not bear the kind of internal relationship to some worldviews that would be necessary to provide reasons for action to adherents of these views. As we have seen, although it may be arguable that someone who accepts the best or most adequate interpretation of a worldview should support the doctrine of human rights, it does not follow that those who accept other interpretations of that worldview have reasons to do so as well. It all depends on the details of the interpretative process that produces progressive convergence and the extent to which acceptance of the results of such a process can be said to be required of adherents of the worldview in question. These matters are complex, but it is clear that we cannot generalize about them across moral cultures. So even if there is some significant sense in which we can be said to tolerate other worldviews by confining human rights to values that are "reachable from" their authoritative tenets, we cannot conclude that adherents of these worldviews will necessarily find reasons internal to their worldviews as they conscientiously understand them to support human rights.

The concern about toleration is important for its own reasons but it is orthogonal to the question we are considering here. We are in search of an answer to the question, "What are human rights?" The candidate answer under consideration holds that human rights are standards for institutions to which all can agree, where agreement is interpreted as falling within a progressive convergence of worldviews. To avoid circularity, we must understand the process by which a progressive convergence might emerge to be driven by interests which are independent of the interest in defining or grounding human rights. Perhaps it is best to regard progressive convergence as a hypothesis about moral progress. We cannot know whether it will turn out true. The most we can do is to imagine as sympathetically as possible how various worldviews might evolve (or be "freshly elaborated") in response to the range of social forces we understand, roughly, as those of modernization, including those associated with the growth of a global

---

[36] I do not mean to say that any of the writers mentioned earlier adopts this view of the justifiability of interference.

economy and culture. If through such a process of sympathetic imagination we can see how a progressive convergence on human rights might emerge, we might acquire a reason to hope for the success of a global human rights regime.[37] But such a basis for hope would not satisfy the aspiration that motivated our initial interest in agreement conceptions, which was the thought that human rights should be recognizable as common concerns among all the world's cultures. The straightforward interpretation of that thought is one we might better simply give up.

---

[37] It would, that is, answer Cohen's question, from Kant: "What may I hope?" "Minimalism about Human Rights," 191.

5

A Fresh Start

BOTH naturalistic and agreement conceptions are efforts to make sense of human rights by treating them as expressions of one or another familiar and more general philosophical idea. I have tried to show how conceiving of human rights according to either of these approaches invites misunderstanding. What I have said is hardly conclusive and it would not be surprising if both conceptions could be given more persuasive interpretations than those I have considered. Still, the fruits of these approaches are sufficiently discouraging that it would be worthwhile to ask whether a different way of grasping the idea of a human right would produce more constructive results.

15. Human rights in *The Law of Peoples*

The alternative approach I shall suggest is implicit in the view of human rights taken by John Rawls in *The Law of Peoples*.[1] Although I shall not endorse this view as Rawls presents it, I believe his way of understanding human rights is instructive in its departure from the more familiar positions we have considered.

Rawls presents a view of human rights as one element of a larger conception of public reason worked out for an international society of liberal-democratic and "decent" peoples organized politically as states. Decent peoples are distinguished, in part, by having a conception of justice which, although not liberal, embodies an idea of the common good and a procedure of consultation for legislation which, although not democratic, affords opportunities for

---

[1] John Rawls, *The Law of Peoples* (Cambridge, MA: Harvard University Press, 1999). Rawls's remarks on human rights and their political significance are scattered throughout the work. See, in particular, 36-8, 65-6, 68, 78-81, 80 n. 23, 81 nn. 25-6, 93, 93 n. 6.

all adult members of society to make their voices heard. Liberal and decent peoples together constitute a "Society of Peoples" whose affairs are regulated by a "Law of Peoples" that defines the content of this society's public reason and serves as a common basis of justification for international political action.

The element of public reason in this conception is indispensable. The Society of Peoples is not simply a collection of political states whose mutual relations consist of self-interested bargaining. Rawls holds that liberal and decent peoples have a "duty of civility requiring that they offer other peoples public reasons appropriate to the Society of Peoples for their actions."[2] These "public reasons" refer to shared principles and norms, of which human rights constitute one class. The availability of principles and norms shared by all members of the Society of Peoples makes it possible for them to carry out their duties of civility and in doing so to stabilize a mutually respectful peace.

The essentials of Rawls's view of human rights can be summarized in four main points:

1. Human rights are "a special class of urgent rights" whose violation is "equally condemned by both reasonable liberal peoples and decent hier-archical peoples." They include rights to life (importantly including "the means of subsistence"), personal liberty (including liberty, though not equal liberty, of conscience), personal property, and equal treatment under law. These rights ("human rights proper") are indispensable to any "common good idea of justice" and therefore not "peculiarly liberal or special to the Western tradition."[3]

2. "Human rights proper" do not include the full complement of the rights found in the international law of human rights. For example, Rawls's list does not include rights to freedom of expression and association (though it does include "freedom of thought" and its "obvious implications") or the rights of democratic political participation. In addition, rights against dis-crimination are limited; for example, human rights are compatible with religious and (perhaps) gender qualifications for higher public office. In Rawls's view the omitted values are "liberal aspirations" or "presuppose specific kinds of institutions."[4]

---

[2] Ibid. 59.   [3] Ibid. 79-80, 80 n. 23; compare 65.

[4] Ibid. 80 n. 23, and the account of a decent society and its "common good" conception of justice at 62-75. The rights mentioned in the text above are found in the Universal Declaration, arts. 2, 19-21; Rawls omits these from his catalog of "human rights proper" (p. 80 n. 23).

3. The world may also contain societies such as "outlaw states" that are neither liberal nor decent. Although human rights may not be compatible with the moral beliefs prevailing in these societies or among their rulers, their "political (moral) force extends to all societies, and they are binding on all peoples and societies, including outlaw states."[5] Human rights, as Rawls conceives them, are "universal" in the sense that they apply (at least) to all contemporary societies.

4. The political significance of human rights is given by their "special role" in the public reason of the Society of Peoples. A society's adherence to human rights is necessary to qualify it as a member "in good standing in a reasonably just Society of Peoples" and "sufficient to exclude justified and forceful intervention by other peoples."[6] On the other hand, a society whose institutions fail to honor its people's human rights cannot complain if it is condemned by world society and it makes itself vulnerable *in extremis* to forceful intervention to protect human rights.

It may not be obvious from these propositions how substantially Rawls's understanding of the idea of a human right departs from more familiar philosophical positions. In contrast to naturalistic views, Rawls does not claim that human rights belong to persons "as such" or "in virtue of their common humanity." He stresses that the Law of Peoples does not try to derive human rights from "a theological, philosophical, or moral conception of the nature of the human person."[7] And although at one point he refers sympathetically to the idea that human rights are in some important way "neutral" between contending conceptions of political justice,[8] the idea of an intercultural or intersocietal agreement plays no part in the definition or justification of human rights. It is true that Rawls describes human rights as falling within an agreement among liberal and decent societies, but one should not be misled by this. It is part of the definition of decent (and liberal) societies that their institutions respect human rights; although there is in this respect an agreement about human rights, an appeal to this agreement to explain the authority of human rights or to determine their proper scope would be circular, and Rawls makes no such appeal. The point of the

[5] Ibid. 80-1.
[6] Ibid. 79-80; also 93-4 n. 6. As examples of "forceful intervention," Rawls mentions "diplomatic and economic sanctions" and "in grave cases . . . military force" (p. 80).
[7] Ibid. 81; cf. 68.   [8] Ibid. 65 n. 4 and the accompanying text.

reference to an agreement among liberal and decent peoples is to characterize the proper scope of international toleration.[9]

The idea that human rights are elements of the public reason of the
Society of Peoples stands in contrast to both naturalistic and agreement
conceptions. Human rights constitute a "political doctrine" constructed for
certain political purposes.[10] The discursive function of human rights (their
"special role") in the public reason of the Society of Peoples is basic: it
defines their nature and explains, or helps explain, why human rights have
the particular content they have. There is no appeal to any independent
philosophical conception of a human right in Rawls's account of the content
or authority of the doctrine. Indeed, there could not be, given that human
rights are values about which liberal and decent societies are supposed to
agree, each for their own reasons.

How might one be led to conceive of human rights in this unorthodox
way? It may be illuminating to consider a speculative analogy with the
approach taken in *A Theory of Justice* to defining the concept of social
justice.[11] There, Rawls suggests that although people may disagree about
the content of principles of justice—that is, they may accept *conceptions* of
justice that differ in their requirements—they may nevertheless agree about
the role these principles play in moral and political thought. The *concept* of
justice is defined by the role its various conceptions have in common. Thus
he argues that the subject of justice is the way in which the basic institutions
of society determine the division of advantages from social cooperation.
Different conceptions of justice, which advance different principles for
evaluating and regulating this division, represent different interpretations
of the concept. Reasoning analogously, one might think that although
people disagree about the content of human rights, they may agree about
the role of human rights in practical reasoning about the conduct of global
political life. This role defines the concept of a human right. As Rawls
understands them, human rights are standards whose satisfaction guarantees

[9] On Rawls's understanding of international toleration, see § 24, below.

[10] Specifically, the purposes listed in point 4 above. On the idea of human rights as a political
doctrine, see the discussion in Peter Jones, "International Human Rights: Philosophical or
Political?" in *National Rights, International Obligations*, ed. Simon Caney, David George, and
Peter Jones (Boulder, CO: Westview, 1996), 183–204. Rawls's reservations about Jones's interpretation of the view do not seem to go to this characterization. *The Law of Peoples*, 81 n. 25.

[11] John Rawls, *A Theory of Justice*, rev. edn. (Cambridge, MA: Harvard University Press, 1999),
§§ 1-2, pp. 5, 9. Rawls's remarks, as he notes, are influenced by H. L. A. Hart's distinction between
a concept and its conceptions in *The Concept of Law* (Oxford: Clarendon Press, 1961), 155-9.

a society against external intervention and is necessary for acceptance as a cooperating member of the Society of Peoples. One might say that substantively different conceptions of human rights are recognizable as interpretations of the same concept in virtue of their common aspiration to play this role.

The analogy suggests two observations, one exegetical and the other critical. First, although Rawls remarks, in *A Theory of Justice*, that the distinction between the concept of justice and its conceptions does not resolve any substantive dispute, various aspects of the role of justice do, in fact, come into arguments about the merits of its rival conceptions. A prominent example is the appeal to publicity in the argument against utilitarianism.[12] The same seems to be true of his view about the content and basis of human rights. Human rights are supposed to be part of the public reason of an international society composed of both liberal and decent peoples. The aim of this Society of Peoples is to achieve conditions in which different peoples can engage with each other peacefully while determining their own individual futures free from the interference of others. In order to secure the stability of the Society of Peoples, the Law of Peoples tries to provide a shared basis of political justification, one on which each participating society can expect the willing cooperation of the others. This aim exerts pressure to confine the principles of the Law of Peoples so that appeals to them can provide reasons for action to members of both liberal and decent peoples. We see the influence of this in the limited scope of Rawls's conception of genuine human rights. I leave aside for now the question of the persuasiveness of this view about the proper contents of the doctrine. The important point is that, according to the approach to human rights found in *The Law of Peoples*, considerations about their discursive role in the public reason of international society might influence thinking about their content as well as their nature.

The other observation pertains to Rawls's characterization of this role. He holds that human rights delineate the boundaries of acceptable pluralism in international affairs: adherence to human rights is necessary for a society to be a member of the Society of Peoples and sufficient to guarantee a society against reform-oriented intervention. In these respects we might say that human rights function as a standard of international legitimacy.[13] But one is

---

[12] Rawls, *A Theory of Justice*, §§ 1, 29, pp. 5, 154-5.

[13] Aaron James, "Constructing Justice for Existing Practice: Rawls and the Status Quo," *Philosophy and Public Affairs* 33 (2005), 311.

bound to wonder why human rights should be assigned these (and only these) roles. In the analogy of social justice, we have both a well-established tradition of thought and a range of contemporary views from which the role of the concept can be inferred. In the case of human rights, however, Rawls makes no reference to the history of thought about international human rights, to other contemporary views about them, or to the nature and development of international practice. The role of human rights in the Society of Peoples is simply stipulated.

The difficulty is that this view of the practical role of human rights is so much more limited than what we observe in present practice (§ 6). For example, Rawls does not describe human rights as entitlements enforceable in national constitutions, as they are sometimes regarded in the regional human rights courts and as they were imagined by some of the framers of the declaration. There is no provision for practices of international monitoring, reporting, and censure (though perhaps there might be). He notices but does not incorporate the broad array of noncoercive political and economic measures used by states and international organizations to influence the internal affairs of societies where human rights are threatened. He does not represent human rights as justifications for individuals and nongovern-mental organizations to engage in reform-oriented political action. Even to describe human rights as "foreign policy imperatives" for liberal and decent societies[14] might overstate their political role as Rawls conceives it: although in his view egregious violations can justify coercive intervention by other states, it is ambiguous whether human rights violations of lesser degrees of extremity would justify other types of action (for example, diplomatic or economic sanctions, commercial pressure, refraining from diplomatic engagement, or providing aid to further respect for human rights).[15]

In these respects Rawls's understanding of the functions of human rights is narrower than what is found in present international practice. The differences are not only of exegetical interest. We noted earlier that considerations about the discursive functions of human rights might come into

[14] Erin Kelly, "Human Rights as Foreign Policy Imperatives," in *The Ethics of Assistance: Morality and the Distant Needy*, ed. Deen Chatterjee (Cambridge: Cambridge University Press, 2004), 180-1.
[15] Rawls suggests that well-ordered peoples may have to bring various kinds of pressure to induce "outlaw regimes to change their ways" (*The Law of Peoples*, 93). Perhaps this licenses political action in response to human rights violations. He also argues that well-ordered peoples have a duty to assist "burdened" societies to develop the capacity to sustain just or decent institutions which would, in turn, honor their people's human rights (pp. 105-13).

Problems :
1) political objections to the practice
2) sympathetic puzzlement about some novel feature of practice
102   A FRESH START

judgments about the contents of the doctrine. To the extent that judgments about the doctrine's contents depend on considerations about the concept's functions, it seems likely that a more expansive understanding of function would generate a broader view of the doctrine's normative range. One's grasp of the discursive role of human rights is of normative as well as descriptive interest.

If our aim were to construct a conception of human rights for an idealized global order of decent and liberal societies, perhaps it would be sufficient simply to stipulate the role that human rights should play within the larger normative order. But our aim is to grasp the concept of a human right as it occurs within an existing practice, and for this purpose we need, not a stipulation, but a model that represents the salient aspects of this practice as we find it. I sketch such a model below (§ 17).

16. The idea of a practical conception

The basic insight implicit in Rawls's way of conceiving of human rights can be detached from the restrictions of function and content found in his account. This insight, as I have described it, is that we might frame our understanding of the idea of a human right by identifying the roles this idea plays within a discursive practice. We attend to the practical inferences that would be drawn by competent participants in the practice from what they regard as valid claims of human rights. An inventory of these inferences generates a view of the discursive functions of human rights and this informs an account of the meaning of the concept.

I shall call a conception of human rights arrived at by this route a "practical" conception. Such a conception differs from both naturalistic and agreement views in the following way. A practical conception takes the doctrine and practice of human rights as we find them in international political life as the source materials for constructing a conception of human rights. It understands questions about the nature and content of human rights to refer to objects of the sort called "human rights" in international practice. There is no assumption of a prior or independent layer of fundamental rights whose nature and content can be discovered independently of a consideration of the place of human rights in the international realm and its normative discourse and then used to interpret and criticize international doctrine. Similarly, it is not assumed that human rights seek to describe what is actually common to all political-moral codes or to state common standards reachable by inference from them. Instead, we take the functional role of human rights in international discourse and practice as basic: it constrains our conception of a human right from the start.

We should not confuse the distinction between naturalistic or agreement conceptions and a practical conception with a different distinction, suggested by Richard Rorty, between foundationalist and nonfoundationalist (or "sentimentalist") conceptions.[16] It is true that naturalistic views, at least, are foundationalist in an obvious sense: they interpret international human rights as the public, doctrinal expression of a distinctive underlying order of moral values conceived as rights. Agreement conceptions might also be seen as foundationalist, if perhaps not so obviously: they hold that the moral force of human rights, considered as norms of international action, derives from the fact of intercultural agreement, under one or another interpretation of this fact. One need not say, however, that practical views are nonfoundationalist, if by this is meant that such views deny that there are reasons to adhere to and support international human rights. Perhaps such a denial is part of Rorty's ("sentimentalist") conception of human rights, but that conception is not the only alternative to the familiar conceptions I have described.

The contrast of interest is this. Naturalistic and agreement theories treat the question of the authority of human rights as internal to the question of their nature: once we understand what human rights are, we understand the range of considerations that determine the content of international human rights doctrine and explain why we should care that it be adhered to. This is because these views interpret international doctrine as an attempt to embody in international law and practice an independently intelligible moral idea. By contrast, because a practical conception prescinds from taking any philosophical view about the nature or basis of human rights, it can distinguish between the problem of conceptualizing human rights and that of understanding their authority. It responds to the first problem by taking the functions of human rights in international practice as basic. On such a view, international human rights is the name of a collective political enterprise—a practice—with distinctive purposes and modes of action. An understanding of these purposes and modes of action is essential to a grasp of

[16] Richard Rorty, "Human Rights, Rationality, and Sentimentality," in *On Human Rights: The Oxford Amnesty Lectures 1993*, ed. Stephen Shute and Susan Hurley (New York: Basic Books, 1993), 115-17.

the nature of human rights. It does not, however, settle questions about their content or basis. Such a view allows that people might agree about the nature of international human rights but disagree about their content or the kinds of considerations that ground them. This does not mean that we need no reasons to care about human rights—only that it is not part of the practice that everyone who accepts and acts upon the public doctrine must share the same reasons for doing so.[17]

The idea of a practical approach invites the following objection.[18] When we inspect the practice of human rights, we observe regularities in behavior and belief. We might find that members of some group tend to perform some action A in circumstances C. We might find, moreover, that these agents perform A in C because they believe there is a norm that agents in C should A. These agents may also believe that someone who finds himself in C but fails to A is vulnerable to criticism for behaving improperly unless he can bring forward some other reason that plausibly defeats the reason he has to A in C. The objection I wish to consider observes that a practical theory of human rights seems to understand statements about human rights as nothing more than references to complicated sociological facts of this nature. But such an analysis is bound to fail because it cannot account for the normativity of human rights. A human right is supposed to provide a reason for action. According to a practical view, however, to say there is a human right to X is simply shorthand for a complex description of regularities in behavior and belief observed among the members of some group. If, having been advised that there is a human right to X, I ask why I should regard this fact as a source of reasons for action, it cannot be enough to reply that members of some group believe there is a human right to X and take this belief to be a source of reasons for action. The reply seems to beg the question. We see this by recalling that people can be wrong in their beliefs about how they should behave.

But the objection as it relates to human rights rests on a confusion. As I observed earlier, the question "What are human rights?" is ambiguous. On

---

[17] Describing a "political" model of human rights, Anthony Langlois characterizes them as representing an "incompletely theorized agreement" that stops short of articulating its own foundations. (*The Politics of Justice and Human Rights: Southeast Asia and Universalist Theory* (Cambridge: Cambridge University Press, 2001), 102-24.) The source of the idea of an "incompletely theorized agreement" is Cass R. Sunstein, *Legal Reasoning and Political Conflict* (New York: Oxford University Press, 1996), ch. 2.

[18] The objection is suggested by some remarks of Joseph Raz in *Practical Reason and Norms*, 2nd edn. (Princeton, NJ: Princeton University Press, 1990 [1975]), 57-8. He does not discuss human rights.

one interpretation, it asks for an analysis of the concept of a human right; on another, for an account of the content of human rights; and on yet another, for an explanation of their reason-giving force. These questions are related but they are not identical. If a practical analysis were brought forward in reply to the question "Why do human rights provide reasons for action?" then the analysis might be open to the objection I have just described. But that is not our question. We inspect the practice of human rights because we are interested in the way participants in this practice understand the practical inferences to be drawn from assertions about human rights. We want to understand how these objects called "human rights" operate in the normative discourse of global political life. Whether we should accept claims about human rights as sources of reasons for action *for us* is a further question. But we cannot think clearly about this further question without first understanding the practice in which these claims are made and responded to.

There is, however, a similar objection that may seem to escape the reply I have just given. This is the objection that a practical conception gives too much authority to the status quo by taking an existing practice as given. One reason we need a theory of human rights is that there is disagreement about various aspects of the practice, importantly including the composition and reach of its normative requirements. Another is that some aspects of the practice—notably, the permission to interfere in a society's domestic life— may seem, from some perspectives, objectionable on their face. But if a theory begins with the practice as we find it, it is hard to see how the theory can be critical.

In response, a practical conception need not take the details of present practice as beyond criticism. A social practice is a pattern of norm-governed conduct whose participants understand it to serve certain purposes. A theory of the practice seeks not only to grasp its aims but also to appraise their importance and to construe the practice in light of this judgment. For example, one might judge that some of the practice's norms are ill-suited to advance its aims or that the conduct required by the norms under typical circumstances is likely to be objectionable. In the case of human rights, surely the most important consideration is that a doctrine of international human rights should be suited to the public political role it is expected to play. An understanding of this public role constrains the content of the doctrine. Whatever else is true of human rights, they are supposed to be matters of international concern in the sense that a society's failure to respect its people's human rights on a sufficiently large scale may provide a reason for outside agents to do something. So, to anticipate, we should construe the doctrine so that appeals to human rights, under conditions that will need to be specified, can provide reasons for the world community or its agents to act in ways aimed at reducing infringements or contributing to the satisfaction of the rights in societies where they are insecure.

This requirement will constrain the content of a plausible doctrine of human rights in several ways. For example, it might exclude from the catalog of human rights protections of interests that would not reasonably be seen as worthy of protection by most members of existing societies. It might also exclude values for which a failure to secure or protect them in a society would not provide any intelligible reason for action to appropriately situated outside agents. And it might exclude values for the deprivation of which no remedy is achievable through some permissible form of international action for which there is a reasonable expectation of success. Obviously, these possibilities need explication. We return to them below (§ 21). I state them now to suggest that a practical approach might achieve some critical leverage on the practice as we observe it by taking seriously the role of human rights in justifying various forms of political action.

17. A two-level model

A practical conception of human rights must rely on a construction of some kind—a "model," as I shall call it—that abstracts from the particulars to describe in general terms the roles played by human rights in the public normative discourse of global politics. Such a model would give an answer to the question "What are human rights?" understood as a request for an account of the meaning of the term within the practice. It would make explicit the kinds of linguistic commitments one would undertake if one were to participate in good faith in the discursive practice.

I shall propose such a model, but first something should be said about the main difficulty one confronts in doing so. Human rights, like any practice, is a social phenomenon whose meaning depends on how it is engaged by its many participants. It is not likely that the members of the discursive community that sustains the practice will be unanimous about its salient elements—for example, the identity of its agents, the character of its norms, the range of responses that failures to adhere to these norms might license, and a general understanding of the point or purpose of the practice in the

1) states — required of political institutions of states to protect
urgent interests of individuals wilin territorial jurisdiction
1) protect from predictable threats
A FRESH START 107

larger context in which it operates. Even when there is not overt disagreement, these elements, as they appear in the empirical materials, may be ambiguous and therefore susceptible to being modeled in more than one way. The opportunities for disagreement and ambiguity about the structure and purposes of a practice are plainly larger when the practice is emergent. This means that a model cannot simply be "read off" from the record. We need some way of moving from the observable facts to a model that identifies the practice's salient elements and assembles them into an intelligible structure.

I know of no good systematic method of interpretation for social practices, so we must proceed informally.[19] The guiding ambition is to frame a reasonably clear and realistic conception of the practice as it presents itself in the range of source materials at hand. These include the major international texts and the reporting and monitoring mechanisms established by them; observations of critical public discourse, particularly when it occurs in practical contexts involving justification and appraisal; evidence of the public culture of international human rights found in its history and in contemporary public expression; and prominent examples of political action justified and reasonably regarded as efforts to defend or protect human rights, such as those which are subjects of historical and ethnographic studies. We surveyed some of these materials earlier (§§ 4–6).

There are several kinds of considerations that might be brought to bear in abstracting from these materials to a model. I note four here. First, in identifying the central elements of the practice, the model should seek to represent a consensus among competent participants, allowing for the fact that the relevant sense of "consensus" need not require unanimity about the practice's normative contents; a consensus in the form of common patterns of usage and a continuity of discursive experience can exist notwithstanding substantial disagreement about the contents of a practice's rules and standards.[20] Second, the model should rely on a conception of the practice's aim or purpose in order to adjudicate among conflicting beliefs

[19] The idea of interpretation in law is in some respects an instructive analogy. See Ronald Dworkin, *Law's Empire* (Cambridge, MA: Harvard University Press, 1986), ch. 2, and its application to Rawls's political theory in James, "Constructing Justice for Existing Practice," 298–308. However, I do not believe that the method of "constructive interpretation" is entirely suitable for the task at hand. I cannot discuss the reasons here. See the illuminating discussion in Gerald J. Postema, "'Protestant' Interpretation and Social Practices," *Law and Philosophy* 6 (1987): 283–319.

[20] Postema, "'Protestant' Interpretation and Social Practices," 315–17.

about the practical significance of its central terms or to resolve ambiguities about their meanings. But it is not necessary, for our purposes, to understand such a conception as a general justification supplied from the point of view of a single participant interested in deciding how a rule or standard would best be construed.[21] What is needed is a facially reasonable conception of the practice's aim formulated so as to make sense of as many of the central normative elements as possible within the familiar interpretative constraints of consistency, coherence, and simplicity.[22] Third, the model should observe a distinction between disagreement about the practice and disagreement within the practice, and, as far as possible, avoid presenting the practice in a way that presupposes one or another resolution of the second type of disagreement. This is because one function of a model is to clarify what is at stake in disagreement about the content and application of the practice's norms. Finally and relatedly, it should allow for the possibility that disagreement of certain kinds may be integral to the practice rather than signs of failure or incompleteness in the model. I do not mean only that a good model should make clear what is at stake in disagreement about the contents of a practice's norms or about the practical inferences to be drawn from them in any particular circumstances (though this is certainly true). The further point is that in some practices it is common to find participants engaged in critical, reflective disagreement about the structure and value of the practice itself. It would not be a criticism of a model aiming to present an abstract but realistic interpretation of such a practice that the model clarifies the subject-matter of this type of disagreement rather than seek to resolve it.

I shall propose a two-level model of human rights. The two levels express a division of labor between states as the bearers of the primary responsibilities to respect and protect human rights and the international community and those acting as its agents as the guarantors of these responsibilities. I present the model in summary form and then offer some comments to elaborate. In later sections I take up some objections that might be brought against the model, considered as an interpretation of the idea of a human right found in contemporary international practice: that it fails to capture the sense in which human rights are rights, that it gives too prominent a place to the state, and that it overstates the interference-justifying role of human rights.

---

[21] As Dworkin suggests. *Law's Empire*, 66.
[22] James, "Constructing Justice for Existing Practice," 302–3.

The model has three elements:[23]

1. Human rights are requirements whose object is to protect urgent individual interests against certain predictable dangers ("standard threats") to which they are vulnerable under typical circumstances of life in a modern world order composed of states.

2. Human rights apply in the first instance to the political institutions of states, including their constitutions, laws, and public policies. These "first-level" requirements may be of three general types: (*a*) to respect the underlying interests in the conduct of the state's official business; (*b*) to protect the underlying interests against threats from non-state agents subject to the state's jurisdiction and control; and (*c*) to aid those who are non-voluntarily victims of deprivation.[24] Governments have limited discretion to choose the means by which they carry out these requirements, the scope of discretion varying with the nature of the underlying interest and the range of threats protected against. The government of a state may be said to "violate" human rights when it fails in any of these respects.[25]

3. Human rights are matters of international concern. A government's failure to carry out its first-level responsibilities may be a reason for action for appropriately placed and capable "second-level" agents outside the state in three overlapping kinds of circumstances: (*a*) the international community may through its political institutions hold states accountable for carrying out the first-level responsibilities listed above; (*b*) states and non-state agents with the means to act effectively have *pro tanto* reasons to assist an individual state to satisfy human rights standards in cases in which the state itself lacks the capacity to do so; and (*c*) states and non-state agents with the means to act effectively have *pro tanto* reasons to interfere in an individual state to protect human rights in cases in which the state fails through a lack of will to do so.

---

[23] I am indebted for the main ideas to Henry Shue, *Basic Rights*, 2nd edn. (Princeton, NJ: Princeton University Press, 1996), ch. 1 and the 1996 Afterword, and James Nickel, *Making Sense of Human Rights*, 2nd edn. (Malden, MA.: Blackwell, 2007), chs. 1–4. For a characterization of human rights similar to that in the text, see Amartya Sen, "Elements of a Theory of Human Rights," *Philosophy and Public Affairs* 32 (2004): 315–56. This model is compatible with the understanding of international responsibility for human rights in International Commission on Intervention and State Sovereignty, *The Responsibility to Protect* (Ottawa: International Development Research Centre, 2001).

[24] For the tripartite distinction of duties, see Shue, *Basic Rights*, 60.

[25] So a government might be said to have violated a human right even when there is no intention to do so (e.g. through a lack of capacity or poor policy planning) and when the proximate cause of the deprivation is something other than government action (e.g. when a government fails to take the appropriate preventive or remedial steps).

Several aspects of this model need explanation. First, the model characterizes human rights as protections of "urgent individual interests" against
"standard threats" to which they are vulnerable. How should we understand
these phrases? An "urgent" interest is one that would be recognizable as
important in a wide range of typical lives that occur in contemporary
societies: for example, interests in personal security and liberty, adequate
nutrition, and some degree of protection against the arbitrary use of state
power. An urgent interest is not necessarily an interest possessed by everyone or desired by everyone: to recognize an interest as urgent, we must be
able to understand why it would be reasonable to regard its satisfaction as
important within some range of normal lives but we need not believe that
all persons value the interest or care about its satisfaction in their own cases.
In this sense the idea of an "urgent" individual interest is distinct from the
idea of a "universal" human interest, understood as one necessarily shared
by all human beings "as such" (a general feature, perhaps, of "human
nature"). As I argued earlier, it is difficult to see how any philosophically
plausible interpretation of the latter idea that can make sense of the wide
normative scope of contemporary human rights doctrine.

When I say that only urgent interests qualify for the protection of human
rights, I mean to generalize from the interests that most of the human rights
recognized in international doctrine seem designed to protect. But it will be
observed that interests can vary in their urgency: urgency is a scalar, not a
binary, property. An obvious question is whether there is a threshold or
lower bound of urgency below which an interest does not qualify for the
protection of a human right. I do not see any determinate analytical reply. It
seems clear that some such threshold must be drawn because the protection
of human rights at both domestic and global levels has costs, and some
justification for imposing these costs is owed to those called upon to bear
them. But whether an interest qualifies for protection, or more accurately,
whether a particular form of protection of an interest qualifies as a human
right, calls for a normative judgment. Such a judgment would take into
account the urgency of the interest, but it would also take into account
various other considerations such as the likelihood that the threat protected
against will actually occur, the feasibility of implementing the protection in
typical circumstances, and the likely cost of making the protection effective.
Judgments of this nature are likely to be more-or-less controversial within
the practice. A model can draw attention to the relevant considerations but
it cannot settle the judgments.

is "standard" the
right word?

Human rights are institutional protections against "standard threats" to urgent interests. A "standard" threat is a threat which is reasonably predictable under the social circumstances in which the right is intended to operate.[26] The human rights of international doctrine are not, for the most part, best understood as unrestricted or blanket protections of urgent interests. It does not seem reasonable, for example, to regard the right to life as a protection of the interest in physical security against all imaginable threats. Similarly, the right to health care is not a protection of the interest in good health against all perils. Most human rights are at least implicitly and often explicitly limited in the range and type of threats against which they require institutions to offer protection. (The fact that these limitations are not always spelled out in the documentary formulations is not necessarily evidence to the contrary: some of the formal and informal political contestation that takes place within international human rights practice consists of dispute about which threats count as standard threats that can justify remedial political action.)

Reflection about the kind of justification that would be required for most institutional rights suggests that it could hardly be otherwise. I shall say more about this below, but for our immediate purposes I anticipate briefly. A facially plausible justification for a claim that human rights doctrine should incorporate some specific protection should make good at least three types of claim. As a first approximation, these are (1) that the interest protected has a kind of importance that it would be reasonable to recognize across a wide range of possible lives; (2) that in the absence of the protections embodied in the right, there is a significant probability that domestic-level institutions will behave, by omission or commission, in ways that endanger this interest; and (3) that there are permissible means of international action such that, if they were carried out, the interest would be less likely to be endangered and that these means would not be unreasonably burdensome for those who have reason to use them.[27] The idea of a "standard threat" comes into this formula at two points: as part of the explanation of the vulnerability of the underlying interests in the absence of the protection embodied in the right and as a way of limiting the exposure of outsiders who might be called upon

---

[26] Shue, *Basic Rights*, 29 ff.; Nickel, *Making Sense of Human Rights*, 70-4.

[27] Broadly similar although in some respects more demanding considerations seem to be required to justify claims about moral rights. See T. M. Scanlon, "Rights, Goals, and Fairness" and "Human Rights as a Neutral Concern," both in *The Difficulty of Tolerance: Essays in Political Philosophy* (Cambridge: Cambridge University Press, 2003), 35 and 115-16.

to act. This shows that the justification of most any human right will be more-or-less dependent on empirical generalizations about the nature of social life and the behavior of social and political institutions. These generalizations can vary in their range of application; plainly, for human rights the range should be relatively broad, because the rights are supposed to be claimable by all members of contemporary societies. But the generalizations no more need to pertain to social life in all times and places than the underlying interests need to be shared by all human beings "as such." The restriction of human rights to protections of urgent interests against predictable dangers *in the modern world* is meant to recognize, albeit roughly, both dimensions of contingency. The inclusion of such a restriction in an analysis of human rights is inescapable.

Secondly, a comment about the description of human rights as protections of "individual interests." There is a long history of criticism of human rights as excessively individualistic in their substantive focus. Usually the criticism has taken one of two forms: either that the particular interests protected tend to produce social disunity (e.g. religious freedom, private property) or that human rights fail to require forms of public action to which high priority should be given (e.g. guarantee of an adequate standard of living).[28] These criticisms seem to me to misrepresent both the content and the aims of the doctrine of human rights, but for the moment I will leave this aside. The question I want to raise is whether the two-level model is objectionably individualistic in a somewhat different sense, by construing human rights in such a way that their use to protect certain important social values would be ruled out from the outset, as it were by conceptual fiat. This would be objectionable in a model of present practice because this practice comprehends rights whose purpose is to protect values with a collective dimension—for example, the right of self-determination and the right to participate in the distinctive linguistic, religious, and cultural practices of a one or another type of social group.[29]

---

[28] Some such criticism of "the so-called rights of man" was expressed by Marx in his early writings and has had considerable resonance in modern thought about human rights. Karl Marx, "On the Jewish Question," in *Selected Writings*, ed. Lawrence Simon (Indianapolis: Hackett, 1994), 1-26. There is a discussion of this line of criticism in Jeremy Waldron, "Can Communal Goods be Human Rights?" in *Liberal Rights: Collected Papers 1981-1991* (Cambridge: Cambridge University Press, 1993), 341-4.

[29] "Group rights" are sometimes regarded as a new idea (a "third [or perhaps fourth] generation" of human rights), but in fact both covenants recognize some such rights, including the examples in the text above (see e.g. ICCPR, arts. 1, 27).

What is it for a value to have a "collective dimension?" We might say, for a start, that these are values whose importance for the individuals who enjoy them can only be explained by referring to the fact of these individuals' group memberships. This is plainly true of the values just mentioned. By contrast, no such reference is necessary to explain the importance of the values protected by, say, the right to life or to an adequate standard of living.[30] The question is whether the two-level model is biased against the recognition of human rights whose purpose is to protect values of the former kind. According to the model, human rights protect interests of individuals. If there is such a thing as a "group interest" which is non-individualistic, in the sense that its importance cannot be seen as deriving from the interests of individual members of the group, then, if we were to accept the two-level model, we could not say that such an interest could be protected by a human right. This might be taken to indicate a kind of bias. So it is important to see that a value can have a collective dimension without being non-individualistic. The value of self-determination, for example, has a collective dimension because its importance to the individuals who enjoy (or wish to enjoy) it cannot be explained without reference to their group membership, but it is still an individualistic value: it is a value *for* the individuals who enjoy it. The same is true of whatever rights there are to cultural membership and participation. What this shows is that the model is not objectionably biased against the possibility of "group rights," understood as rights that can be claimed by individuals in virtue of their interests in membership in various kinds of groups. I believe it is clear that there are such interests (e.g. interests in cultural identity), although for the present I am agnostic about whether there is a sufficient justification for protecting these interests with the mechanism of a human right.[31] All I mean to say for now is that the two-level model is framed so as to allow the question whether international doctrine should include rights aimed at protecting these interests to be treated as a normative question arising within the practice rather than as a matter to be settled by definition.

Thirdly, according to the two-level model, human rights express requirements that apply in the first instance to states. By "in the first instance" I mean that the institutional protection called for by human rights is to be provided by

---

[30] For a further discussion of the definitional problem, see Waldron, "Can Communal Goods be Human Rights?" 344-59.

[31] For some doubts, see David Miller, "Group Rights, Human Rights and Citizenship," *European Journal of Philosophy* 10 (2002): 178-95.

means of the laws and policies of the states of which the beneficiaries of these protections are citizens or in which they reside. States have the primary or "first-level" responsibility to ensure the satisfaction of the human rights of their own residents.[32] However, the model does not require that states carry out this responsibility by incorporating guarantees of human rights in their constitutions or basic laws. This is a departure from the expectations of some of the framers and contemporary practitioners. The question is whether we should regard the purpose of the enterprise as to promote the enactment of human rights protections in state-level constitutional laws or to bring about effective protection of the underlying interests (of individuals) by whatever permissible means the state commands. For several reasons I believe the second better represents the point of the enterprise. First, this idea fits better with the normative heterogeneity of human rights doctrine. Some of its elements, of course, could hardly be achieved at all without appropriate legal provision (e.g. the right against arbitrary arrest or detention), but others can be achieved by a variety of policy measures that do not require enactment as a legal right (an adequate standard of living). The declaration's allowance that economic, social, and cultural rights are to be realized "in accordance with the organization and resources of each State" (art. 22) seems to recognize this fact. Second, the "effective protection" idea provides a better rendering of the political practice of human rights since the declaration. As we have seen, both within and beyond the treaty-based human rights system, the objective of international action has been to secure enjoyment of the substance of human rights rather than (only) the enactment of protections in municipal law. Finally, this idea allows a more transparent distinction between ends and means, so that the question of the desirability and importance of constitutional protection can be seen as one of contingent judgment rather than conceptual necessity.

Some people have entertained a view that seems to contrast with the conception of human rights as standards that apply in the first instance to states. According to what Thomas Pogge calls an "interactional understanding," human rights are grounds of claims that individual persons may make upon other persons: everybody has human rights and everybody has responsibilities to respect human rights. Pogge himself rejects this view. He proposes instead an "institutional understanding" according to which human rights justify claims directly against those institutions and shared

---

[32] Later we consider whether it is a fault of the model that it excludes the possibility that non-state agents might have primary or non-derivative responsibilities (§ 19).

practices of which the claimant is a part and indirectly against those who support these institutions.[33]

I believe that Pogge is correct to regard human rights as standards that apply in the first instance to institutions and to distinguish this view from individualistic conceptions. Failure to observe this distinction is perhaps another result of the conflation of international human rights with the natural rights tradition. Pogge's conception of an "institutional understanding," however, says more than this. It combines a view about the primary agents of human rights with a further substantive claim about the grounds of concern about them. Pogge holds that it is a form of wrongdoing to support an institutional scheme that avoidably allows people to suffer the kinds of deprivations that human rights protect against. To do so is to violate a "negative duty"—a species of a more general duty not to harm.[34] This means that responsibilities to respect and protect the human rights of a population are held only by those who participate "in the same social system" with that population.[35] Now, it is a substantive question whether a view of this kind provides a sufficient account of the grounds of duties to respect human rights. Below, I express doubt, but for the moment I pass the question by.[36] The point here is that an interpretation of contemporary human rights doctrine as consisting of standards for institutions need not commit itself to a further view about the nature or basis of the duties human rights impose on individual agents.

Fourth, the two-level model does not restrict responsibility for the protection of the human rights of persons to the states in which these persons reside. It represents human rights as matters of international concern by holding that appropriately placed and capable outside agents may have *pro tanto* reasons for action when states fail in their "first-level" responsibilities. As I have emphasized, this is a distinctive feature, perhaps the most distinctive feature, of contemporary human rights practice. Even if we confine ourselves to the expectations of the framers as represented in the declaration and

---

[33] Thomas Pogge, *World Poverty and Human Rights* (Cambridge: Polity, 2002), 44-8, 64-7. Describing an "institutional understanding," he writes: "Human rights are, then, moral claims on the organization of one's society. However, since citizens are collectively responsible for their society's organization and its resulting human rights record, human rights ultimately make demands upon (especially the more influential) citizens. Persons share responsibility for official disrespect of human rights within any coercive institutional order they are involved in upholding" (p. 64).

[34] Ibid. 66.   [35] Ibid.

[36] For a discussion, see Alan Patten, "Should We Stop Thinking about Poverty in Terms of Helping the Poor?" *Ethics and International Affairs* 19/1 (2005): 19-27.

the covenants, it is clear that *some* international role was contemplated; otherwise the references to international cooperation and the provisions for international monitoring would be inexplicable. Moreover, as we have seen, in contemporary global politics violations are regularly treated as reasons for action by other agents than international organizations, including other states and nongovernmental organizations, and are understood as capable of justifying a wider range of actions than those open to the international human rights institutions. To be sure, these modes of political action are not recognized or authorized by the human rights treaties themselves, but they are plainly visible in the practice of states, international organizations, and nongovernmental organizations. The model seeks to recognize these features of human rights practice by distinguishing between the primary role of states and the *pro tanto* reasons for action generated for outside agents when human rights are threatened because states fail in this role.

I shall say more about *pro tanto* reasons in a moment, but first a further observation about the kinds of international action for which human rights might provide reasons. I have said that the interference-justifying role of human rights is central to understanding their discursive functions. But it bears recalling that, even in its most generous interpretation, the idea of interference for human rights does not exhaust the range of measures for which human rights violations might provide reasons. The structures and practices of global governance have grown more complex and consequential since the time of the declaration and these may either impede or enhance the capacities of individual states to protect the human rights of their residents. Consider, for example, international trade rules that allow states to restrict trade in goods with poor countries, intellectual property rules that increase the cost of essential medications, and norms for labor practices established by transnational, nongovernmental standard-setting bodies. To be realistic, an understanding of human rights as imposing responsibilities on third-party states and international organizations should recognize that the most effective remedy for some human rights failures within states may be reform of rules and structures at the global level rather than interference in the state in any familiar form. The idea of external assistance in the third part of the model should be interpreted so as to embrace the paradigm of "external adaptation" as well as those involving more familiar forms of political interference (§ 6).

Finally, a comment about *pro tanto* reasons for action. The conventional contrast is with conclusory reasons. Conclusory reasons require us to act, regardless of the other considerations in play. These reasons override other considerations, whatever their content. *Pro tanto* reasons are genuine reasons for action, but they do not necessarily override competing reasons that may also be in play. According to the model, when a state's institutions fail to respect human rights, appropriately placed outside agents have *pro tanto* but not necessarily conclusory reasons to act. This means that, in the general case, a human rights failure in one society will not *require* action by outside agents. Although there may be some sense in saying that such agents would have "*prima facie*" duties to act, it would not necessarily be true that they have such duties, all things considered.

It is true that violations of certain human rights might provide conclusory reasons to act, or perhaps very strong *pro tanto* reasons (ones that overrule most other reasons in the circumstances in which they typically arise). Someone might believe that this is true, for example, of genocide and torture.[37] The model does not rule out this possibility. But we must regard cases like these as special if we seek a model capable of representing the normative breadth of contemporary human rights doctrine. The threats protected against by the human rights of existing international doctrine vary in degrees of urgency and we should expect, and the model allows, that these threats will give rise to reasons for action of varying strength.

18. "Manifesto rights"

The two-level model is an interpretation of the idea of a human right found in contemporary human rights practice. Looked at this way, the model is open to several objections. Among the most troubling may be that by characterizing human rights as giving rise to *pro tanto* reasons rather than to requirements that override most other consideration, the model fails to register an essential element of the idea of a right.

The most familiar moral rights are bases of claims against specific other agents that they perform or refrain from performing relatively specific types

---

[37] Article 4 of the ICCPR allows states to take measures derogating from their obligations when strictly necessary in times of public emergency but designates certain requirements as non-derogable (e.g. the right to life, freedom from torture, the right to recognition before the law, and freedom of conscience and religion). Arguably the distinction of these rights from other rights tracks the distinction between *pro tanto* and conclusory reasons. For a discussion, see Sarah Joseph, Jenny Schultz, and Melissa Castan, *The International Covenant on Civil and Political Rights*, 2nd edn. (Oxford: Oxford University Press, 2004), §§ 25.49-66.

of actions. Moreover, although it is not generally true that a right can never be overridden by other considerations, the reasons for action a right supplies have a special status for the agents to whom they apply. They are not simply reasons to be balanced against whatever other reasons might be present; rights exclude some competing reasons as irrelevant and impose special conditions on our consideration of other reasons. The objection holds that any plausible conception of human rights should inherit these features. The two-level model may appear to fail this test because it holds that a government's failure to satisfy human rights requirements does no more than generate *pro tanto* reasons for protective or corrective action by outsiders. Human rights as the model construes them may seem to be rights *manqués*.

The objection trades on an oversimplification. The model distinguishes between the practical interferences to be drawn from human rights claims for the deontic situations of the governments of the states in which such claims arise and those of outside agents which are in a position to act. There is no serious indeterminacy about the location of the first-level responsibilities: they rest with the governments of states. And, although the model's characterization of the required actions is relatively abstract, it is no more so than is true for various other kinds of rights which are not usually taken to be similarly problematic (for example, constitutional rights like that to free expression). It is true that the model allows for the possibility of conflicts among rights, or more accurately, among the obligations associated with them, but once again this should be no more troubling for human rights than for other rights of constitutional stature. Of course, the analogy should not be pressed too far: as I have observed, human rights practice does not consistently adhere to a juridical paradigm of implementation, even at the domestic level. It is not plausible to read every human right as a requirement that a corresponding constitutional provision be enacted in every state. But this does nothing to vitiate the fact that the holder of the primary responsibility to act is easy to identify and the content of the responsibility not extraordinarily difficult to make out.

The objector might accept this point but reply that it avoids rather than responds to the objection. Human rights are supposed to be "universal" not only in their reach but also in the character of the associated obligations. As Onora O'Neill puts it, we should not say that "there are some universal rights" unless we can specify "counterpart [universal] obligations."[38] In her view, this stricture is violated by any conception in which the obligations to

[38] Onora O'Neill, "The Dark Side of Human Rights," *International Affairs* 81 (2005), 433.

respect someone's ("universal") human rights are held only by members of that person's own society or by its government. The two-level model appears to be such a conception; although it allows that a domestic government has obligations to respect human rights, the most it can say about other agents in general is that they may have *pro tanto* reasons to act that lack the specificity and force of obligations. The specter of rights *manqués* seems to have returned.

The first thing to be said in response is that the model seeks to describe an existing discursive practice, and the respects in which human rights as the model characterizes them are less rigorous than ordinary rights are respects in which human rights are typically treated differently from ordinary rights within the practice. Human rights doctrine does not present a set of standards that can always be expected to be satisfied simultaneously and it does not include priority rules for settling conflicts when they arise. It has no clear principles and no process for assigning specific obligations to specific external agents when human rights are violated. If one were to think of claims of right as conveying information, then one might say that, ordinarily, a valid claim of right is information-rich. It conveys information about the nature and importance of the benefit that would be provided or the harm avoided by compliance with the right's requirements, the identity of the agents whose conduct is regulated by the right, the conduct required of them, and the kinds and range of circumstances in which it could be permissible not to comply. In contrast, within the practice of human rights, a valid claim of right is less information-rich. It conveys information about the nature and importance of the benefit or harm, the likelihood that eligible agents will have reasons to act, and the aims at which their action should be directed, but in the general case it tells us less about the identity of the agents whose conduct is regulated and the circumstances in which it would be permissible not to comply. Considered in relation to ordinary rights, human rights leave more to be worked out at the point of application. One can imagine a model of human rights that brings them closer to the idea of a claim-right, but such a model would not be faithful to a substantial portion of contemporary human rights doctrine.

The objector may not be satisfied with this reply. Human rights as they are understood in contemporary international practice are supposed to be action-guiding. But if a human right is such that there is no criterion or process by which specific agents can be identified whose action is to be guided, then the right cannot play this role. Its pretension to guide action may come to appear as little more than a flourish. The objector may think that we cannot have it both ways: we cannot regard human rights as having the kind of normative authority usually claimed for them yet maintain that their violation is no more than a source of *pro tanto* reasons for unspecified agents to act. If we must retain the second of these conditions to be faithful to the practice as we observe it, then we should let go the first and settle for an "aspirational" view of human rights.[39]

Joel Feinberg takes what has sometimes been understood to be a similar view when he describes "economic rights"—for example, the right to an adequate standard of living—as "manifesto rights."[40] Since this characterization has been influential (and because I believe it has been misunderstood), it is worthwhile to consider his understanding of these rights. "Manifesto rights," in Feinberg's view, "are not necessarily correlated with the duties of any assignable persons" because "under widely prevalent conditions of scarcity and conflict, [they may] be impossible for *anyone* to discharge."[41] Feinberg appears to assume that there is no possible assignment of duties such that their fulfillment would result in the satisfaction of certain economic rights. Whatever may have been the case when Feinberg wrote, this is not obviously true today. For our purposes, however, the more important point is that, even if it is impossible or impractical to satisfy a "manifesto right" in the present, it might still be action-guiding. Feinberg is clear about this. He writes that we should understand "manifesto rights" as

> real claims, if only upon hypothetical future beings not yet in existence.
> I accept the principle that to have an unfulfilled need is to have a kind of claim against the world. . . . Such claims, based on need alone, are "permanent possibilities of rights," the natural seed from which rights grow. Manifesto writers are easily forgiven for speaking of them as if they are already actual rights, for this is but a powerful way of expressing the conviction that they ought to be recognized by states as potential rights and consequently as determinants of present aspirations and guides to present policies.[42]

I quote at length to challenge the impression that classifying a value as a "manifesto right" is somehow to disparage it as normatively inert. Feinberg

---

[39] Ibid. 432-3. I consider O'Neill's position further below (§ 25).

[40] Joel Feinberg, *Social Philosophy* (Englewood Cliffs, NJ: Prentice Hall, 1973), 67, 95. O'Neill uses the phrase in "Women's Rights: Whose Obligations?" in *Bounds of Justice* (Cambridge: Cambridge University Press, 2000), 99-100.

[41] Feinberg, *Social Philosophy*, 94 (emphasis in original).   [42] Ibid. 67.

holds that a "manifesto right" can guide action even if it is not correlated with a duty on any assignable agent to see to the satisfaction of the right for any particular person. It can do so by establishing as a goal of political action for agents appropriately situated the creation of conditions in which it would be possible to satisfy the right, and hence, to assign duties to see to its satisfaction.

Another way to put the point is this. A government's failure to prevent or remediate a rights deprivation might give rise to two different types of reasons for action for outside agents. "Direct" reasons are reasons to act in ways whose success would bring about enjoyment of the substance of the right for those deprived. Reasons of this type can call for various kinds of action. These might include, for example, ceasing activities that bring about or contribute to the deprivation, offering protection against threats of deprivation by other agents or by natural forces, and providing aid that would offset or compensate for the effects of the deprivation.[43] (It should be observed—a point Feinberg omits—that circumstances might be such that one has direct reasons with respect to some people under a threat but not to others, perhaps because resources are sufficiently scarce that only some can be helped.) "Indirect" reasons are those that count in favor of actions by which an agent can help establish conditions in which those deprived, or their successors, could enjoy the substance of the right in the future. A particularly important kind of indirect reason is the reason one may have to contribute to the establishment and operation of cooperative schemes designed to undertake such actions. An agent's situation would be analogous to what it might be in an unjust society: although there would be no duty to comply with the rules that would apply if the society's institutions were just, yet one might have a duty to help establish just arrangements with which one would have a duty to comply once established, at least when this can be done without excessive sacrifice.[44]

The idea of a "manifesto right" shows that a right can be action-guiding even when no agent is in a position to perform a sequence of actions that would result in enjoyment of the substance of the right for those deprived. Although I shall not use Feinberg's phrase, this fact will be important when we turn to questions about the "supply side" of human rights (§ 25).

---

[43] Shue, *Basic Rights*, 51–60.
[44] I adapt Rawls's formulation of the natural duty of justice. *A Theory of Justice*, § 19, p. 99.

19. The role of states

The model may also seem objectionable for the prominent role it assigns to states. There are two dimensions. First, according to the model, human rights apply in the first instance to states, in the sense that the protections guaranteed by human rights are supposed to be achieved, for any state's residents, by means of the laws and policies of that state. Second, in this model, states are the principal guarantors of the human rights performance of other states, both through their collaborative activities in international organizations and by unilateral action.

These features prompt the question whether the model is excessively state-centric.[45] There are empirical reasons for thinking it might be. The main forms of global political and economic life are different today than in the postwar years. For example, as transnational firms have developed since World War II, their activities have become more resistant to effective regulation by their home states and by host states in which they operate. There has been a proliferation of nongovernmental organizations with independent influence and a capacity to organize political action "horizontally," by coordinating activities across borders. International organizations and treaty-based regimes have grown in number and functional complexity, and might now be thought to have sufficiently independent political significance to be treated as directly subject to human rights requirements. Systems of global and regional regulation have been elaborated, for example by means of globalized administrative law and within transnational networks of state-level officials, which adhere to norms that cannot be analyzed as expressions of the sovereign power of states. At the same time, some states have suffered a deterioration of their capacities to govern, often in the face of challenges from sectional and separatist political forces. These various developments draw into question some of the background assumptions that made the assignment to states of primary responsibility for human rights seem plausible. It is not always clear that governments can be relied upon to protect their residents against the threat of infringement by non-state actors. It is also not clear that states, acting alone or collaboratively, are typically in the best position to act effectively to bring about human rights compliance

---

[45] It is a distinct question whether the centrality of states in the contemporary organization of world order is in some way undesirable. For a comprehensive theory of global justice this question would be essential, but for the conception of human rights set forth here, it need not arise (§ 20).

in other states. An objector might therefore hold that the two-level model is deficient in its failure to take account of the fact that the actors whose behavior is or should be regulated by human rights norms include various types of non-state actors (such as business firms or political networks) and that those with responsibilities to enforce also include non-state actors (all of those mentioned, plus nongovernmental organizations).[46]

I shall comment about this objection shortly, but let me note first that our question about the role of states in the model might be asked from quite a different perspective as well. The model describes states acting alone or collaboratively as the principal guarantors of the human rights performance of other states. This "interference-justifying" feature of the two-level model is an interpretation of the idea that human rights are matters of international concern. Someone might say, however, that this idea is open to another interpretation under which human rights infringements in state A do not provide a reason for state B to interfere. Perhaps the content of the idea of international concern is exhausted by the statement of human rights standards in declarations and treaties with the authority of international law with the responsibility for compliance reserved exclusively for individual states. Thus it might be said that although states have duties to satisfy human rights standards within their jurisdictions, other states and international organizations have not only no reason (not even *pro tanto*) but no right to interfere when these duties are not complied with. They are stopped from acting by considerations of either collective self-determination or national sovereignty. This is not an esoteric view: it is, for example, the position of the Chinese government and is held in some form by other governments whose adherence to human rights norms is combined with an insistence that the principle of non-intervention limits transnational action to protect human rights.[47] This objection leads to a conclusion that is in a way the opposite of

---

[46] The pertinent literature is extensive. On business firms, see Steven R. Ratner, "Corporations and Human Rights: A Theory of Legal Responsibility," *Yale Law Journal* 111 (2001): 443–545; David Weissbrodt and Muria Kruger, "Norms on the Responsibilities of Transnational Corporations and Other Business Enterprises with Regard to Human Rights," *American Journal of International Law* 97 (2003): 901–22. On global administrative law and network governance, see Benedict Kingsbury, Nico Krisch, and Richard B. Stewart, "The Emergence of Global Administrative Law," *Law and Contemporary Problems* 68 3-4 (2005): 15–61; and Anne-Marie Slaughter, *A New World Order* (Princeton, NJ: Princeton University Press, 2004). On transnational issue networks, see Margaret E. Keck and Kathryn Sikkink, *Activists beyond Borders* (Ithaca, NY: Cornell University Press, 1998), esp. ch. 1.

[47] For the Chinese government position, see China, Information Office of the State Council, *Human Rights in China* (Beijing: Information Office of the State Council, 1991); and the discussion in Ann Kent, *China, the United Nations, and Human Rights* (Philadelphia: University of Pennsylvania

what follows from the objection canvassed in the previous paragraph: not, so to speak, that the model claims too little for the practice, but that it claims too much.

I do not believe that either objection provides a good reason to revise our statement of the model. One need not dispute the accuracy of the observations that motivate the first objection to hold that contemporary human rights practice has not (or not yet) responded to them. The human rights treaties all place the primary responsibility for compliance on states and rely on states to regulate the behavior of non-state actors. The formal mechanisms for monitoring human rights violations are overwhelmingly constituted of states and their reporting procedures rely primarily on states (nongovernmental organizations have an important but subsidiary role).[48] It is true that there have been efforts to frame human rights principles directly applicable to business firms,[49] but thus far these efforts have lacked the independent structure and regularity to justify considering them as elements of an ongoing global practice. Of course, an important feature of global human rights practice is its emergent and evolutionary character, so that what appear to us today as irregular and episodic political efforts could develop into more highly structured elements of practice in the future. If that occurred, it would argue for a revision of the model. But it has not occurred yet.

The response to the second objection is similar although historically more complex. As we have seen, the question of the scope and limits of permissible international action to protect human rights has been disputed from the beginning. The Charter commits the UN and its members to protect and promote human rights while withholding authority to interfere in matters falling within the domestic jurisdiction of states, and the covenants include affirmations of the rights of "all peoples" to self-determination (§ 4). Yet both covenants and every subsequent international human rights instrument have included some type of machinery of implementation, typically a

---

Press, 1999), 158-9. For a defense of a similar position, see Li Buyun, "International Protection of Human Rights and the State Sovereignty," *Constitutionalism and China* (Beijing: Law Press, 2006), 447-60 [first published 1995].

[48] For a further discussion, see Jack Donnelly, "The Social Construction of International Human Rights," in *Human Rights in Global Politics*, ed. Tim Dunne and Nicholas Wheeler (Cambridge: Cambridge University Press, 1999), 85-8, 91-6.

[49] E.g. UN Human Rights Commission, Subcommission on the Promotion and Protection of Human Rights, *Norms on the Responsibilities of Transnational Corporations and Other Business Enterprises with Regard to Human Rights*, August 26, 2003 (E/CN.4/Sub. 2/2003/12/Rev. 2).

procedure for the international monitoring of the human rights practices of the parties. A substantial body of international opinion holds that coercive intervention to protect against the worst human rights abuses by governments may be justifiable.[50] (Even the government of China, while holding as a general principle that "human rights are essentially matters within the domestic jurisdiction of a country," also holds that "to effect international protection of human rights, the international community should interfere with and stop acts that endanger world peace and security, such as gross human rights violations caused by colonialism, racism, foreign aggression and occupation, as well as apartheid, racial discrimination, genocide, slave trade and serious violation of human rights by international terrorist organizations."[51]) There is an extensive record of transnational political action short of the use of force aimed at protecting human rights (§ 6). The idea that international concern for human rights is exhausted by the authoritative statement of human rights standards, leaving the responsibility for compliance exclusively in the hands of individual states, is not consistent with these facts. The contestable issue is different: not whether infringements of human rights generate reasons for outside agents to act, but what forms of action by which agents would be permissible for various types of violations. Dispute of this kind is common in the public discourse of human rights. Here, again, a model aiming for descriptive accuracy should leave room for it.

[50] This is reflected in International Commission on Intervention and State Sovereignty, *The Responsibility to Protect*, and is substantially affirmed in UN General Assembly, 60th Session, *Resolution 60/1 [2005 World Summit Outcome]* (A/Res/60/1), October 24, 2005. Neither, of course, has the force of international law.

[51] China, Information Office of the State Council, *Human Rights in China*, pt. X.

6

Normativity

A PRACTICAL approach seeks to distinguish between the problems of conceptualizing human rights and of grasping their basis and determining their content. The two-level model is a response to the first problem, not the second or third. These problems need to be considered separately.

The normative questions of interest arise at several levels of generality. At the most general level, the issue is this. We have before us an existing normative practice and we must decide what orientation to adopt toward it. Considered in general and as an element of a larger global normative order, we want to know if the practice is of a kind we have reason to endorse and support. What desirable purposes might such a practice seek to achieve and why, if at all, should we regard their achievement as a sufficiently important objective of global political life to justify imposing costs on those agents whose contributions the practice claims to enlist? Stepping down a level, we want to know whether the norms of the practice as we find it make up a justifiable instantiation of the practice's general kind. So we must ask by what criteria we should select among the various requirements that might comprise a practice seeking to achieve these justifying purposes, and how well the norms actually embodied in existing international doctrine satisfy these criteria. At a third level, the problems involve the related questions of the types and identities of the agents who might be called upon to defend and advance the norms properly considered to belong to the practice and the kinds of reasons why these agents should do so. Who should act when human rights are threatened, and why?

I have distinguished these questions for clarity but it will be obvious that they are closely related. The selection criteria for the substantive requirements of human rights should be compatible with a persuasive view of the practice's justifying purposes. These criteria should take account of the

kinds of reasons for action probably available to those agents most likely to
be in a position to act when various of the practice's norms are breached.
And, of course, these reasons will depend on the kinds of actions likely to
be available to these agents and on their prospects of success, costs, and
risks.

We consider the normativity of human rights in this chapter and the next.
I begin in this chapter with a sketch of a view about the value of a practice
with the functional features of human rights. It should be stressed that our
interest at this initial stage is in a practice of a certain kind, not necessarily in
the practice as it now exists. The idea is to work from a generalized
understanding of the value that this kind of practice might have to a more
discriminating account of the considerations that bear on judgments about
the practice's normative content, a subject I turn to next. I shall present
these considerations in the form of a schema that seeks to relate them to the
functional features of human rights represented in the two-level model and
a view about the justifying purposes of the practice, so conceived. Among
other considerations, the schema holds that any value counted as a human
right should be such that a government's failure to respect it could give rise
to reasons for external agents to act in its defense. A grasp of the nature and
variety of these reasons is the beginning of an account of international
responsibility for human rights. (We return to that subject in the next
chapter, where we consider some hard cases about the contents of human
rights.) With the schema in hand, I turn briefly to the common belief that
human rights are in some way "minimalist" and the opposing view that they
restate the requirements of social justice, and explain why neither position
seems correct. The remainder of the chapter is devoted to the idea of
international toleration. Many people think this idea should play an independent role in reasoning about the contents of human rights. The schema
makes no explicit reference to it, so I should explain why I believe its import
has been misunderstood.

The account of normativity I shall suggest displays two features worth
noting in advance, both of which are consequences of taking a practical
approach. First, on this account, human rights do not appear as a fundamental moral category. For any particular human right, it is always possible
to ask why *this* right should be part of a global normative doctrine and to
expect a reply that brings forward further moral (and other) considerations.
Human rights operate at a middle level of practical reasoning, serving to
organize these further considerations and bring them to bear on a certain

range of choices. Moreover, these further considerations are diverse. According to the view I shall suggest, human rights need not be interpreted as deriving their authority from a single, more basic value or interest such as those of human dignity, personhood, or membership. The reasons we have to care about them vary with the content of the right in question and the nature of our relationship, if any, with various classes of potential victims of abuse. Human rights protect a plurality of interests and require different kinds and degrees of commitment of different agents. These rights have a distinctive identity as normative standards, but this identity is not to be found in their grounds or in the nature of their requirements for action. We find it, instead, in their special role as norms of global political life.

20. What human rights are for

Human rights are standards for domestic institutions whose satisfaction is a matter of international concern. As I have observed, a practice of human rights, so conceived, might be described as "statist" in at least two senses: its standards apply in the first instance to states, and they rely on states, individually and in collaboration, as their principal guarantors. This does not mean that human rights impose no constraints on other agents or that only states have responsibilities as guarantors. But the centrality of states to the practice of human rights cannot be denied. Perhaps there would be analogous institutional standards in a world that was differently organized, but if there were, the political role and substantive content of these standards would very likely be different. The practice of human rights as it has developed so far can only be understood as a revisionist appurtenance of a world order of independent, territorial states.

The significance of this is not only descriptive; it means that any plausible view of the justifying purposes of a practice of human rights must be compatible with the fact that the state constitutes the basic unit of the world's political organization. A theory of human rights is not a theory of ideal global justice. At the most general level, the relevant question is not whether, within the ideal political constitution of the world, a practice of human rights would have a place. Instead we take certain basic facts about the world's political structure as fixed and consider the purposes of a practice of human rights within this structure. In doing so, we need not commit ourselves to a more inclusive judgment one way or the other about the

acceptability or legitimacy of the states system itself, regarded as a question
of ideal theory; for our purposes, that question does not arise.

The basic facts are clear. The political structure of the world consists of a
system of territorially defined political units, each claiming to exercise
legitimate political authority within its borders. These states comprise a
political order, a "society of states."[1] Although not organized on the
model of domestic-level societies, the global order is constituted by a system *economic ties*
of norms that facilitates states' interactions and organizes cooperation to
supply collective goods. Among other things, these norms define a sphere of
autonomous domestic authority within which each state is secured against
coercive external interference. Although this structure does not ordinarily
sustain itself by enlisting the wills of the individual members of states, it
claims a kind of acceptability: its norms present themselves as regulative for
states and in some respects for individuals and non-state actors, and noncompliance is generally regarded as a reason for criticism and perhaps
sanctions.

Historically, the argument for a global practice with the functional
features of human rights turns on an empirical thesis about the pathologies
of a global political structure that concentrates power at dispersed locations
not subject to higher-order control. Such a thesis was a commonplace
among the framers and early advocates of modern human rights doctrine
(§ 4). They regarded World War II and its precipitating events as evidence
of a structural deficiency in the system of states as it then existed. By
embracing a broad sphere of autonomous domestic authority, the system's
norms provided a safe haven for governments that mistreated or failed to
protect their populations in ways that had devastating consequences for
those affected. They believed, moreover, that the prospects for domestic
misconduct could be reduced by international cooperation to establish and
implement a set of common standards. The framers also believed, as a
further empirical thesis, that the institutional and cultural features that
caused or enabled governments to engage in these forms of mistreatment
also contributed to a tendency to pursue aggressive foreign policies. Human
rights, considered as a set of standards for governments together with an
international means of implementation, were a remedy for both deficiencies, a way to repair a structural fault of the prewar system of states.

[1] The phrase is Hedley Bull's. See e.g. "Society and Anarchy in International Relations," in
Diplomatic Investigations, ed. Herbert Butterfield and Martin Wight (London: George Allen and
Unwin, 1966), 35–50.

What is the significance of these ideas? One way to assess their force is to consider an informal thought experiment. Suppose we were in a position to choose principles for a "society of states." We recognize that the global order disposes various international and transnational legal and political capacities, some of which are only latent, that might be employed to regulate the domestic conduct of governments. We then ask whether any defensible purpose would be served by establishing a system of standards for the domestic conduct of governments that might be implemented through the development and use of these regulative capacities. Why should *any* standards for domestic-level institutions be recognized as matters of international concern? Why not leave individual states to their own devices?

The nature of the appropriate reply depends on the perspective from which we consider the question. The idea of a "society of states" leaves it ambiguous whether the appropriate perspective is that of states in their corporate capacities (as, perhaps, the classical international jurists might have imagined) or that of individuals whose circumstances would be affected by the compliance of states and subordinate actors with the system's norms.[2] The empirical theses speak to both perspectives: the contention that neglect of human rights by states increases the likelihood of aggression appeals primarily to the corporate interests of states, whereas the contention that it allows predictable forms of official abuse and neglect appeals to the interests of individuals. The main question about the first contention concerns its empirical premise, to which I return briefly below. Assuming its plausibility for the moment, the reasoning for the desired conclusion is straightforward. The second contention might be thought more problematic. Returning to our thought experiment, suppose we regard the choice of principles for a global order of independent states from the perspective of individuals who recognize the historical possibility that the actions and omissions of governments, shielded from external interference by norms that protect a broad sphere of domestic autonomy, can have disastrous

---

[2] The ambiguity is present in Bull's remarks about human rights in *The Anarchical Society*, 3rd edn. (New York: Columbia University Press, 2002 [1st edn., 1977]), ch. 2. He treats human rights as subversive of the organizing principles of the "society of states" because of the possibility of conflict between a state's political values and the values embodied in human rights. He does not, however, endorse the principles of the "society of states" as the only valid norms of global political life; he also recognizes the pertinence of what he describes as "individual or human justice" (pp. 79-80), which on his view serves as the basis of human rights, and argues that in practice a system of states can accommodate these values (although perhaps in a distorted or incomplete way). Consider also Bull's Hagey Lectures, *Justice in International Relations* (Waterloo, Ontario: University of Waterloo, 1984), esp. p. 13.

consequences for the most urgent of the interests of their people. We then ask, taking the structural features of such a political order as more-or-less fixed, under what conditions it would be reasonable to expect people to accept and support it.[3] If we assume that it is reasonable to care about protecting one's most important interests against predictable forms of official abuse and neglect, then, recognizing that the global order disposes a capacity for self-regulation, it seems, *prima facie*, that a condition of its acceptability would be the establishment of an apparatus by which the domestic juris-diction of states could be limited and its exercise regulated so as to guard against such a threat. A global practice of human rights might be understood as such a precautionary apparatus.[4]

This *prima facie* position is open to some challenges. Before turning to them, two comments to elaborate. First, the account I have rehearsed locates the significance of a practice of human rights in two different aims: to protect important individual interests against predictable threats and to deter societies from developing certain features that might cause their governments to pursue policies that threaten international order. Assuming, still, that the empirical premise of the second aim is true, it should be observed that there is no *a priori* reason to believe that these two purposes justify the same catalog of protections. For example, although there may be a superficial plausibility to the thought that genocidal regimes are likely to be aggressive as well, it is much less plausible that the same association holds for various other failures (e.g. to satisfy minimum welfare standards). There is also no reason to assume that these two rationales allow the same range of preventive and remedial responses to violations. Indeed, it seems more likely that concern to accomplish these purposes would produce diver-gences in both respects. So they make an unstable combination. The question is whether and in what respects this might present a problem.

In general, there is nothing untoward about characterizing a practice as advancing more than one value. Even as ostensibly simple a practice as the exchange of gifts is notoriously complex in the aims it seeks to accom-plish. The issue posed when a practice seeks to advance multiple values is how to choose when circumstances force a choice among alternatives that

---

[3] For the most part, the political expression of acceptance and support must be indirect; it takes place through the policies of one's government. But this fact does not diminish the force of the question.

[4] Compare the discussion of "conditional sovereignty" in Henry Shue, *Basic Rights*, 2nd edn. (Princeton, NJ: Princeton University Press, 1996), 174-5 (in the 1996 Afterword).

contribute differently to the different values. Problems of this kind might arise for human rights at several levels: for example, in thinking about which protections should count as human rights or which features of a particular domestic violation might justify international action. There is no question that dilemmas of these kinds can occur in practical deliberation. The point for now is that they arise "downstream" from questions of purpose: unless the conflict between the underlying values is systematic and pervasive, its possibility does not give us reason to resist attributing multiple purposes to the practice.

The more important observation is that the empirical premise required for the argument that encouraging respect for human rights promotes international peace is notably insecure. To date, there is very little systematic evidence that governments that abuse their people's human rights pose a greater threat than other governments to international order, and it is not at all clear what causal mechanism could explain such a regularity, if it were found to exist.[5] Even in the cases of prewar Germany and Japan, it would be speculative to suppose that the features of these regimes that explain their various forms of domestic misconduct were also responsible in any substantial way for the decisions that led to war. And it would be a further step to the proposition that the forms of action available to international agents in response to a regime's domestic misconduct could also reach to the underlying features supposed to influence the regime's foreign policy. We cannot resolve the historical and political questions here, but in the absence of better evidence it is difficult to see how a persuasive account of the justification of a practice of human rights can be developed from a generalized concern to protect international stability. This, of course, does not

---

[5] One relevant study is David Sobek, M. Rodwan Abouhard, and Christopher G. Ingram, "The Human Rights Peace: How the Respect for Human Rights at Home Leads to Peace Abroad," *Journal of Politics* 68 (2006): 519–29. These authors find that pairs of states, both of which respect human rights, tend not to fight each other. But neither the causal mechanism nor the inference about individual state behavior outside of rights-respecting dyads is obvious. Notwithstanding the absence of more robust evidence, the belief that there is a relationship between noncompliance with human rights norms and a tendency to aggression in foreign policy seems to be widely held. For example, Rawls's account of human rights in *The Law of Peoples* (Cambridge, MA: Harvard University Press, 1999) relies at some points on such a belief (e.g. p. 81). One might think the belief is made plausible by analogy with the hypothesis of a "democratic peace." That hypothesis is controversial, but even if one takes it to be persuasive, it is, at best, only of indirect relevance to human rights, because regimes that score badly on measures of democracy need not also score badly on measures of human rights compliance. So even if it is true that nondemocracies are more likely to initiate wars, there is no straightforward inference that regimes that abuse human rights are also more likely to do so.

exclude the possibility that there may be cases in which a regime's domestic misconduct might contribute to international instability; consider, for example, domestic abuse that prompts massive cross-border flows of refugees. In such cases, considerations about international stability might supply a reason for international action to stop the domestic misconduct. But this kind of case, in which the cause of instability is the misconduct itself rather than those aspects of the domestic society and culture that bring it about, is not what the original argument contemplates.

The second comment is this. In framing the *prima facie* argument for regarding a practice of human rights as a precautionary apparatus, I refrained from describing the practice's purposes in relation to the norm of sovereignty or to the distinction sometimes drawn between "statist" and "cosmopolitan" conceptions of global justice. Human rights are often described in terms that recall this distinction—for example, as the entering wedge of a more comprehensive form of cosmopolitan concern, as an expression of "individual" as opposed to "international" justice, or as evidence for the proposition that individuals are or should be regarded as subjects of international law in their own right. There is no question that human rights have a cosmopolitan purpose in the limited sense that they represent certain aspects of the internal structure and conduct of governments as properly subjects of international concern. Perhaps it is illuminating to think of them as imposing conditions on the permissible exercise of the prerogatives traditionally associated with the norm of sovereignty. But I do not believe it is accurate or constructive to adopt a view of the justifying purposes of the practice that requires a commitment to one or another larger conception of global justice. The conventional distinction between such conceptions, although perhaps illuminating for other purposes, is a distraction here and might distort our view of the justification of the practice when it is considered as an element of the existing global normative order.

Let me turn to two challenges to the *prima facie* account of the purposes of the practice given earlier. The first derives from a position I shall call the "anti-imperial view." This view accepts the empirical thesis that a system of states with no central authority is vulnerable to potentially egregious forms of domestic misconduct by governments, but it does not accept the inference that a global practice of human rights is a suitable remedy. This is because the view adopts the further thesis that, when inequalities of power among states are sufficiently great, hegemonic states are likely to use whatever devices are at their disposal to advance their interests regardless of the consequences for weaker states and their people. A global practice of human rights, according to this view, would in fact offer opportunities for imperial self-aggrandizement through the self-interested and perhaps hypocritical manipulation of the mechanisms established by the practice for exercising influence in other societies. This, in turn, would present a greater risk of damage than benefit to urgent human interests. One inference is that a more desirable alternative—one that might be seen as responding to both empirical theses—would be a practice like that of human rights, but with the element of "international concern" limited to the declaration of global norms and perhaps establishment of some non-intrusive form of international monitoring. Any further responsibility for implementation would be reserved exclusively to domestic governments.[6]

The question is whether the anti-imperial view is better understood as a challenge to the precautionary account of the purposes of human rights or as a form of argument occurring within a practice that seeks these purposes. If the (first) empirical thesis is accepted, then it is hard to resist the thought that some kind of global apparatus designed to deter or limit certain forms of misconduct by governments would be preferable to none, when the matter is considered from the perspective of individuals concerned to protect their most important interests. The real point of the dispute between the anti-imperial and the precautionary views seems to concern the nature of this apparatus. To what extent and in what ways should it license external agents in acting to deter or prevent, or to seek remedies for, harmful domestic conduct by governments? A resolution of the dispute turns on broadly instrumental considerations about how a global practice of human rights might be structured, whether global institutions might be developed to contain pressures for hegemonic corruption within the practice, and what results might be expected from the alternatives. The result of taking these considerations seriously might be revisionary; we consider them later (§ 29). For now, the important point is that one can recognize the anti-imperial view's reservations about the uses to which human rights might be put by hegemonic powers without being driven to reject a precautionary account of the justifying purposes of the practice, provided it is left open for determination at a later stage which forms of international action, and by

---

[6] This position, with the local responsibility reserved for the government, might be associated with the conception of human rights advocated by the government of China and discussed earlier (§ 19).

which agents, are acceptable in response to violations of the practice's various norms.

The other challenge arises from the possibility of conflict between a precautionary human rights regime and the exercise of collective self-determination in individual societies. It seems clear that such a conflict could occur. For example, nothing rules out the possibility that the government of a constitutional democracy, say, or for that matter the society's laws or constitution, could violate internationally recognized human rights.[7] In such a case it might appear that action by external agents seeking to bring about a change in the offending law or policy would be an objectionable interference in a society's exercise of collective self-determination. A conception of the justifying purposes of human rights that allows interference in such cases might therefore seem implausibly permissive.

This challenge raises large issues, although perhaps not as large as it may appear. Here, as before, the force of the challenge depends on how the details of the practice are filled in, in particular the demandingness and scope of its norms and the forms of international action their violation is taken to justify. It depends, also, on how the idea of collective self-determination is understood: although it is clear that this idea has a content that restricts its application—as the paradigm case of colonial rule suggests, not every kind of regime can be regarded as expressing the self-determination of its people—we have no unambiguous, pre-theoretical conception of the conditions a government or constitution should satisfy to be so regarded. We can imagine views about all three of these subjects—the content of the practice's norms, the forms of action the practice takes to be justifiable in response to violations, and the conditions for collective self-determination—such that, when these views are taken together, objectionable interference by outside agents to protect against violations of human rights norms would seem likely to occur frequently and in a wide variety of circumstances. Imagine, for example, the combination of an extensive list of protections, a principle justifying coercive international action in any case of substantial violation and a conception of self-determination whose conditions could be satisfied by most any actually occurring type of regime. If one took these

---

[7] Unless, of course, one takes the view that no political society should be considered democratic unless its constitution protects its people's human rights. In that case the possibility of conflict would still arise, but at an earlier stage of reasoning about the requirements of political legitimacy. Seyla Benhabib, *Another Cosmopolitanism* (New York: Oxford University Press, 2006), 32-6.

starting points as given, the prospect of frequent, objectionable interferences would be hard to deny. But of course we need not take any of the starting points as given. The substantial content of human rights, the forms of action for which their violation supplies reasons, and the circumstances under which these reasons should be allowed to be decisive are all matters internal to a theory of the practice. And, although it is a separate question how we should conceive of the conditions of collective self-determination, it is reasonable to expect that under any plausible conception, only certain types of regime would be recognizable as genuinely self-determining, and—though it is plainly a contingent matter—that regimes of these types would be more likely than others to respect at least some human rights. So it may be that, once the details of the practice have been worked out and the conditions for self-determination have been filled in, the chances that the practice would generate frequent, objectionable interferences with self-determination would be considerably less than it first appears. At this stage, of course, we must leave this as a hypothetical possibility. We shall have to return to this challenge later, when we consider the grounds and requirements of some specific human rights (Chapter 7). But it is important to see that the nature and extent of the possible conflict between international concern for human rights and respect for collective self-determination are not, so to speak, fixed *ex ante*: they depend on the details of the practice in its most justifiable form and on the conditions under which there is reason to respect the processes through which a society's government reaches decisions that affect the well-being of its people.

21. A schema

What I have said about the purposes of the practice frames the second question we distinguished earlier. Someone claims there is a human right to some protection P. The claim is meant to be normative: it is not the observation that international doctrine recognizes a right to P but rather an assertion that it should do so. How should we decide whether to agree? To answer this question, we must consider the functional role of human rights in light of a generalized conception of their purposes. The two-level model explicates this functional role by showing what one would be committed to if one accepted the claim that there is a human right to P.

An argument for the claim should be responsive to all three elements of the model.

We might therefore imagine a schema for justifying claims about the content of human rights doctrine with three parts.[8] An argument for any such claim should make good three contentions:

1. That the interest that would be protected by the right is sufficiently important when reasonably regarded from the perspective of those protected that it would be reasonable to consider its protection to be a political priority.

2. That it would be advantageous to protect the underlying interest by means of legal or policy instruments available to the state.

3. That in the central range of cases in which a state might fail to provide the protection, the failure would be a suitable object of international concern.

Each of these contentions needs explanation. Beginning with the first: to account for the importance of an interest, one must explain why it would be reasonable for the agent whose interest it is to consider it an especially bad thing for the interest to be threatened or set back. The required notion of a setback's being a "bad thing" is objective. It is not sufficient and might not be necessary to establish that the agent's preferences would be disappointed if the interest were set back. The judgment in question involves the urgency of the interest, and this is best explained by considering why an agent might reasonably regard the satisfaction of the interest as an important matter. At the same time, to explain why the interest should be made a priority of political action for others, one must account for the importance of the interest in a way that those who might be called upon to protect it could reasonably recognize. Since human rights are supposed to provide reasons for action for agents external to the societies in which they might be violated, the account should not depend exclusively on beliefs and norms that are specific to a single culture or way of life. This requirement can be satisfied in more than one way. For example, some interests are sufficiently generic that it would be reasonable to expect anyone to recognize their

---

[8] The general form of this schema was suggested to me by T. M. Scanlon's remarks about the backing of claims about rights in "Rights, Goals, and Fairness," in *The Difficulty of Tolerance: Essays in Political Philosophy* (Cambridge: Cambridge University Press, 2003), 35. The content of the schema given here is different.

importance (e.g. the interests in physical security and adequate nutrition). In other cases, although the interest when specifically described might not be widely shared, it may be able to be brought under a more abstract description that enables its importance to be recognized even by those who do not share it (e.g. "being able to follow one's religion").[9] In still other cases, the importance of the interest may be derivative; for example, it may be that under contingent but currently prevalent historical circumstances, the satisfaction of the interest would be instrumental to the satisfaction of other interests already identified as important (e.g. perhaps, interests in political participation or in the nondiscriminatory application of the law). Perhaps there are other ways as well. What is essential is that the importance of the interest, seen from the standpoint of a reasonable beneficiary, should be intelligible to reasonable persons who might be called upon to protect it. (This does not amount to a showing that any prospective agent has sufficient reason to undertake protective action. That is a further consideration, taken up in the third part of the schema.)

Some people believe that human rights are best understood as protecting or deriving from a single underlying interest or value. For reasons given earlier (§ 10), I do not believe it is plausible to think of the human rights of international practice in this way. The interests that might be suitable for this role (for example, those in human dignity, personhood, or membership) seem likely either to be too abstract to settle disagreement about the contents of human rights doctrine or arbitrarily to constrain the doctrine's substantive scope. Moreover, there is no clear reason to hold that human rights *should* be explicable in terms of a single master value. Perhaps the pressure to regard them in this way derives from a desire to see them all as standards of the same generic kind. But if we take the discursive functions of human rights as primary, then an account of their normativity need not be embarrassed to appeal to a variety of distinct justifying considerations.[10]

By extension, it also does not seem necessary to identify a list of relatively specific interests or values to serve as the grounds or subject-matters of

---

[9] This is T. M. Scanlon's example. "Value, Desire, and Quality of Life," in *The Difficulty of Tolerance* (Cambridge: Cambridge University Press, 2003), 184. See also Scanlon, "Preference and Urgency," in *The Difficulty of Tolerance*, 74-7.

[10] I do not mean to suggest that values of the kind sometimes thought to play a unique foundational role have no place in an account of the basis of individual human rights. If, as some philosophers believe, it would be reasonable to regard any of these values as sufficiently important that it would be reasonable to make their protection a priority of political action, then that value might have a place within the schema.

human rights. The aim of the schema is to characterize the argument required to support claims about the substance of human rights. It does so, in part, by requiring that the interests that would be protected by some candidate human right be intersubjectively recognizable as important or urgent. Any list that might be proposed would be the result of applying such a requirement, not an alternative to it. There is also a danger that any relatively specific list of interests to be protected by human rights might be undesirably exclusive. A schema that seeks to organize our reasoning about the contents of human rights should identify the standards of judgment appropriate to the subject-matter without artificially constraining the normative open-endedness we have observed in the practice.

The second main contention is that it would be advantageous to protect the underlying interest by means of legal or policy instruments available to the state. Whether or not this is true will not normally depend only on the importance of the underlying interest; not every threat to an important interest is best made the subject of a right.[11] One must also consider the nature and likelihood of the threats to which the interest is likely to be vulnerable and their amenability to political and legal protection. International human rights are not best understood as protections against all perils; they are responses to "standard" threats that can be protected against or remediated by public measures (§ 17). This contention accordingly has two elements. It requires a showing that (a) under some range of reasonably likely circumstances the underlying interest is vulnerable to certain predictable threats; and (b) under these circumstances it would be desirable for the state to protect against or remediate these threats by means of constitutional provision, law, or policy. Both elements depend on more-or-less substantial empirical generalizations about human social behavior and the capacities and dynamics of social institutions. Since human rights are supposed to apply widely, these generalizations should have broad scope. On the other hand, the fact that they interject a dimension of historical and social contingency is not itself an objection; it seems to be generally true of institutional rights that their justification depends to some extent on

---

[11] This adapts J. S. Mill's remark about the proper subjects of legal rights in *Utilitarianism* [1861], in *Essays on Ethics, Religion, and Society* [*Collected Works of John Stuart Mill*, x], ed. J. M. Robson (Toronto: University of Toronto Press, 1969), ch. 5, para. 13. Similarly, Amartya Sen observes that a suitable subject of a human right should be open to some form of "social help." "Elements of a Theory of Human Rights," *Philosophy and Public Affairs* 32 (2004), 329.

contingent empirical beliefs of this kind and there is no obvious reason why we should expect human rights to be different.

Finally, since human rights are supposed to be capable of guiding political action by agents external to the societies in which they are breached, it must be shown that any candidate human right is a suitable object of international concern. Whatever its importance regarded from the perspective of potential beneficiaries and however appropriate it would be as a requirement for domestic institutions, a protection cannot count as a human right if it fails to satisfy a requirement of this kind. What should be true of a value to satisfy this condition? Offhand there are at least four considerations. First, the value should be such that first-level failures to satisfy its requirements are amenable to correction or remediation by means of some sequence of actions that could be carried out by political agents outside the society in question. This is a requirement of feasibility. Second, any such actions should be permissible: they should satisfy whatever general standards of political morality are pertinent and should have reasonable prospects of success. The analogy is to the *jus in bello*. Third, in the central range of cases, there should be some outside agents (not necessarily the same in every case) that, in virtue of their location, capabilities, and resources, would be in a position to carry out these actions. Finally, again in the central range of cases, at least a proper subset of these eligible agents should have reason to bear the burdens that would be imposed by taking the actions.[12] In the general case, it will not be enough simply to point to the reasons why the interest protected by a right is important for the prospective beneficiaries; there is no general obligation to contribute to the satisfaction of other people's interests. Various other factors may also need to be taken into account. These include the nature and importance of the threatened interest, the source and explanation of the likely threat, the burdensomeness of the actions contributors would be called upon to perform in order to protect it, the likelihood of harm to both beneficiaries and third parties, and the nature of the historical and present relationships, if any, between beneficiaries and eligible contributors. Taken together, these four factors aim to establish that there is a practical

---

[12] This is inexact, but it is difficult to put the point more precisely. Nothing would be accomplished by including a protection in the public doctrine if the circumstances in which a failure of the protection would generate a reason for outsiders to act were so unusual or eccentric that in practice the right would never justify action. On the other hand it would be too strong to require that a failure should always justify action. We need something like the idea of reasons that would be decisive for some set of outside agents in some nearby possible world. I am grateful to Ryan Davis for conversation about this point.

point to counting a protection as an international human right: its object should be a value the deprivation of which is open to some permissible and constructive form of international action that some class of agents could have reason to carry out.[13]

In referring to these three contentions as a "schema" I do not mean to overstate their import. By itself a schema does not settle anything. It is simply a framework or outline of the reasoning that would be necessary to arrive at judgments about the protections that should make up a public doctrine of human rights. The details of this reasoning will vary with the nature of the protection in question. This is best illustrated by considering in detail some candidates for recognition as human rights, a task we turn to in the next chapter. Before doing so, I comment about two topics of more general interest for the question of the normativity of human rights. The first is the idea that there is some ethically important sense in which we should be able to regard human rights as a "moral minimum." The second is the thought that the substantive contents of any justifiable doctrine of human rights should respect the value of international toleration.

22. Minimalism and social justice

The position I have sketched starts from an interpretation of the purpose and functions of human rights derived from an inspection of the practice: they are standards for domestic institutions whose widespread recognition as matters of international concern is a condition of the acceptability of the system of states. The schema represents the normative problem as one of identifying the values for which there is sufficient reason to treat them in this role. But this may appear to be objectionably open-ended: it seems to invite a proliferation of human rights. Many people suppose that human rights must be in some way "minimalist," but this approach does not appear to set any limit to the normative range of human rights.[14] The question is whether this is a defect of the schema.

[13] This is the international analog of the observation quoted from Sen in n. 11, above.
[14] See e.g. James W. Nickel, "Poverty and Rights," *Philosophical Quarterly* 55 (2005), 386 (human rights aim to ensure conditions "of a minimally good life"); Michael Ignatieff, *Human Rights as Politics and Idolatry* (Princeton, NJ: Princeton University Press, 2001), 56 (human rights are minimum conditions "for any life at all").

The idea that human rights are or ought to be "minimalist" is hardly univocal. A doctrine might be considered to be minimalist according to any of several different dimensions of variation—for example, in the scope or urgency of the protections it contains, the cost of implementing these protections, the intrusiveness of the means of action it authorizes, or—the simplest possibility—the number of threats protected against. Obviously these are not the same. Perhaps the most plausible interpretation of the idea is that a doctrine of human rights should be limited to protections of the most urgent of interests against the most likely of threats. Someone who took such a view might say, for example, that there is a human right to the means of subsistence but not to a fair wage; to protection against arbitrary arrest but not to freedom of occupation; to collective self-determination but not to democratic institutions; to sufficient primary education to be a productive member of society but not to higher education.

Such a position should be puzzling to anyone who takes contemporary practice seriously (§ 5). Even limiting ourselves to the rights listed in the declaration, human rights are not in this straightforward way "minimalist." They include standards bearing on most significant dimensions of a society's basic structure, from protections against the misuse of state power to requirements for the legal system and political process, the organization of the economy, and the level of public provision. On the face of it, these standards do not seem significantly more minimal than the requirements of many theories of social justice. Indeed, one might be tempted to hold that human rights simply *are* the rights of social justice.[15]

This, however, cannot be right. The best reply to the "minimalist" objection is to say why. Human rights are matters of international concern and it is not plausible that the international community should take responsibility for the justice of its component societies.[16] For one thing, requirements of justice are grounded in interests of different degrees of urgency and therefore exert claims of different weights. There is a difference, for example, between the interest in having a standard of living adequate for a decent life and the interest in not feeling ashamed or humiliated by one's

[15] There is some resonance of this idea in the contemporary practice. One observer holds that "The human rights movement is now concerned with global social justice." Andrew Clapham, *Human Rights: A Very Short Introduction* (Oxford: Oxford University Press, 2007), 162. In the past I have had some sympathy for this idea. "What Human Rights Mean," *Daedalus* 132 1 (winter 2003), 39.

[16] Someone might plausibly believe there is a general duty not to obstruct or undermine the functioning of just institutions, where they exist. But that is a separate matter.

material situation considered in relation to those of others. Both interests are urgent in the sense that their satisfaction would be important in a wide range of lives. But if we suppose that the international resources available for advancing human rights are scarce, then if the first interest could somehow be satisfied with international help for everyone, the demand for a further international investment to satisfy the second would be less pressing. Secondly, some requirements of justice may not be achievable by means of any permissible form of action available to outside agents. Consider, for example, the difference between assisting a society to develop its economy sufficiently to eliminate the worst forms of poverty and causing it to attain an income distribution that satisfies some more ambitious standard of distributive justice. Finally, it is not unreasonable to expect the requirements of social justice, at the level of institutions, laws, and policies, to vary across societies in ways that respond to differences in the economic, social, and cultural background. One example is the question of whether the value of effective political participation in a society's affairs requires special provisions for the representation of minority groups; another involves the details of the constitutional provisions required to protect religious freedom. This need not be a "relativist" thesis, of course; it is consistent with the idea that the same abstract moral requirements might be capable of being instantiated in various different ways at the level of institutions. The point is that judgments about the requirements of justice at this level sometimes turn on complex assessments of the significance of the pertinent background facts. The nature of these judgments may be such that outsiders are at a disadvantage in making them reliably.

Each of these reasons to limit the scope of human rights to something less than the requirements of social justice derives its force from an appreciation of the practical role of human rights as sources of reasons for transnational political action. They follow from a grasp of the functional aims of the practice. On the other hand, these considerations do not argue that human rights are in any other way "minimalist"—for example, they do not support the idea that human rights are protections of conditions for "a minimally good life" or "for any life at all." If human rights can be said to be "minimalist" in any sense, it is that they constitute only a "proper subset" of the rights of social justice.[17] But to say this is not to say very much. The

---

[17] This is Rawls's phrase. *The Law of Peoples*, 81. Also see Joshua Cohen, "Minimalism about Human Rights," *Journal of Political Philosophy* 12 (2004), 210-13.

question of the composition of this subset is a separate question of global
political theory, to be settled in a way that takes account of the special role of
human rights in the normative discourse of global political life.

23. Toleration (1): the domestic analogy

The considerations I have suggested to guide judgments about the contents
of human rights do not refer to the value of international toleration. Many
people have thought this to be an independently important consideration
that limits what human rights can require. But it is not clear what international toleration means or why we should regard it as an independent
value.

Historically the idea that toleration is a value in international relations
arose as an application of the domestic analogy. For example, in the most
influential modern formulation, Vattel holds that each state is a "moral
person having an understanding and a will peculiar to itself." Like individuals in a state of nature, nations are "free and independent." Each should
therefore "be left to the peaceable enjoyment of that liberty which belongs
to it by nature." It follows that each nation "has the right to govern itself as it
thinks proper. . . . No foreign state may inquire into the manner in which a
sovereign rules, nor set itself up to judge of his conduct."[18]

Vattel's formulation has the merit of expressing the domestic analogy
especially clearly but it is insufficiently qualified to be taken seriously today.
Few would agree, for example, that it is a virtue to tolerate regimes that
violently repress religious minorities. Still, the idea that we have reason to
accept a high degree of variation among constitutions and political, moral,
and religious cultures has been the majority view in modern international
thought. The distinguishing feature of the idea is that societies organized as
states are both objects and agents of toleration: they have duties to tolerate

---

[18] Emerich de Vattel, *The Law of Nations* [*Le Droit des gens*] [1758], trans. Charles G. Fenwick
(Washington, DC: Carnegie Institution, 1916), iii, Introduction, §§ 2, 15; bk. II, ch. 4, §§ 54-5.
See also bk. II, ch. 3, §§ 35, 38. Vattel does not deny that everyone has a right of conscience. He
holds that where there is more than one religion with significant numbers of adherents, the state
has a duty to tolerate; where there is a majority religion and one or more small minorities, the state
has a duty not to obstruct emigration. But none of this implies that outsiders have rights to
interfere; a state's citizens must work out their own terms of association. Bk. I, ch. 12, §§ 128-31,
135; bk. II, ch. 4, §§ 7, 58-9.

other states and in turn have rights to be tolerated by them. For this reason we might call this the "societal conception" of international toleration.

This is not, however, the only way to think of international toleration. We get a different conception by thinking of the international principle as an extension of the principle of toleration in the domestic case rather than as its analog. According to this second conception, individuals are the primary objects of toleration, whereas its agents are political actors at any level, from the local to the global, with the capacity to provide the protection of individual liberties that toleration requires. Societies or states might be objects of toleration as well, but they would be so only derivatively, just in case tolerating a state is the most effective way of ensuring the protection of the liberty interests of its individual members. We might call this the "individualistic conception."

It will be obvious that these conceptions bear differently on the doctrine of human rights. Unless substantially restricted in scope, a societal conception could require refraining from interfering in states whose domestic institutions are intolerant or otherwise disrespectful of the liberties of their own people; an individualistic conception, on the other hand, allows various international actors to take steps to protect individuals against abuses of liberty by their own government. A societal conception might therefore argue for a less demanding doctrine of human rights than an individualistic conception.

One strategy for choosing between these conceptions would be to investigate the reasons for toleration at the domestic level and then to ask how these reasons apply to international conduct. The strategy is complicated by the fact that people disagree about the grounds of toleration in the domestic case. Since it is not our aim to resolve the disagreement, I shall try to avoid it by recalling two different (though not necessarily incompatible) views and asking what plausibly follows for the international case. I do not claim that these exhaust the possibilities.

Both views locate the grounds of toleration in considerations about the autonomy of persons, or, as I shall sometimes say, in the value of self-direction. Suppose we say that a person is autonomous if she has a developed capacity to exert some significant degree of control over her destiny by means of a succession of decisions taken throughout her life. As Joseph Raz puts it, such a person has the capacity to make her life her own.[19] There are

[19] Joseph Raz, *The Morality of Freedom* (Oxford: Clarendon Press, 1986), 369. I am indebted here and elsewhere to Hans Oberdiek, *Tolerance: Between Forbearance and Acceptance* (Lanham, MD: Rowman and Littlefield, 2001), ch. 8.

two ways to understand the relationship between the value of autonomy
and toleration. They differ according to whether the interest in autonomy
which is taken to be fundamental belongs to the agents who are tolerated
(a "first-party interest") or to others who benefit from living in a tolerant
regime (a "third-party interest"). These perspectives generate different
accounts of the value of toleration. Both produce a view of international
toleration in tension with the societal one, but they do so in different ways.

The first argument is the legacy of Kant but I shall present it in a form
suggested by Rawls in *A Theory of Justice*. He observes that persons choosing
principles for their institutions would be concerned to "secure the integrity
of their religious and moral freedom." They would understand that those
who recognize religious and moral obligations regard them as having the
most fundamental importance and would not qualify these obligations "for
the sake of greater means for promoting . . . other interests."[20] He does not
claim that everyone recognizes such obligations in their own lives; it suffices
that some may do so and that anyone can acknowledge that for such persons
it is of the greatest importance to be left free to act on them. The principle of
toleration is a principle of mutual respect among persons who understand
the significance of this interest.[21]

This argument locates the importance of toleration in the centrality of the
first-party interest in the development and expression of a conception of the
good. As Rawls observes, the idea that persons have a capacity for such a
conception is not exclusive: "[t]here is no race or recognized group of
human beings that lacks this attribute."[22] If we accept this as an empirical
truth of human nature, then we are led to one form of the individualistic
view for the international case. The international-level principle would
have an asymmetrical structure: it would require deference to societies
whose domestic institutions are tolerant but would allow toleration-
improving interference in those that are not.[23]

Someone might think that the extension of the argument to the international realm misconstrues its motivating idea. Kant himself held that the

---

[20] John Rawls, *A Theory of Justice*, rev. edn. (Cambridge, MA: Harvard University Press, 1999),
§ 33, pp. 181-2.
[21] Ibid., taking together §§ 40 ("The Kantian Interpretation") and 77 ("The Basis of
Equality").
[22] Ibid., § 77, p. 443.
[23] For an elaboration of this argument to which I am indebted, see Kok-Chor Tan,
Toleration, Diversity, and Global Justice (University Park: Pennsylvania State University Press, 2000),
80-3.

proper expression of respect for individuals' capacities for self-direction at the level of states was to be found in adherence to a principle of non-intervention in each state's internal affairs.[24] It is not clear if Kant's position simply reflects an application of the domestic analogy or if it is the conclusion of an argument (not actually formulated by him) originating in a concern for individual liberty. Perhaps he believed, as a historical matter, that free institutions are most likely to develop in a society as an expression of a deeper social process of cultural growth and enlightenment. Either way, however, I believe the objection is unsuccessful. If it is taken as an analogical argument, it is open to the familiar rejoinder that such an argument is only persuasive when the objects of the analogy are relevantly similar. This is not true of persons and states. If the view is taken as an application of a concern about individual liberty, then, in the absence of (implausible) empirical assumptions about the direction of historical change, the conclusion is overly broad, because it would apply to states whose institutions do not respect the capacities for self-direction of their members and manifest no tendency for autonomous reform (intolerant autocracies, for example).

But perhaps the analogical argument points to a more complicated conception of the moral personality of states that would vindicate the view that considerations about individual autonomy, transported to the international level, lend support to a principle of societal toleration. Mervyn Frost has advanced such a conception, elaborating a view taken by Hegel.[25] According to Frost, just as individuals recognize each other as free persons within domestic society, so states should recognize each other as legislatively self-determining entities in international relations. This is because "political states" are the political forms of national communities: their institutions harmonize individuals and groups in their interactions and supply shared loci of identification that enable people to recognize one another as members of a self-determining whole. Membership in such a state which is recognized as autonomous by other states is essential for the full self-realization of free individuals.[26]

---

[24] Immanuel Kant, "Toward Perpetual Peace" [1795], in *Practical Philosophy*, trans. Mary J. Warnock (Cambridge: Cambridge University Press, 1996), Ak. 8:344, 346 (the second and fifth "preliminary articles"). Compare the last paragraph of the essay, "On the Common Saying: That May Be Correct in Theory, But It Is of No Use in Practice" [1793], ibid., Ak. 8.312-13.

[25] Mervyn Frost, *Ethics in International Relations* (Cambridge: Cambridge University Press, 1996), esp. ch. 5. Compare G. W. F. Hegel, *Elements of the Philosophy of Right* [1821], trans. Allen Wood (Cambridge: Cambridge University Press, 1991), paras. 323, 331, 349.

[26] Frost, *Ethics in International Relations*, 150-1.

What is not clear is how the recognition of a state by other states bears on the freedom or autonomy of the state's individual members. Perhaps some light is shed by the condition Frost suggests for a polity to count as a "political state:" it "must be one in which the people recognize each other as citizens in terms of the law which they in turn recognize as being both constituted by them and as constitutive of them as citizens."[27] A political state is a self-governing unit whose members recognize each other as co-participants in determining the laws. One state's failure to tolerate another—for example, by denying it recognition or by interfering in its affairs—would be an affront to the second state's members because it would deny their status as politically free or self-directing persons. It would be, at least, an insult (in the case of nonrecognition) and possibly also an infringement of their political liberties (in the case of coercive interference).

The problem is that this converts the principle of international toleration from one that applies generally to one that applies selectively. One state's interference in another is an affront to the second state's members only if the interference actually obstructs or frustrates a shared capacity to determine the content of the law. But this depends on whether the second state is self-determining in an ethically significant way. The last phrase needs interpretation, but we may bracket this for the moment. If we only suppose that the idea of collective self-determination has some content—enough, say, to rule out classifying dictatorships as instances of collective self-determination—then we can see that the principle of collective self-determination will not support a principle of international toleration that applies to all states. To put it roughly, international toleration will plausibly apply to states whose institutions enable their individual members to exercise some form of political freedom by participating in a process of self-determination, but not to those that do not.[28] We seem, therefore, to have arrived back at a position closer to an individualistic than a societal conception.

A second understanding of the relationship of autonomy and toleration emphasizes the value of tolerant institutions for third parties—persons other than those who might be threatened with harm because they, themselves, hold heterodox beliefs or embrace despised ways of life. This understanding

---

[27] Ibid. Compare Hegel, *Philosophy of Right*, para. 349.

[28] One respect in which this formulation is rough is that it does not recognize what might be called transitional cases—ones in which a state is not self-determining at present, but features of its domestic life are such that it is more likely to become self-determining if left alone than if outsiders interfere. See Frost, *Ethics in International Affairs*, 211; compare 155.

derives from J. S. Mill and has been influentially reformulated by Raz.[29] There are two components. The first is the contention that autonomous control of a life can only be achieved in social circumstances in which individuals confront and are free to choose among a reasonably broad range of potentially incompatible options. These options represent, so to speak, alternative possible lives with different prospective achievements and rewards. The second component is the thesis that any society containing a sufficiently diverse range of alternatives to satisfy this condition is likely to generate friction among its constituent groups. To sustain itself, such a society needs mechanisms that protect against the prospect of intolerance to which its own diversity gives rise. This includes, as the central case, the prospect of coercive interference by the state in the conduct of minority cultures and religious communities. Together these considerations yield an argument for a robust principle of toleration, although significantly limited in scope: there is no case for tolerating beliefs or ways of life that nobody could reasonably wish to have available as an option.

Assuming that this sketch can be plausibly filled out, we should ask what we might infer for the international case. As before, the answer seems clear: someone who accepts a view of this kind about toleration at the domestic level should reject societal conceptions of international toleration as incompatible with it. What is important, according to this argument, is that *persons* should confront a reasonably broad range of options, and this can only be assured when domestic social institutions tolerate certain kinds of differences among individuals. A commitment to the value of toleration provides reasons to tolerate tolerant states, but not necessarily intolerant ones. Once again, the international-level principle is asymmetrical.

Is this too quick? Someone who thinks so might observe that toleration can take a variety of forms within a society. The liberal idea of individual freedom of conscience and expression, familiar from the resolution of the religious wars, is only one of these. Another form of toleration—found, for example, in the millet system of the Ottoman Empire—takes groups rather than individuals as units of analysis and expresses itself in institutions that protect each group's capacity to conduct its internal life as it sees fit.[30] The millet system was stable over a long period of time and effectively protected a range of ways of life against destructive interference by outsiders. This

[29] I abstract here from the argument given by Raz in *The Morality of Freedom*, chs. 14-15.
[30] Will Kymlicka, *Multicultural Citizenship* (Oxford: Clarendon Press, 1995), 156-8.

general form of toleration might be seen as peculiarly appropriate to multi-national empires, of which international society today is the evolutionary product—the result of the decomposition of multinational empires into separate national states.[31]

The question is whether the comparison with the millet system offers any reason to favor the societal conception for international relations. As Will Kymlicka observes, toleration of groups as it occurred in the millet system was not *liberal* toleration.[32] It did not respect the third-party autonomy interests of individuals: although groups were left more-or-less free to organize their internal lives as they saw fit, the state did not protect individual members of these groups against whatever forms of inducement the groups themselves employed to bring about conformity with their internal norms. Nor did it take steps to ensure that individuals within groups confronted any substantial range of alternative possible lives. An analogous point applies in the international case. Although there is a descriptive sense in which we might say that a world order of sovereign states represents a regime of toleration, the form of toleration embodied in this regime will not be of interest from a point of view that accords high importance to the value of (personal) autonomy.

Perhaps a shift of focus to the case of toleration within a multicultural domestic society will yield a more sympathetic view of the societal conception. After all, there need be no inconsistency in maintaining that a society's governing institutions should be tolerant of minority subcultures whose internal practices are in some respects intolerant or otherwise incompatible with political values associated with autonomy. There is no reason to deny that tolerating some such subcultures might produce the values for third parties that motivate the more general argument for toleration that we are considering. If this is plausible in the domestic case, perhaps the international analog will be plausible as well. Why should we not believe that the prospects for personal autonomy would be enhanced in a world whose global institutions and practices tolerate a diverse array of local cultures, including some whose internal practices are incompatible with liberal toleration?

The answer is that a plausible argument that proceeds from considerations of personal autonomy to the toleration of internally intolerant minority

---

[31] Michael Walzer, *On Toleration* (New York: Yale University Press, 1997), 19-22.
[32] Kymlicka, *Multicultural Citizenship*, 157.

subcultures in the domestic case must assume that various conditions are satisfied in the background. Prominent among these are that intolerance within subcultures should not manifest itself in ways that do harm to individual persons without their consent and that there should be a reasonable chance of exit from the intolerant subculture for those who wish to leave. These limiting conditions are required to ensure respect for the autonomy of persons.[33] It is possible to imagine these conditions being met in domestic societies. But it is unrealistic to believe that analogous conditions are likely to be satisfied at the global level in the absence of global institutions (like a practice of human rights) that enforce them. Unlike minority subcultures within a liberal state, an intolerant society which is itself a state disposes a coercive apparatus with the capacity to harm those who are not tolerated. In most cases there will be no chance of exit available at reasonable cost—indeed, restrictions on exit may be among the ways intolerance is expressed.[34] Whatever third-party benefits are produced for outsiders by tolerating an intolerant regime would come at the expense of those members of internal minorities whom the regime does not tolerate or protect. So the argument for tolerating intolerant minority subcultures, whatever its persuasiveness in the domestic case, will not lend much support to the societal conception of toleration at the international level, unless that conception is limited in a way that renders it practically equivalent to the individualistic view.

The general point illustrated here is that the considerations about autonomy that might be thought to explain the value of toleration within a domestic society do not scale to a general principle of toleration among societies. Both first- and third-person considerations produce an asymmetrical view about international toleration. They argue for the toleration of states that tolerate their own people and (perhaps) when it would be a way of respecting the outcomes of an ethically significant domestic process of self-determination.[35] These considerations do not argue for toleration of other states. There is also a further and more basic point. Considered as features of social institutions, toleration and self-determination are distinct and need not travel together. There is no guarantee that a self-determining regime will also be tolerant. So even if we confine ourselves to self-determining

---

[33] Oberdiek, *Tolerance: Between Forbearance and Acceptance*, 129-32.
[34] As Tan observes. *Toleration, Diversity, and Global Justice*, 42-4.
[35] I continue to bracket the question of the meaning of self-determination; we come to it later (§ 26).

societies, it appears that considerations related to the value of individual autonomy will fall short of justifying a principle requiring toleration of all such societies. More needs to be said to justify such a principle, even if it is qualified so as to apply differently to regimes that are self-determining and those that are not.

24. Toleration (2): the autonomy of peoples

Perhaps more can be said. Societal toleration might be justified by other considerations than those which are salient in the case for toleration in domestic society—the interests of peoples in political autonomy, perhaps, or the value for their individual members of membership in a cohesive, common culture. Some of these are suggested in Rawls's discussion of international toleration in *The Law of Peoples*. In his view, these considerations constrain the permissible content of a doctrine of human rights. What should we make of them?

Rawls argues that liberal peoples should tolerate societies that satisfy certain conditions of "decency." Among these are the following. Decent societies do not have aggressive aims. They are governed according to a comprehensive and widely shared conception of political right and justice which embodies an idea of the common good. They have institutions that make it possible for individuals to participate in law-making and provide opportunities for political dissent. And, importantly, they respect certain basic human rights (§ 15). In these respects, decent societies resemble liberal ones.[36]

There are also differences. The political institutions of decent societies, although allowing for the participation of all, need not do so on the basis of political equality and may provide for the representation of citizens as members of groups rather than as individuals. Moreover, these groups participate in political life primarily as agencies of consultation and, although they can be expected to have influence, they may not exercise control over the selection of public officials or the enactment of legislation. Although no religion may be persecuted, there may be an established church, religious doctrine may be taken as controlling on certain political matters, and access to some political offices may be limited to members of

---

[36] Rawls, *The Law of Peoples*, 60-1, 78-80.

the dominant faith.[37] In these ways a decent society is less tolerant than a liberal one. Liberal and decent societies may also differ in the treatment of women: although decent societies respect the basic human rights of men and women equally, the status of women in other respects is left to be specified by each society's "common good conception of justice" and it is not intrinsic to such a conception that people be treated as free and equal individuals.[38]

Rawls argues that the governments of liberal societies should tolerate decent ones as "equal participating members in good standing of the Society of Peoples" in spite of their shortfall from liberal standards of justice.[39] His conception of what international toleration requires is expansive. Among other things, it rules out military, economic, and diplomatic interference aimed at changing the conditions of a society's internal life and prohibits the offering of incentives (either by liberal societies or by international organizations) to induce reform. Members of liberal peoples are permitted to criticize nonliberal decent societies, but the public posture of liberal governments towards these societies is constrained by the duty to extend to them "a due measure of respect" and to recognize them as "*bona fide* members of the Society of Peoples" with the capacity "to reform themselves in their own way."[40]

The requirement of toleration applies to relations among liberal and decent societies. There is no obligation to tolerate societies which are neither liberal nor decent. This limitation is integral to Rawls's view and produces a conception which, although similar in form, is significantly different in content from the traditional position found in Vattel. As a result, Rawls's position is more progressive than it may appear; indeed, the consequences for international conduct might be similar to those of some individualistic conceptions. But the convergence would not be complete because the Law of Peoples requires toleration of societies that do not adhere to liberal standards of toleration or of political justice.

What is the basis of this requirement? There are various strategic reasons in its favor. For one thing, as Rawls observes, interfering in the internal lives of decent peoples is likely to produce resentment, bitterness, and perhaps conflict. This would be undesirable for its own sake and also because it

---

[37] Ibid. 65 n. 2, 74.
[38] Rawls plainly hopes that the political systems of decent societies would be sufficiently open to bring about a progressive improvement of the status of women over time. Ibid. 75, 78.
[39] Ibid. 59.   [40] Ibid. 61, 84.

might be counterproductive. Decent societies might be more likely to develop liberal political cultures if they are accepted and tolerated by liberal societies than if they are subjected to coercive pressure. Secondly, the international resources available for humanitarian or reform-oriented political action are likely to be limited and should be focused on the worst forms of injustice. But decent societies do not manifest the worst forms of injustice; although their institutions are not fully just, they are not simply mechanisms of oppression, either. We may do better to concentrate limited resources on relieving more urgent forms of distress. Thirdly, intervention to promote internal reform is fraught with well-known possibilities for error and miscalculation. A comparison of the potential costs and benefits would argue against intervention in most cases other than those where the harms that would be prevented are severe and widespread.[41]

These strategic reasons for toleration of decent societies are plausible and in many practical contexts might be decisive. However, these considerations cannot exhaust the reasons for international toleration, as Rawls understands them. In his view, what is required of liberal peoples is not only that they refrain from interfering in decent societies, but that they "accept" them as social forms capable of determining their futures according to their own religious, moral, and political standards. The strategic considerations I have mentioned do not explain this requirement.

What else can be said? Rawls suggests at least two further arguments. The first invokes an analogy with the reasoning for toleration of religious and philosophical pluralism in domestic society. This argument proceeds from the observation that a diversity of individual conceptions of the good develops within societies as the inevitable result of the operation of human reason in free institutions. Its analog at the international level is a plurality of reasonable (or at least not unreasonable) "cultures and traditions of thought" including comprehensive religious and philosophical views which have definite implications for the character of political order. Considerations of reciprocity require us to accept this degree of pluralism in international life just as in the life of our own society.[42]

---

[41] Ibid. 61, 83-4. The last point was not lost on Vattel, who argued against intervention to protect people against outrageous conduct by their rulers on the grounds that a permission to intervene "opens a door to all the ravages of enthusiasm and fanaticism, and furnishes ambition with numberless pretexts." *The Law of Nations*, bk. II, ch. 1, § 7.

[42] Rawls, *The Law of Peoples*, 11, 19. For the domestic case, see John Rawls, "The Idea of Public Reason Revisited," in *The Law of Peoples*, 136-7; and *Political Liberalism* (New York: Columbia University Press, 1996), §§ 3.2-3.4.

In both the domestic and the international cases the persuasiveness of this argument depends on a restriction of its range of application to conceptions of the good (in the domestic case) or to "cultures and traditions of thought" (in the international case) that qualify as sufficiently reasonable. Conceptions that fail to qualify are not entitled to be tolerated. Confining our attention to the international case, Rawls observes that, although decent hierarchical societies are not "as reasonable and just" as liberal societies, they are also "not fully unreasonable," either.[43] The difficulty is that we have no systematic account of the idea of reasonableness as it applies to conceptions of political justice; the judgment that a decent society's conception is sufficiently reasonable to qualify for toleration is offered as a matter of first impression about which, Rawls must suppose, most people would agree. But this is plainly not the case. We need some further reason to accept that judgment.[44]

The second argument might be seen as explaining the sense in which decent societies are sufficiently reasonable to warrant toleration. Recall that decent societies, although not democratic, provide for the representation of people's interests and admit dissent. These societies are not tyrannies or groups of individuals ruled by brute force; they are collaborative enterprises guided by a shared conception of the common good. Their people generally identify with this common-good conception of justice and believe themselves obligated to comply with the norms of their institutions. Decent societies have their own distinctive capacities for self-government and political reform. They are in this sense self-determining. Because self-determination is a good for people, these "institutional features deserve respect:" "[d]ecent societies should have the opportunity to decide the future for themselves."[45]

Why should these features "deserve respect?" There appear to be two reasons. The first is that these societies are assumed to satisfy various minimal conditions of political morality including respect for a core of basic human rights. Presumably this reflects the people's commitments duly expressed through their institutions. The second is that these societies' institutions provide a way for their people to take part in political life which is consistent

---

[43] Rawls, *The Law of Peoples*, 83, 74. For a contrasting interpretation see Erin Kelly, "Human Rights as Foreign Policy Imperatives," in *The Ethics of Assistance: Morality and the Distant Needy*, ed. Deen Chatterjee (Cambridge: Cambridge University Press, 2004), 177–92.

[44] For a discussion, see Tan, *Toleration, Diversity, and Global Justice*, 30–8.

[45] Rawls, *The Law of Peoples*, 84, 85; also 61–2.

with a widely shared conception of the common good. Participation in these institutions enables each person to identify with others as members of a common culture, affirm their inherited norms, and influence (though perhaps not control) public decisions. We can appreciate these values even in relation to societies the substance of whose political norms we cannot accept.

I believe that an argument of this kind provides the strongest available reason in favor of a doctrine of international toleration like that advanced by Rawls. If it were plausible to think of the members of a decent society as being more-or-less unanimous in their acceptance of a common-good conception of justice and of the political and legal institutions based on it, then the argument might be decisive. Perhaps there are, or anyway might be, such societies. But one has only to consider the possibility of disagreement about constitutional arrangements within a decent society to see the argument's limits.

Suppose the government of a decent society faces an indigenous opposition movement committed to the reform of the society's political institutions. Perhaps the movement wishes to abolish discrimination on the basis of religion or sex in laws regulating access to higher political office. Suppose the movement seeks support from other societies, nongovernmental agents, or an agency of the international community. How should these agents respond?

On Rawls's view, the outside agents, recognizing the decent society as an "equal participating member in good standing" of the Society of Peoples, have no choice but to decline to help. The decision is simple, because the outside agents are blocked by their adherence to the Law of Peoples from engaging with the forces of reform within the decent society: they are required to respect the decent people as a self-determining social entity even though its political system might reasonably be believed by its own reformers to place them at a disadvantage.[46]

There is, however, another way to think about the case. Suppose one accepts an individualistic conception of international toleration while acknowledging that strategic considerations like those identified earlier should carry weight. Now the outside agents' reasoning must be more complicated.

---

[46] Rawls stresses that a decent society should allow political protest, but protest should stay "within the basic framework of the common good idea of justice." Ibid. 72. But what if the object of protest is an element of this very idea?

They must hope that the forces of reform will eventually prevail and estimate the chances that providing help to those seeking it would effectively advance this process. An important component of this estimate would be an accounting of the chances that whatever forms of political action are available would bring about a sufficient change in the society's political culture to sustain the reforms. Surely they must consider the possibility that outside interference would generate a counterproductive reaction from within. The outside agents must also assess the opportunity costs of helping, calculated in help not provided elsewhere, for other purposes. And they must consider whether interference would have adverse consequences for global order. Obviously, it will not be easy to combine these disparate considerations to decide how to act. Certainly there is no formula. What is clear is that, though it might turn out that noninterference is the best policy, this would not be simply because there is a value in international toleration that blocks the influence of the political values spoken for by the reforming minority. Instead, it would reflect an instrumental judgment of the general form that the gains from interference, discounted by its probability of success, would be less than its likely costs, including the opportunity cost of being unable to help elsewhere where more good might be done.

This is imprecise, but I believe it more accurately describes the range of considerations that bear on a decision whether outside agents should offer assistance. If this is right, then it seems that the argument from considerations about communal autonomy to a principle of societal toleration faces significant limits. It will have force in cases where a society's institutions satisfy conditions of self-determination and where a common-good conception of justice is, indeed, widely shared, so that the important interests of all, including potentially vulnerable minorities, are reliably taken into account in policy-making. The appeal to the values of self-determination or communal autonomy will have less force in cases where there is division within the society, because in these cases it can no longer be argued that refraining from interference shows respect for a widely accepted conception of the common good or for political processes embedded in a culture with which most people identify. Strategic considerations will argue against interference in some such cases but probably not in all. In these latter cases, which are the more likely ones for interference to protect human rights, there seems to be no alternative to a case-by-case judgment about the gains and costs of interference.

We began with the question whether an appreciation of the value of international toleration argues for constraining the substantive scope of international human rights. It now appears that this question was ill-formed. The attempt to extend the familiar reasons for toleration to the international level does not produce a single, univocal principle. The familiar reasons for toleration in the domestic case—that is, those deriving from considerations about the autonomy of persons—have their place, but they argue for *international* toleration only in cases which are unlikely to be of practical interest. Various strategic and instrumental considerations specific to the international realm argue for toleration in a wider range of cases, but there is likely to be substantial room for variation among the cases. In one class of cases, there is a strong presumption of societal toleration—specifically, cases in which a society is self-governing in a morally significant sense and the basic interests of its members, particularly those of vulnerable minorities, are reliably taken into consideration in public decision-making and are believed to be so by those potentially disadvantaged. In a second class of cases, in which one or the other of these conditions is not met (for example, when local processes of self-government fail to protect the important interests of vulnerable minorities), the familiar reasons are ambiguous—on balance they might argue either for noninterference or for interference, depending on the details of the case. In a third class of cases, in which neither condition holds, the familiar reasons are likely to argue for remedial interference, at least when there are means available with reasonable prospects of success. The source of the incoherence is the fact that at the international level we are concerned with both individual and collective agents, and it is a contingent matter whether the toleration of collective agents will produce outcomes in which the value of toleration is achieved for the individuals who compose them.

It is therefore puzzling how an appreciation of the value of international toleration could be brought to bear in a systematic way on reflection about the proper scope and contents of human rights. It does not seem, for example, that one can inspect the catalog of human rights found in international doctrine and identify those that are ruled out by considerations of international toleration and those that are not. If the idea of toleration bears on the scope of human rights, it bears less directly than this thought suggests. Consider, for example, the first part of the schema, which requires a showing that a putative human right would protect an interest which is sufficiently important to warrant international political action when it is

endangered. The idea of international toleration calls attention to differences among culturally specific worldviews that might affect reflection
about the nature and urgency of these underlying interests. Or consider
the problem of deciding how to act when human rights are infringed.
According to our model, infringements of human rights provide *pro tanto*
reasons for political action. But the forms of action for which infringements
provide reasons and the weight of these reasons as against other relevant
considerations depend on the context. Considerations associated with international toleration might influence our judgments on both points. For
example, coercive means might be ruled out as unacceptable interferences
with rights of collective self-determination whereas others, which do not
involve the use of coercion (for example, providing political assistance to a
dissenting group), might be allowed.

We took up the subject of international toleration because it seemed
that the value of toleration should constrain the content of a public doctrine
of human rights. But it now appears that international toleration is not
so much a value in itself, as our beginning question seems to presuppose, as
it is a way of calling attention to considerations which are largely independent of the value of toleration as we understand it in the more familiar
domestic case. The main significance of the idea of international toleration
is heuristic.

7

International Concern

IN the last two chapters I argued that international human rights constitute a distinct class of norms. They are neither principles for individuals of the sort that might be said to regulate behavior in the absence of institutions nor principles for domestic political institutions, adherence to which is sufficient for the justifiability of those institutions to their own members. Human rights are, peculiarly, matters of international concern: they are norms worked out for one among many possible situations of human interaction, that found in a world order in which political authority is vested primarily in territorial states. As I have noted, a consequence of this fact is that their normative range is more restricted than that of the requirements of social justice. Another is that the grounds of human rights may be pluralistic: we have no reason to assume *ex ante* that human rights protect a single value (on the demand side) or that they count in favor of action for a single typical reason (on the supply side).

These observations are abstract. In this chapter I try to show their significance by considering three hard cases—those of anti-poverty rights, rights of political participation, and the human rights of women. Each represents an innovation of the twentieth century in human rights doctrine and there is growing, though hardly unanimous, agreement in the discourse of the practice that all three are properly taken to be matters of international concern. At the same time, in each case we encounter a distinct problem in trying to explain why, if at all, this should be true. In the case of anti-poverty rights, the problem is to say how and why these rights can supply reasons for action for agents outside the society in which the rights are violated, given the diversity of causes of severe poverty and the variety of relationships among states and the members of their populations. In the case of political rights, the issue is the relationship between the interests that serve as grounds of political rights and the relatively specific institutional requirements of these rights as many interpret them today. Finally, in the case of the human rights of women, the central question concerns the degree to which the global practice should defer to recalcitrant local norms and conventional beliefs.

Although their salience varies from case to case, these problems are generic. In taking each case as an illustration of only one problem, I do not mean to suggest that it is the only problem we encounter in reflection about the case or that the same problem might not arise in connection with other putative rights as well. What unites the problems is their bearing on the plausibility of the claim that an international doctrine of human rights should embrace the rights in question. Taken together they illustrate the main respects in which the fact that human rights are peculiarly matters of international concern can influence judgment about the content and conduct of human rights doctrine and practice.

25. Anti-poverty rights

Contemporary human rights doctrine contains a series of protections against [right to health in UDHR] the most devastating of the consequences of poverty—malnutrition, lack of clothing and shelter, disease, and ignorance. We might call the interests in these protections "subsistence interests." The protections are summarized in the Universal Declaration's guarantee of a standard of living "adequate for the health and well-being of [oneself and one's] family, including food, clothing, housing and medical care and necessary social services" and in the separate guarantee of free elementary education (arts. 25(1), 26).[1]

These rights have several notable features. First, they establish noncomparative standards of well-being. It should be possible to determine if they have been satisfied in the case of any one person without needing to refer to the situation of anyone else. In this respect anti-poverty rights differ from various other human rights that import equality as a value directly into human rights doctrine—for example, the rights to equal protection of the law, equal suffrage, and equal access to public positions (UDHR, arts. 6, 21).

[1] The declaration also holds that every person is entitled to "the realization" of these rights "through national effort and international co-operation and in accordance with the organization and resources of each State" (UDHR, art. 22). The Covenant on Economic, Social and Cultural Rights adds that states should "take steps, individually and through international assistance and co-operation, especially economic and technical, to the maximum of its available resources, with a view to achieving progressively the full realization" of economic rights (ICESCR, art. 2).

In contrast, anti-poverty rights set thresholds. Their requirements should therefore be compatible with a range of conceptions of (domestic-level) distributive justice, from the more to the less egalitarian, provided that the implementation of each conception would result in the thresholds' being met.[2]

Second, anti-poverty rights state objectives for policy while leaving the choice of means for local determination. The clear expectation conveyed in the declaration is that in the normal case persons would purchase the goods required for subsistence with income earned from work against a background of social policies guaranteeing employment opportunities for all and fair standards of compensation. (Separately, the declaration requires that provision be made for those unable to provide for themselves due to "circumstances beyond [their] control" (art. 25(1).) The space left for local determination suggests that we need not regard anti-poverty rights as requiring that states enact schemes of constitutional welfare rights or their statutory equivalents.[3] They are better interpreted as setting standards by which state policies and the conduct of governments should be oriented and assessed.

direction for authorities

Third, although an international role is plainly contemplated, its details are also left open. There is an abstract responsibility to act when a local government fails to achieve the outcomes defined by the rights. This embraces a responsibility to cooperate internationally to remove obstacles or disincentives for local governments.[4] Perhaps there is also a responsibility to contribute to a system of international transfers, but it would be a mistake to interpret anti-poverty rights as if such a requirement were straightforwardly implied. The types of international or transnational action for which a government's failure supplies reasons depend on the background circumstances of the society under consideration, the reasons for the government's

local ⟷ international

[2] This does not, of course, rule out that the reduction of economic and political inequalities could be instrumental to the satisfaction of anti-poverty rights that are in principle noncomparative. As I understand it, this is one of the lessons of Paul Farmer's reflections about "structural violence." *Pathologies of Power: Health, Human Rights, and the New War on the Poor* (Berkeley: University of California Press, 2005), ch. 1.

[3] The Covenant on Economic, Social and Cultural Rights states a preference for "the adoption of legislature measures" as means of realizing economic rights, but even this text, which is more fully under the sway of the juridical paradigm of implementation than the declaration, refers to these measures with inclusive rather than restrictive language (ICESCR, art. 2(2)).

[4] Nutrition is treated specially: the covenant includes a requirement that states cooperate "to ensure an equitable distribution of world food supplies in relation to need" (ICESCR, art. 11(2)(b)).

transnational action is allowed to address
INTERNATIONAL CONCERN failures of
local
governments?
163

failure, and the range of policy measures available. To reach the conclusion that resource transfers are required, we would need reason to believe that the resources could be delivered in ways likely to produce a greater sustainable improvement in living standards for those below a threshold of "adequacy" than would be produced by the various other measures likely to be open to outside agents—for example, investment in a society's physical infrastructure, reform of trade practices, relaxation of immigration restrictions in wealthy countries, and so forth. A choice of means would be a complex judgment of policy, not a direct inference from the assertion of a right.[5]

Why should we consider anti-poverty rights a hard case? The interests protected by these rights are among the most uncontroversially urgent of all human interests and the least open to variation by culture. Moreover, there is no doubt that, under a variety of reasonably likely circumstances, these interests can be threatened by the actions and omissions of governments. Looked at from the point of view of their prospective beneficiaries, the case for counting protections against the harms associated with severe poverty as human rights seems easy.

The case is not so straightforward, however, when regarded from the perspective of the outside agents who might be called upon to act when a government fails in its first-level responsibilities. The difficulties are of two kinds. First, in the nature of the case, it is not clear how it should be decided which outside agents have reasons to act. Second, it is not clear what kinds of reasons might arise for these agents or whether they would normally be weighty enough to require action. As the schema suggests, an explanation of the normativity of human rights needs to show how and why their violation might be action-guiding for outside agents, so each point should have a response. Where might this function in just war theory?

Beginning with the first difficulty, suppose that a government fails for some reason to protect against threats to its people's anti-poverty interests. Human rights doctrine contains no criterion for calibrating and apportioning ("second-level") responsibilities to come to their assistance. Moreover, the global political system does not include any authoritative mechanism for

"outside agents"

---

[5] The point would not need emphasis but for the tendency of both advocates and critics of anti-poverty rights to underestimate the distance between principles and policy. For an analysis recognizing this distance while still advocating certain forms of international action to reduce severe poverty, see Paul Collier, *The Bottom Billion: Why the Poorest Countries Are Failing and What Can be Done about It* (Oxford: Oxford University Press, 2007), part 4.

implementing or enforcing such a criterion, even if one were present. This means that those whose anti-poverty interests are threatened due to a failure of their own government have no basis for identifying those outside agents against which to press claims, and those agents which are in a position to act have no way to decide if they are obligated to do so. But if this is true, it might be doubted that anti-poverty rights have any practical point. What could be the value of a right, if there is no way to identify the holders of correlative responsibilities?

A skeptical view of this kind has been pressed by Onora O'Neill. She distinguishes between "normative" and "aspirational" views of rights and argues that a value cannot count as a right, on a "normative" view, unless it can be seen as the ground of a claim that specific others have obligations to act or refrain from acting in ways that would result in the claimant's having or being able to enjoy the value. "We normally regard supposed claims or entitlements that nobody is obligated to respect and honour as null and void, indeed undefined."[6] The values expressed in such claims are better conceived of as "aspirations:" they describe resources or conditions that their beneficiaries have reason to want but that no identifiable agent has an obligation to provide. O'Neill thinks it obvious that the familiar "rights of man" to freedom, property, and security can count as rights on a "normative" view because the inferences about the deontic situations of other agents are clear: everybody has an obligation to respect them. The same cannot be said about "abstract rights to goods and services, now seen as universal human rights," such as rights to food and health care. This is because it is not clear how these supposed rights can generate obligations for everyone, the performance of which would result in the satisfaction for all of the interests which the rights protect. But without a basis for assigning obligations to specific agents we cannot know that a right has been violated. We must therefore regard rights of this latter kind as "merely aspirational" and normatively inert.[7]

Two observations in response. First, it is not clear why one should think that rights to goods and services cannot have counterpart obligations. It is true that contemporary human rights practice does not provide a mechanism for assigning second-level obligations to specific agents when anti-poverty

---

[6] Onora O'Neill, "The Dark Side of Human Rights," *International Affairs* 81 (2005), 430. Compare O'Neill, "Women's Rights: Whose Obligations?" in *Bounds of Justice* (Cambridge: Cambridge University Press, 2000), 101-5.

[7] O'Neill, "The Dark Side of Human Rights," 428, 430.

rights are violated at the first level. The question is what to make of this fact. O'Neill writes as if the nature of rights to "abstract goods and services" is such that they are not amenable to having counterpart obligations assigned. But why should this be? One possibility is that, in view of the overall scarcity of resources in our world, there is no feasible assignment of obligations such that, if they were carried out, everyone would enjoy the substance of anti-poverty rights. O'Neill does not make this argument, and in any case, it is a complex empirical question whether its premise is true. Without engaging the question here, we might at least observe that the obstacles to the satisfaction of these rights are more likely to be found in the indigenous features of certain poor societies, particularly in the quality of their institu-tions, than in a global shortage of resources.[8] Another possibility is that the causes and social circumstances of poverty are so diverse that any attempt to generalize about second-level responsibilities to contribute to preventive and remedial measures would be too abstract to be practically helpful. But while the antecedent is plausible, what follows is that principles defining obligations would have to differentiate among types of cases, not that they cannot be devised. Since it has not been established that no reasonable assignment of obligations is possible, we are not forced to conclude that there is any conceptual error in thinking that subsistence interests are an appropriate subject of human rights.

The other observation is that, even if one could make sense of the idea that it is not possible to assign obligations to specific agents—so that anti-poverty rights would not count as "normative" in O'Neill's sense of the term—it still would not follow that these rights are "merely aspirational" and therefore normatively inert.[9] O'Neill's conception of the normative is narrower than it may at first appear. A "right" counts as "normative" only if it has "well-specified counterpart obligations."[10] It appears that a "well-specified obligation" must satisfy two conditions. First, it should identify a set of actions such that, if the actions were performed, the right-holder

---

[8] See Dani Rodrik, *One Economics, Many Recipes: Globalization, Institutions, and Economic Growth* (Princeton, NJ: Princeton University Press, 2007), ch. 1, for a summary of evidence, and the acute discussion in Mathias Risse, "How Does the Global Order Harm the Poor?" *Philosophy and Public Affairs* 33 (2005), 355–9.

[9] "In effect, we would concede that the rhetoric of universal human rights to goods or services was deceptive, but defend it as a noble lie that helps to mobilize support for establishing justiciable rights of great importance." O'Neill allows that there is something to be said for such a view but holds that many would see it as "cynical." "The Dark Side of Human Rights," 429–30.

[10] Ibid. 431.

would enjoy the substance of the right. Second, it should identify the agent or agents required to perform these actions. But it is no more clear that a claim failing to satisfy these conditions would necessarily be "merely aspirational" than it is that "manifesto rights" cannot be action-guiding (§ 18). A violation might supply a reason for action whose performance would not result in immediate enjoyment of the substance of the right but would increase the chances that right-holders would enjoy the substance of the right in the farther future (for example, when the reason counts in favor of contributing to a development assistance program). Or it might supply a reason for action for agents whose identity depends on facts about the case (for example, where a fixing of responsibility depends on ad hoc judgments about proximity and capacity). The distinction between the "normative" and the "merely aspirational" leaves possibilities like these aside.

Of course, one might hold that contemporary human rights practice is ill-conceived in allowing claims whose practical consequences are in this way indirect. Perhaps one believes that the practice generates a culture of recipience rather than of self-reliance, or that it fails to concentrate political energy on the most damaging of social evils, or that the language of human rights is too abstract and unspecific to mobilize political action when it is most needed. But these arguments need to be made and their empirical premises, which in the case of anti-poverty rights are implausible on their face, need substantiation.

We have not yet answered our question about the distribution of second-level responsibilities to act. To do so we must consider the second problem identified earlier, about the grounds of any such responsibilities. This problem arises from a recognition that international action to stop or redress local failures to ensure the satisfaction of anti-poverty rights may be costly to its agents. The question is whether prospective agents are likely to have reason to incur these costs. If no such reason can be identified, or if the reason is such that it would usually be trumped by competing reasons, then one might resist the view that human rights should include anti-poverty rights because, except in special cases, prospective international agents would lack sufficient reason to be motivated by them. The third condition of the schema would not be satisfied.

Why might this difficulty seem serious? As I observed earlier, there is no doubt about the urgency of the subsistence interests that anti-poverty rights are supposed to protect. One might suppose that considerations of urgency would be enough, in themselves, to provide the reason we are seeking. Such a reason would be one of beneficence: it would count in favor of an action just in case the action would contribute to the satisfaction of another person's interests, independently of considerations about any historical or contemporary relationship one might have with that person. However, it is controversial whether reasons of beneficence are strong enough, in themselves, to require anyone to undertake substantial sacrifices for the benefit of persons unknown to them, particularly when the sacrifices take the form of continuing commitments rather than one-off transfers.[11] The skeptical temptation is easy to see.

The truth in the skeptical position is the perception that considerations of beneficence are not, in general, enough to justify attributions of responsibilities to act when the costs of action would be significant to the agent. But the position is vulnerable in at least two ways. The first and more straightforward involves the application of the perception about beneficence to the case of global poverty. It is a modern prejudice to think that reasons of beneficence are always in some way discretionary or less weighty than other types of reasons for action.[12] Although considerations of beneficence may not, in general, be enough to justify attributions of responsibilities to act, they may be in special cases. I shall refer to the special cases as ones of "strong beneficence." These are cases that satisfy three conditions. First, the threatened interest is maximally urgent, in the sense that the realization of the threat would be devastating to the life of anyone exposed to it. Second, there is a set of "eligible" agents with the resources, position, and capacity to act so as to alleviate the threat or mitigate its consequences. (Stipulate for the moment the existence of whatever international institutional infrastructure is required for effective action.) Third, the costs of action, if shared among these agents and regarded from their perspectives, would be only slight or moderate, and when added to the costs previously borne by these agents for similar purposes would not be unreasonably great.[13] In cases satisfying these conditions, I shall say that the eligible agents have a reason of beneficence

[11] For some doubts, see Richard Miller, "Beneficence, Duty and Distance," *Philosophy and Public Affairs* 32 (2004): 357–83. For contrary views, see Peter Singer, "Famine, Affluence, and Morality," *Philosophy and Public Affairs* 1 (1972): 229–43, and Garrett Cullity, *The Moral Demands of Affluence* (Oxford: Clarendon Press, 2004).

[12] Recall again the natural-law principle, found familiarly in Locke, that those with pressing wants have a "*right* to the surplussage" of others' goods (§ 11, emphasis added). And see the perceptive critical remarks in Allen Buchanan, "Charity and Justice," *Ethics* 97 (1987): 558–75.

[13] Peter Singer advances a similar view in "Famine, Affluence and Morality," although with less restrictive conditions than those given above. Compare T. M. Scanlon's remarks on the "Rescue Principle" in *What We Owe to Each Other* (Cambridge, MA: Harvard University Press, 1998), 224.

normally strong enough to require them to act.[14] I do not say that the reason is conclusory or non-defeasible, since we cannot rule out that eligible agents will face even stronger reasons to act on some other front. On the other hand, it would be an understatement to represent these reasons simply as ordinary reasons of beneficence, since under normal circumstances (that is, in the absence of weighty conflicting reasons) we would judge that eligible agents ought to take the beneficent actions open to them. Their reasons to act, while not conclusory, are sufficiently weighty to overcome the conflicting reasons they are apt to face in the normal course of events.

The conditions of strong beneficence are probably satisfied in the poorest societies today. To see this, one has only to take note of the extent of severe poverty in these societies and of the fact that, in most of them, economic growth will almost certainly be insufficient, without international action (usually, in combination with local reforms), to produce sustainable improvement in living standards. Moreover, in these cases the cost to the wealthy countries of policy measures that would be sufficient, with local cooperation, to bring about a sustainable improvement in standards of living would most likely be modest.[15] If this is right, then eligible outside agents normally have relatively strong *pro tanto* reasons to contribute regardless of the extent and nature of their past or present political and commercial relationships with these societies.

The most likely objection to this position is practical rather than philosophical. It proceeds from the observation that the forces that sustain severe poverty are most often local, having to do with political culture, government corruption, and more generally with incompetent institutions. If this is true, the objection continues, then those outside agents that appear as "eligible" are actually not so. Eligible agents are those that have the position and resources to act effectively to remove or compensate for a human rights violation. But if the causes of severe poverty are as described, then it is not

Elizabeth Ashford proposes a more demanding interpretation of the "Rescue Principle" in "The Demandingness of Scanlon's Contractualism," *Ethics* 113 (2003), 287-92.

[14] Someone might think that another condition is also necessary, to the effect that there are no other agents with a relationship to those threatened that generates special responsibilities to act. I believe this is too strong: we can have general responsibilities to act in response to urgent needs even when these needs result from the failure of other agents to satisfy their special responsibilities. The difficult question is to say under what conditions the general responsibilities exist.

[15] Views differ about the extent of these costs. Jeffrey Sachs reports a range of estimates, with varying assumptions as to the kind and extent of investments required, between 0.5% and 0.7% of the GDP of the rich countries. *The End of Poverty: Economic Possibilities for Our Time* (New York: Penguin, 2005), ch. 15. See also Collier, *The Bottom Billion*, ch. 11.

likely that any actions open to outside agents, no matter how generous, will actually bring about a sustainable improvement. Therefore there are no actually eligible agents.

As a general matter, this does not seem persuasive. From the fact—if it is a fact—that the forces that sustain poverty are primarily local, it does not follow that outside agents lack opportunities to act effectively. There may, for example, be strategies available that would reduce or remove local obstacles to growth (for example, establishment of incentives for transparency in government, assistance in the development of legal institutions, perhaps even intervention after civil wars to maintain stability). There may be forms of assistance that can be delivered directly to their intended beneficiaries without reliance on local institutions. And it may be possible to reduce external barriers (for example, by opening foreign markets to trade in local products).[16] These possibilities are illustrative. The general point is that it is a mistake to conclude from the fact that the primary causes of a deprivation are local that the only agents which are in a position to prevent or compensate for the deprivation, or to reduce the chances of its recurring, are indigenous.

I have argued so far that in some cases of severe poverty considerations of ("strong") beneficence may be enough to give potential donors strong reasons to contribute, but matters should not be left there. Part of the force of the skeptical position is exclusionary: it denies that in typical cases other kinds of reasons for action are likely to exist. Beneficence is all there is. But we might wonder whether the denial is justified. Much depends on the details of that which is denied. There are two positions. Someone might hold that, for all typical cases of poverty and for all eligible outside agents, no other single reason exists that can always be expected to count in favor of action. Alternatively, one might hold that, for any typical case of poverty (allowing that there might be more than one kind of "typical" case), no other reason exists for any eligible agent that counts in favor of action. The first position denies that severe poverty is susceptible to a uniform diagnostic analysis under which it can be shown that, beneficence aside, eligible agents always have one and the same reason for action. By contrast, the second position denies that there is any set of diagnostic analyses of typical cases under which, for each type of case, and beneficence aside once again, there is some subset of eligible agents that have a reason for action.

[16] Collier, *The Bottom Billion*, chs. 9–10; Rodrik, *One Economics, Many Recipes*, esp. chs. 5, 8.

One might be attracted to the first position by thinking about the diversity of societies. The conditions that generate and sustain severe poverty are very likely different in different societies. Suppose for simplicity, though obviously contrary-to-fact, that for each poor society there is one dominant factor that explains its poverty. One society may be trapped in social and institutional circumstances inherited from previous generations that obstruct economic development. A second may be trapped in similar circumstances, but they are legacies of colonial or neocolonial exploitation. A third may be prevented by the trade policies of potential trading partners from marketing its exports. A fourth may have a tropical location where life expectancies are shorter without access to pharmaceuticals whose price is kept high by the global intellectual property regime. A fifth may suffer from a dearth (or an excess) of natural resources. Each of these possibilities suggests a reason for external action, but the reasons differ in their grounds and reach. There is no single reason for action that applies to all cases and all eligible agents. If one insists that there can be no anti-poverty rights unless the reasons for action available to potential outside agents are the same in all typical cases, then, again, one will be tempted by skepticism.

The trouble is that the "no single reason" view is implausibly strong. Human rights constitute a public normative practice. Within the practice, human rights operate in the same way that middle-level principles operate in other branches of political discourse. Normally, we expect public principles to rest on some deeper level of reasoning in which various ethical concerns are brought together with facts about the world in a way that shows that our principles are reliable guides to action in the range of circumstances we are likely to confront in practice. So, for example, the principle of freedom of expression might be thought to summarize and bring into focus an array of underlying ethical and pragmatic considerations lying at a more fundamental level of practical reasoning. It is not an objection that the range of circumstances to which the principle applies may vary in their morally significant features—consider, for example, the differences in the grounds for protecting political and commercial speech, and between both of these and the grounds for protecting artistic expression—or that, as a result, different elements of the principle's basis will motivate its application in different circumstances. This is simply how principles operate in practical reasoning.

If, however, we move to the more plausible "no reason for any agent" view, skepticism is less tempting. This is because, as our earlier examples suggest, it is likely that in many typical cases some eligible agents will have reasons, although not always the same reasons, to act. To see why this is plausible one has only to consider the various patterns of interaction that might exist between severely poor societies and more affluent ones and ask in each case what kinds of reasons for action would be available to external agents.[17] The possibilities begin with two limiting cases. One is autarky; here, by hypothesis, there are no reasons other than those of beneficence in play. The other is benign interdependence, in which poor and non-poor societies cooperate as equals. The most important reasons in this case have to do with the fairness of individual transactions and of whatever cooperative practices and institutions there are. These polar cases are, however, unlikely. There are several intermediate and, on the whole, more likely possibilities which I hope can be suggested with descriptive labels: for example, harmful interaction,[18] historical injustice,[19] non-harmful exploitation,[20] political dependence.[21] Each pattern evokes a different kind of reason for action: for example, not to cause harm, to compensate for the results of harm done earlier, not to exploit one's bargaining advantage, to respect the interest in collective self-determination. This does not exhaust the possibilities but it will illustrate the point. The relationships that characterize the various dyads of interacting poor and affluent societies are diverse, not only in the patterns of interaction they instantiate but also in the reasons why these patterns are morally salient. It seems reasonable to conjecture—though I can only advance it as a conjecture—that most such dyads are characterized by one or more of these or similarly salient patterns. Except for autarky, each

reasons

[17] One might think of this exercise as an attempt to be more specific about the patterns of interaction that exist in a world economy whose structure allows for various forms of interdependence among societies but lacks the properties of closure and completeness that apply to an autarchic, internally interdependent system. Compare A. J. Julius, "Nagel's Atlas," *Philosophy and Public Affairs* 34 (2006), 189–90.

[18] To simplify excessively: a rich country trades with a poor country and invests in it. As a result of their participation in these relationships people in the poor country are worse off than they would have been in the absence of the relationship. (The impact on the rich country does not matter.)

[19] There was harmful interaction in the past. Today there is benign interdependence. But as a result of past interactions the poor country's position today is worse than it would have been if harmful interaction had not taken place.

[20] A rich country trades with a poor country and invests in it. As a result, both are better off than they would be under autarky, but the poor country's gain is less than its fair share of the social product of the relationship. Alan J. Wertheimer calls this pattern of interaction "mutually advantageous exploitation." *Exploitation* (Princeton, NJ: Princeton University Press, 1996), 14.

[21] Termination of their economic relationships would be asymmetrically costly for the poor country. The vulnerability thus induced renders the poor country effectively unable to defend its interests.

pattern suggests a different reason for action that would arise for citizens of the rich country from poverty in the poor country. This means that members of affluent societies are likely to have some reason to act to reduce poverty or to mitigate its effects in most poor societies with which they actually interact, but that these reasons will vary in strength and perhaps in the forms of action for which they are reasons.

Two further considerations reinforce this conjecture. The first concerns uncertainty. There is disagreement about the causes of societal poverty and wealth. The disagreement manifests itself at the aggregate level and in connection with many individual cases.[22] In any dyadic relationship it may not be known to what extent the parties' present or past interactions contribute or contributed to the affluence of one or the poverty of the other. A workable public practice of human rights must abstract from these uncertainties. The parties' asymmetrical vulnerability to error supplies a reason to resolve the uncertainty in favor of the party more vulnerable to error.[23]

The other consideration concerns the international structure. I presented the diversity of reasons for action as arising from a range of patterns of dyadic interaction among individual agents. But, of course, these patterns are organized and facilitated by international property law and the international institutions that regulate trade and finance. To the extent that features of the international structure enable or facilitate patterns of interaction that are objectionable in one of the ways we have distinguished, those in a position to benefit may come under pressure from an additional kind of reason for action, one requiring them to reform the structure or compensate for its undesirable effects on those who cannot avoid them at reasonable cost. It is important to add that the institutions that comprise the structure, considered as agents, may also have reasons to act that do not derive in any straightforward way from the reasons available to their members taken individually. Because they have capacities to coordinate action and apportion costs, these institutions are not constrained in the same way as individual agents may be (for example, by concerns about competitive disadvantage).[24]

---

[22] One way to see this is to consider the difficulties in devising a theory of economic growth capable of explaining intercountry differences in growth rates in sufficiently specific terms to guide policy. There is an instructive survey in Rodrik, *One Economics, Many Recipes*, ch. 1.

[23] I am grateful to Thomas Pogge for this observation.

[24] On the last point, see Michael J. Green, "Institutional Responsibility for Global Problems," *Philosophical Topics* 32 (2002): 79-95.

If my conjecture is correct, then if we accept the two-level model's characterization of the role of human rights, we can say that there are anti-poverty rights even if there is no single distinctive reason or category of reasons for action that explains why eligible agents should contribute to the relief of severe poverty wherever it occurs. Consider again the analogy with freedom of expression. When one asserts a right to free speech, one is saying, among other things, that there are reasons why institutions should make available some reliable form of protection against various interferences with expression that could reasonably be anticipated under a society's general circumstances. Different kinds of interferences might be objectionable for different reasons and might call for different kinds of protection. The nature and strength of the reasons, and the kind of protection required, are matters to be worked out, so to speak, at the point of application. Similarly, when one asserts a human right, one is saying, among other things, that international agents have reasons to act when domestic governments fail. In the case of severe poverty, it is plausible to believe that in typical cases there will be reasons for action available of significant weight, even if the contents of these reasons and the nature and extent of required action depend on features of the individual case.

Let us return to the question of the attribution of second-level responsibilities for action when governments fail to (or cannot) perform their first-level responsibilities. If I am right about the grounds of anti-poverty rights, then this is in one way not a simple question, for the attribution of responsibilities depends on the details of the case in question. For example, we would fix responsibility differently in cases in which poverty in a society is the result of contemporary or historical policy choices made by other governments than we would in cases in which domestic institutions are insufficiently developed or transparent. We would fix responsibility differently in cases of natural disaster than in cases of chronic malnutrition or epidemic disease. The prospect is of a complex, uneven web of disaggregated responsibilities to act.[25] In a world lacking institutions capable of determining and enforcing responsibilities, it must be left to individual agents, alone or in coalitions, to recognize their eligibility and the reasons

---

[25] I believe the position suggested here is broadly sympathetic in substance to that set forth in greater detail in David Miller, *National Responsibility and Global Justice* (Oxford: Oxford University Press, 2007), ch. 9. I do not, however, share Miller's confidence that the conventional distinction between obligations of justice and those of humanity is reliable in establishing priorities among these responsibilities.

Where does responsibility lie?

that apply to them. Agents often may have to decide how and when to act without knowledge or assurance about the plans of others. There are analogs of the familiar problems associated with providing public goods under anarchy. This means that judgments about responsibilities to act will have to be pragmatic.[26] But this fact does nothing to reduce or cancel the force of the reasons to act.

26. Political rights

The declaration's provisions about the political constitutions of states and the parallel provisions in the Covenant on Civil and Political Rights were drafted so as to be compatible with noncompetitive (that is, one-party) as well as competitive electoral systems.[27] They might once have seemed too ambiguous to impose any significant constraints.[28] Since the end of the Cold War, however, the idea that international law includes a right to democratic government has gained currency.[29] The Human Rights Committee interprets the covenant as establishing a "right to democracy" and has set forth a detailed analysis of its requirements.[30] There is now a pattern of international action aiming to encourage the emergence and support the development of democratic movements and regimes and to protect established democratic governments against internal threats.[31] Although it is not a consensus belief, the idea that there is a human right to democratic institutions is now a commonplace in international doctrine and practice.

[26] Or, as Henry Shue says, "strategic." *Basic Rights*, 2nd edn. (Princeton, NJ; Princeton University Press, 1996), 160-1; the remarks on the complexity of duties (pp. 161-5) are also pertinent.

[27] "Everyone has the right to take part in the government of his country. . . . The will of the people shall be the basis of the authority of government; this will shall be expressed in periodic and genuine elections which shall be by universal and equal suffrage" (UDHR, art. 21).

[28] "[I]t is, so far at least, axiomatic that international law does not guarantee representative, still less democratic, governments." Henry J. Steiner, "Political Participation as a Human Right," *Harvard Human Rights Yearbook* 1 (1988), 55.

[29] Gregory H. Fox, "The Right to Political Participation in International Law," *Yale Journal of International Law* 17 (1992): 539-608; Thomas M. Franck, "The Emerging Right to Democratic Governance," *American Journal of International Law* 86 (1992): 46-91. For a skeptical view, see Brad R. Roth, *Governmental Illegitimacy in International Law* (Oxford: Clarendon Press, 1999), ch. 8.

[30] UN Human Rights Committee, "General Comment Adopted by the Human Rights Committee under Article 40, Paragraph 4, of The International Covenant on Civil and Political Rights: Addendum, General Comment 25 (57)," CCPR/C/21/Rev.1/Add.7 (August 27, 1996).

[31] Roland Rich, "Bringing Democracy into International Law," *Journal of Democracy* 12 (2001): 20-34. One study counts thirteen cases in the 1990s of international action to protect or restore democratic regimes facing local threats. Morton H. Halperin and Kristen Lomasnay, "Guaranteeing Democracy: A Review of the Record," *Journal of Democracy* 9 (1998): 134-47.

A human right to democratic institutions would be different from anti-poverty rights in a way that explains why some distinctive difficulties about its justification arise. Anti-poverty rights require the protection of a series of urgent interests but leave it open how they should be protected. The main questions involve the reasons why various agents should contribute to the costs of protecting these interests and the availability of potentially effective strategies of international action. A right to political democracy, by contrast, not only requires protection of some underlying interests but also prescribes a particular kind of institutional mechanism for the purpose. The difficulties we shall consider occupy the space between the underlying interests and the institutional principles. They illustrate that the interests that a human right aims to protect can be suitably general without the form of protection embodied in the right being similarly so.

There are two main difficulties. They are forms of a more general problem that arises in the attempt to generalize familiar views about the moral basis of democratic institutions to social settings that differ from those presupposed by these views. In the first case, the differences pertain to the material conditions and degrees of economic development of societies. In the second, they pertain to prevailing norms of political legitimacy. Reflection about these difficulties converges in doubt about whether a public doctrine of human rights should embody protections as specific in their institutional requirements as a right to democratic institutions.

The most familiar justification of democratic institutions has an instrumental structure.[32] It accounts for the desirability of democratic institutions in terms of the results, broadly construed, they are likely to produce. This is true, for example, of the views of J. S. Mill and John Rawls. Mill holds that popular institutions are desirable because they are more likely than others to protect people's present interests and because the activity of political participation encourages the development of a vigorous, responsible character among citizens.[33] Rawls's account of political justice as a case of "imperfect procedural justice" is formally similar although it adopts a

---

[32] There are also other views about the moral basis of democratic institutions including, importantly, proceduralist ones that derive democratic requirements for institutions from a conception of political fairness. I believe these views are open to similar doubts about their generalizability, but I cannot discuss the matter here.

[33] J. S. Mill, *Considerations on Representative Government* [1861], in *Essays on Politics and Society II* [*Collected Works of John Stuart Mill*, xix], ed. J. M. Robson (Toronto: University of Toronto Press, 1977), ch. 3, 404. For an exposition see Dennis F. Thompson, *John Stuart Mill and Representative Government* (Princeton, NJ: Princeton University Press, 1976), ch. 1.

can HR only exist in democracies?

different conception of the results at which just political institutions should aim.[34]

Those who regard democracy as a universal value often rely on a generalization of this kind of view. For example, Amartya Sen holds that democratic institutions are to be preferred, in part, because they enable people to act effectively to protect their most important interests. To illustrate, he refers to a study of the causes of famines showing that no independent democratic country with a reasonably free press has ever suffered a substantial famine. He believes the explanation is to be found in the incentives created by the electoral mechanism: "Democracy [spreads] the penalty of famines to the ruling groups and political leaders.... This gives them the political incentive to *try* to prevent any threatening famine, and since famines are in fact easy to prevent . . . the approaching famines are firmly prevented." It is not inconsistent to hold that democratic institutions have other kinds of value as well and, again like Mill, Sen argues that the practice of democracy advances a broader developmental interest by encouraging and rewarding active, critical participation in public life.[35]

To come to the first difficulty: it is significant that neither Mill nor Rawls holds that democratic institutions would be desirable, or required by more abstract considerations of political justice, under all circumstances. A society's economic and social conditions might be such that another form of government would be more desirable.[36] One need not accept the details of these views to recognize that the persuasiveness of an instrumental justification of democratic institutions is likely to depend on empirical contingencies regarding the society at which the justification is directed. Once we see this, however, it is natural to wonder why we should have confidence that the justification generalizes.

---

[34] John Rawls, *A Theory of Justice*, rev. edn. (Cambridge, MA: Harvard University Press, 1999), § 36. Rawls also holds that instrumental reasoning about the essentials of the constitution should be constrained by egalitarian considerations (the "principle of equal liberty").

[35] Amartya Sen, *Development as Freedom* (New York: Knopf, 1999), 146–59, 178–84; quotation at p. 180 (emphasis in original). Compare Jean Drèze and Amartya Sen, *Hunger and Public Action* (Oxford: Clarendon Press, 1989), 277–8; and Amartya Sen, "Democracy as a Universal Value," *Journal of Democracy* 10 (1999), 7–8. A similar instrumental argument (although framed in relation to "basic rights") can be found in Shue, *Basic Rights*, 75–7.

[36] For Mill, see *Considerations on Representative Government*, ch. 4, and the remarks on circumstances in which despotic rule might be advantageous, towards the end of ch. 2. For Rawls, see *A Theory of Justice*, §§ 11 and 39.

Perhaps one supposes that the incentive mechanism functions effectively outside of familiar settings. The famine study is sometimes cited as evidence.[37] Its relevance, however, is more ambiguous than it may appear. An electoral incentive mechanism is likely to operate effectively only when voters are in a position to judge whether the government has made the best choices among the alternatives available.[38] The occurrence of a readily avoidable famine whose effects are plainly visible might be enough to inform such a judgment. But the abrupt and discontinuous character of most famines distinguishes them from many other adverse conditions, for which a government's responsibility may be less clear. Indeed, the same study found that the authoritarian regime in China was more effective in combating endemic deprivation than democratic India.[39]

We need more systematic evidence before accepting the inference from the special to the general case. For this we might look to the comparative study of democracy and democratic transitions in developing societies. In these cases the central questions are whether democratic institutions exhibit any systematic tendency to protect urgent interests more effectively than other types of regime and whether democratic transitions are more likely to be successful in more- rather than in less-developed societies. In the present state of knowledge any replies would have to be speculative, but let me offer an observation about each question.

The first concerns the policy performance of regimes. In general, democratic regimes tend to score at least as well as nondemocratic ones on most measures of economic performance (for example, rates of growth, investment, and employment). Indeed, democracies perform better in some respects, but the difference appears only at higher levels of development. In poor societies (those with per capita incomes below about $3,000 per year—that is, about two-thirds of the world's countries containing about 70 percent of its population)—the economic performance of both regime types is about the same. If we look, instead, at measures of social outcomes—for example, infant and child mortality—we find that, notwithstanding better performance in the aggregate, among the poor, democracies seem to

[37] E.g. by Allen Buchanan, *Justice, Legitimacy, and Self-Determination: Moral Foundations for International Law* (Oxford: Oxford University Press, 2004), 143-4, and William J. Talbott, *Which Rights Should be Universal?* (Oxford: Oxford University Press, 2005), 150-1.

[38] For a discussion, see Bernard Manin, Adam Przeworski, and Susan C. Stokes, "Elections and Representation," in *Democracy, Accountability, and Representation*, ed. Adam Przeworski, Susan C. Stokes, and Bernard Manin (Cambridge: Cambridge University Press, 1999), 42-3.

[39] Drèze and Sen, *Hunger and Public Action*, 214.

perform no better than nondemocracies.[40] Democratic regimes also tend to be less stable in poor than in wealthy countries (though the reasons are disputed).[41] On the other hand, societies with democratic institutions are more likely to respect civil liberties, tolerate religious diversity, and allow dissent, though the relationship is weak or nonexistent for transitional or partially democratic regimes.[42]

The second observation involves the success of democratic transitions. The stability and policy performance of newly established democratic regimes appear to depend on the prior successful establishment of institutions like an impartial judicial system and a competent administrative apparatus, a reasonably free press, and a pluralistic social infrastructure. Since the 1970s, more than eighty societies have experienced the replacement of a nondemocratic regime by a regime with some formal features of democracy such as contested elections for office and freedom of association sufficient to allow party competition. But only about one-third of the transition cases resulted in stable and fully "consolidated" democracies, mostly in higher-income countries.[43] The more common outcome is sometimes conceptualized as an incomplete transition: a regime achieves some but not all of the features sufficient to classify it as democratic. It is then described as "stalled" or "limited."[44] Since there appears to be no

[40] Michael Ross, "Is Democracy Good for the Poor?" *American Journal of Political Science* 50 (2006): 860-74. For the demographic data, see World Bank, *World Development Report 2006: Equity and Development* (Washington, DC: World Bank, and New York: Oxford University Press, 2005), table 1, 292-3.

[41] Adam Przeworski, Michael E. Alvarez, Jose Antonio Cheibub, and Fernando Limongi, *Democracy and Development: Political Institutions and Well-Being in the World, 1950-1990* (Cambridge: Cambridge University Press, 2000), chs. 2 (stability) and 3 (economic performance). Compare David L. Epstein, Robert Bates, Jack Goldstone, Ida Kristensen, and Sharyn O'Halloran, "Democratic Transitions," *American Journal of Political Science* 50 (2006): 551-69. See also Barbara Geddes, "What do We Know about Democratization after Twenty Years?" *Annual Review of Political Science* 2 (1999), 117-21, and the sources cited there.

[42] "It takes full-fledged democracy, culminating in a system with multiparty competition, before there is reliable improvement in respect for human rights." Bruce Bueno de Mesquita, George W. Downs, and Alastair Smith, "Thinking Inside the Box: A Closer Look at Democracy and Human Rights," *International Studies Quarterly* 49 (2005), 440. See also Casey B. Mulligan, Ricard Gil, and Xavier Sala-i-Martin, "Do Democracies Have Different Public Policies than Nondemocracies?" *Journal of Economic Perspectives* 18 (2004), 22; and Christian Davenport and David A. Armstrong II, "Democracy and the Violation of Human Rights: A Statistical Analysis from 1976 to 1996," *American Journal of Political Science* 48 (2004), 551.

[43] Geddes, "What do We Know about Democratization after Twenty Years?," 115-16.

[44] Jeffrey Herbst, "Political Liberalization in Africa after Ten Years," *Comparative Politics* (2001), 358. For the post-Communist cases, see Michael McFaul, "The Fourth Wave of Democracy *and* Dictatorship: Noncooperative Transitions in the Postcommunist World," *World Politics* 54 (2002): 212-44.

systematic tendency for these regimes to consolidate as democracies, they are better understood as representing a less familiar "hybrid" political form combining some features of democratic institutions with patterns of personalistic rule that perpetuate the influence of entrenched elites and are relatively unresponsive to popular demands for policy changes. These types of regime can exhibit a variety of political pathologies, including domestic political instability, a propensity to violate the personal and civil rights of their people, and a tendency to adopt aggressive foreign policies leading to war.[45]

What follows about the question of a human right to democracy? Stable democratic regimes occur less frequently in poor societies, but the economic performance of those that exist is hard to distinguish from that of authoritarian regimes in otherwise comparable societies. Moreover, in the aggregate, democratic regimes tend to display a higher level of respect for civil and political liberties. So a possible view is that, all things considered, democratic institutions are likely to perform at least as well as other types in most any society. If this is right, it argues in favor of generalizing the instrumental argument for democratic institutions.

This, however, may be too sanguine. There are two points. First, the findings about the economic and political performance of regimes are generalizations that aggregate from many cases. Suppose one were asked to choose, on the basis of these findings, whether it would be better to live in a democratic or an authoritarian regime, knowing only that one's society is poor by global standards. Without knowing more about the distribution of the cases along some aggregate measure of expectations and about the distribution of expectations within the cases, one would not know how to choose. The worst-case outcome of a choice for democracy might be significantly worse than the worst-case outcome of a choice for authoritarianism. Or the median expectation under democracy might be lower than under authoritarianism. We do not know whether these possibilities are

---

[45] So far there has been little systematic study of the performance of hybrid but not fully consolidated democratic regimes. The most prominent recent work is Edward D. Mansfield and Jack Snyder, *Electing to Fight: Why Emerging Democracies Go to War* (Cambridge, MA: MIT Press, 2005), ch. 3 and *passim*. Compare Thomas Carothers, "How Democracies Emerge: The 'Sequencing' Fallacy," *Journal of Democracy* 18 (January 2007): 12–27. On the policy performance of newly established democratic regimes, see Dani Rodrik and Romain Wacziarg, "Do Democratic Transitions Produce Bad Economic Outcomes?" *American Economic Review* 95 (2005): 50–5. On respect for human rights, see Davenport and Armstrong, "Democracy and the Violation of Human Rights," 551–2.

actual or only hypothetical. But the fact that they cannot be ruled out means that the findings rehearsed above do not settle the question of the empirical basis of the generalization thesis. The empirical uncertainties are too great.[46]

The second point is a consequence of the greater instability of transitional regimes in poor societies. Although it appears that democratic regimes, once securely established, are likely to produce better economic outcomes and to respect civil rights more consistently than nondemocratic ones, it also appears that processes of democratic transition at low levels of economic development are more likely to be truncated. If our question were whether it would be better for a society to have authoritarian or stable democratic institutions, the more plausible answer would likely be the latter. However, if the question is whether it would be a good thing for outside agents to support or attempt to stimulate a movement for democratic reform in a nondemocratic society, the answer would have to be more cautious. Efforts at reform might produce an incompletely democratic (or "hybrid") regime, and at the present stage of understanding we do not have good evidence that such a regime will respect its people's rights or satisfy their interests more effectively than a traditional authoritarianism. So although perhaps there is an "ideal" sense in which democratic institutions might be said to be better justified by considerations about their likely performance than others, it is uncertain, taking relatively poor societies as a group, that any practically available strategy of political action would bring about a successful transition.

Both points illustrate that the empirical basis of the generalization of familiar arguments for democracy to unfamiliar cases is more unsettled than one might have believed. It is difficult to be confident that efforts to promote the democratic reform of political institutions in poor societies have a reasonable probability of producing a sustained improvement in the satisfaction of people's basic interests in personal and material security. This is true, anyway, in the general case; perhaps there are cases about which enough is known to warrant more confident predictions. But for human rights it is the general case that matters.

Let me turn now to the second difficulty. Societies differ not only in their economic characteristics but also in their political cultures. The public political cultures of democratic societies are distinctive in several respects

[46] I am grateful to Robert Taylor for helping me to see this point.

and we may doubt, as Mill did, whether the familiar arguments for democracy would apply with the same force in societies lacking such a culture.

Considerations about political culture could bear on the justification of a human right to democracy in more than one way. For example, there might be cultural preconditions in whose absence democratic institutions would be unlikely to function in the way the instrumental view anticipates. The evidence, however, is that the development of a distinctively democratic culture is a product of a larger process of social and institutional change in which the establishment of constitutional democratic forms usually comes first. Since change in political culture is at least partially endogenous, the absence of "cultural preconditions" need not be counted as an obstacle to generalizing the reasons for democracy.[47]

There is, however, another way that cultural diversity might be significant: it might bear on the justifiability of acting to promote democratic reform in societies whose histories and political cultures favor some other type of regime. The question is whether there is a culturally-neutral sense in which the establishment of democratic institutions can be said to be the most reasonable means of protecting the interests on which their justification depends.

Recall Rawls's view that although we may regard "decent hierarchical" regimes as unjust, they are sufficiently reasonable to be, in Joshua Cohen's phrase, "beyond reproach."[48] How should we understand the status of being unjust but "beyond reproach?" One reply proceeds from a distinction between the norm of democratic political justice and that of collective self-determination. Let us say, following Cohen, that a society is self-determining in a morally significant sense if its political arrangements satisfy three conditions: political decisions result from and are accountable to a process in which everyone's interests are represented, there are rights of dissent for all, and public officials explain their decisions in terms of a widely held conception of the common good.[49] These conditions make it clear that self-determination is a normative idea which is distinct from the idea of a politically independent society: the members of a society whose institutions

---

[47] Terri Lynn Karl, "Dilemmas of Democratization in Latin America," *Comparative Politics* 23 (1990), 4-5. For a review of more recent empirical findings, see Larry Diamond, *Developing Democracy: Toward Consolidation* (Baltimore: Johns Hopkins University Press, 1999), 174 ff.

[48] John Rawls, *The Law of Peoples* (Cambridge, MA: Harvard University Press, 1999), 64-72; Joshua Cohen, "Is There a Human Right to Democracy?" in *The Egalitarian Conscience: Essays in Honour of G. A. Cohen*, ed. Christine Sypnowich (Oxford: Oxford University Press, 2006), 228.

[49] I simplify Cohen's more complex formulation in "Human Right to Democracy," 233.

fulfill the conditions might plausibly be said to govern themselves. Yet a regime need not be democratic in order to satisfy the conditions; the institutions of a decent hierarchical society would do so as well.

It is important to see that, although both democratic and decent hierarchical regimes might satisfy the requirements of collective self-determination, it is not necessarily the case that these requirements would be equally satisfied by either type of regime in any one society. This depends on the content of the society's political culture. One condition of self-determination is that people be governed according to a conception of the common good that is in fact widely shared in their society. The content of this conception must correspond to the structure of the society's political institutions. Suppose that "democratic ideas lack substantial resonance in the political culture, or the history and traditions of the country."[50] Instead, most people conceive of society as an ordered unity of social groups and believe that the common good is best achieved through a system of consultation. In such a society, the right to collective self-determination would not be satisfied by democratic institutions. Indeed, as Cohen observes, an attempt to impose democratic institutions would violate the society's right of collective self-determination. Among other things, the right of collective self-determination is a right not to be (forced to be) democratic. The possibility this suggests is that the appropriate object of international human rights doctrine, to the extent it seeks to regulate the political structures of regimes at all, may be a requirement of collective self-determination rather than the more demanding (and more exclusionary) requirement of democracy.

Should we accept the suggestion? Suppose we ask what exactly would be lost if human rights doctrine incorporated a right of collective self-determination but not a right to democracy. The answer has two parts. First, in most of its contemporary conceptions, democratic institutions satisfy the principle of political equality. So, for example, the system of voting and representation affords equal procedural opportunities to all citizens, public offices are equally open to all, and there is equal access to the public arena. However, in a self-determining but nondemocratic society individual interests need not be given equal weight in political decision-making, higher offices may be restricted to members of an established church, and representatives of the dominant group may have preferential

---

[50] Ibid. 234.

access to the public arena. Political equality is not intrinsic to collective self-determination.

Second, in a democratic constitution there is a formal connection between the expressed political preferences of individual citizens and the outputs of public decision-making.[51] This abstract condition can be satisfied in various ways but some such connection is essential: the influence of individual political preferences on public decision-making must come about by means of fixed, rule-governed procedures rather than, say, as a result of the discretionary judgment of a higher-order political authority. By contrast, in a consultation hierarchy, although there is a procedure for the representation of interests, there is not necessarily a formal connection between the expression of interests within this procedure and the choice of public policies.[52] The idea of self-determination requires that political decisions be responsive to people's interests but it is not inherent that this responsiveness should be guaranteed through fixed procedures that harness outcomes to expressions of individual preferences.

How are these contrasts relevant to the question of a human right to democracy? Beginning with the shortfall from equality: someone might argue that we have two reasons to accept an inegalitarian but self-determining regime as decent ("beyond reproach"), even if not just. First, because its inegalitarian features express aspects of a common-good conception of justice in fact widely accepted in the society, nobody will feel demeaned or insulted because they have fewer political opportunities than others. They will understand these inequalities as justified by the conception of justice they accept. Second, by hypothesis, such a society acknowledges its people's fundamental interests in personal and material security and provides access to adequate nutrition, shelter, health care, and education for all, including members of

---

[51] I borrow from Brian Barry, who writes that in any democratic procedure "the preferences of the citizens have some formal connection with the outcome." As he explains, this rules out "cases where the decision-making process is *de facto* affected by the preferences of the citizens but not in virtue of any constitutional rule." "Is Democracy Special?" *Democracy, Power, and Justice: Essays in Political Theory* (Oxford: Clarendon Press, 1989), 25-6.

[52] There are two points in a Rawlsian decent consultation hierarchy at which such a connection might exist: in the selection of a group's representatives and in the choice of public policies. Rawls's descriptive remarks are vague as to institutional details, but it does not appear that individuals have rights to exercise a share of control (although they are entitled to have a say) in the choice of those who are authorized to represent their groups in the consultation process. And even if there were provisions to elect representatives of groups, there does not appear to be any constitutional rule requiring that the preferences expressed by these representatives must determine choices of public policies (though, again, they may influence them). *The Law of Peoples*, 71-8.

minority groups who do not share the majority's religious or cultural identity. Historically one of the most important reasons for objecting to political inequality has been its role in perpetuating poverty and insecurity. But when the goods just listed are reliably accessible to all, this objection does not apply.

What might be said about the other shortfall from the standard of democracy—the absence of a procedural guarantee that political outcomes will be determined by individual political preferences? This is more difficult. It is not enough to say that such a guarantee would have little value, given that there are well-established expectations that decision-makers will consult widely, respond to expressions of dissent, and take into account everyone's interests. The protective value of a procedural guarantee is not simply its actual contribution to the satisfaction of each person's interests. We appreciate its value by considering counterfactual possibilities: for example, that decision-makers might become corrupt or inattentive or that their attention would be captured by one part of the population. These possibilities are predictable dangers in most societies regardless of the details of their political cultures.[53] The instrumental argument would have this much force even in societies with cultures in which democratic ideas lack resonance.

The weight to be attached to the argument is, however, another question. The argument depends on an assignment of significance to counterfactual possibilities that would not be shared by members of the society in question. We assumed that the society has a widely shared common-good conception of justice and well-established procedures of consultation in which people's interests are effectively communicated to the political authorities, by whom they are taken seriously and who can be required to account for their decisions. In such a society there is likely to be a high level of trust in the established procedures of legislation and administration. Moreover, it would be reasonable to expect that the introduction of democratic procedures, with their individualistic features and reliance on political competition, would be destructive of this trust. So, even if one agrees that there may be circumstances in which certain individual interests would be dangerously insecure without the protective leverage afforded by democratic institutions, one cannot infer that it would be reasonable, all things considered, to attempt to promote their development in self-determining but nondemocratic societies.

---

[53] Henry Shue has emphasized this to me.

Neither of these difficulties is any threat to the familiar justifications of democracy for standard cases, or for that matter to the idea that outside agents could have reasons to support or protect democratic institutions in such cases. What is threatened is the idea that the familiar justification extends to all contemporary societies. Since human rights must be both universal and action-guiding, the proper inference from the fact that there are circumstances in which the absence of democratic institutions would not generate (even *pro tanto*) reasons for outside agents to act is that the doctrine of human rights should not embrace such a right. If the underlying concern is to protect against the threat posed by political oppression or indifferent government to the satisfaction of urgent interests like those to physical and material security, as the instrumental argument holds, then a better candidate for a human right to regulate the political constitutions of societies would be a right of collective self-determination.

I conclude with three observations. First, it is a nontrivial question whether such a right can be rendered with enough precision to serve the practical purposes of human rights. I must leave this important problem aside. It should be clear, however, even from what has been said, that such a requirement stands in contrast to the idea found in classical international law that a society's political constitution falls within the sphere of domestic jurisdiction: self-determination has a content that restricts the range of allowable variation among types of regime. For example, in the Rawlsian variant of the view, liberal democracies and decent consultation hierarchies satisfy the requirement but authoritarian regimes do not. Neither do what Rawls calls "outlaw states." A requirement that societies should be self-determining would be a demanding one.

Second, an affirmative argument for a human right of collective self-determination would face similar empirical uncertainties as a human right to democratic institutions. Indeed, in the present state of knowledge the uncertainties may be even more formidable because the performance and political dynamics of self-determining regimes have been the subject of even less systematic study. The most one can do is to conjecture that, because collective self-determination is compatible with a wider range of institutional forms, the comparison with non-self-determining regimes may be more favorable.

Finally and of the greatest practical consequence, it should be emphasized that it does not follow from the proposition that there is no human right to democracy that the promotion and defense of democratic institutions where they are contested should not be an important goal of international political action. To agree that there is a human right of collective self-determination is to agree that violations provide reasons for political action. In social circumstances in which the satisfaction of this right can only come about through democratic institutions, threats to such institutions would supply reasons for outside agents to defend them.

27. Human rights of women

Human rights treaty law has developed more substantially since 1948 with respect to the rights of women than in any other area excepting possibly the rights of the child. The declaration and covenants address the situation of women in only a few passages—primarily in their omnibus antidiscrimination clauses, providing *inter alia* that human rights belong equally to women and to men and in provisions guaranteeing free choice of marriage partner, equal rights in marriage, and "special assistance" for motherhood (UDHR, arts. 2, 16, 25).[54] In comparison, the Convention on the Elimination of all Forms of Discrimination against Women (CEDAW) is significantly more ambitious. Its antidiscrimination provision is the most sweeping of any to be found in the major international human rights instruments: it rules out "any distinction" on the basis of sex which "has the effect or purpose" of impairing or restricting the exercise or enjoyment by women of human rights "in the political, economic, social, cultural, civil or any other field" (art. 1).[55] This prohibition extends beyond state action: states are required to take steps to "eliminate discrimination against women by any person, organization or enterprise" and to "modify or abolish existing laws, regulations, customs and practices" that sustain discrimination anywhere in society (art. 2 (e)–(f)). The convention provides specifically that women should have the same rights as men to vote and to participate in government, and equal access to education

[54] In addition, the framers went to considerable lengths—unusually at the time—to avoid the terminology of the "rights of man" and to frame human rights as belonging to "everyone" and "all" rather than to "all men." The issue was pressed most vigorously by the Indian delegate, Hansa Mehta, and by Eleanor Roosevelt and the representatives of the Soviet Union. Mary Ann Glendon, *A World Made New: Eleanor Roosevelt and the Universal Declaration of Human Rights* (New York: Random House, 2001), 90, 111–12.

[55] The parallel provision in the Convention on the Elimination of All Forms of Racial Discrimination (1969)—on which the CEDAW was modeled—ends with the phrase "or any other field *of public life*" (art. 1, emphasis added).

(including participation in sports and physical education), preparation for careers, employment, health care, and the courts. It includes a series of stipulations aimed at eliminating discrimination against women in laws governing marriage and family relations and protecting women against the consequences of gender-discriminatory social practices (including betrothal and marriage of children). Most remarkably, it requires states to take measures "to modify the social and cultural patterns of conduct of men and women, with a view to achieving the elimination of prejudices and customary and all other practices which are based on the idea of the inferiority or the superiority of either of the sexes" (art. 5(a)).

Human rights doctrine before the CEDAW might plausibly have been criticized for paying insufficient attention to the circumstances of women. That criticism has been made since, as well, particularly with respect to the omission of explicit protection against violence and related forms of mistreatment within the household.[56] No doubt international doctrine is incomplete in its recognition of the basic interests of women and its requirements are certainly less widely accepted in practice than it might appear from the number of ratifications of the women's convention (185 at this writing).[57] Still, what is most striking about the expression of women's rights in contemporary human rights doctrine is the radicalism of its aspirations considered in relation to social norms as these actually existed and continue to exist in much of the world. This of course is no criticism. Its significance is to point out the most general problem that occurs in reflection about the grounds and contents of the human rights of women: it concerns the degree of deference that a public doctrine of human rights should show towards the moral beliefs and practices embodied in existing cultures.

Before taking up this problem, let me comment briefly about the threshold question of why we should think of women's human rights as a special subject at all. There is an obvious reply. According to what we might call the "nondiscrimination view"—a view encouraged by the approach taken in the declaration and in the preamble to the women's convention itself— the human rights of women are simply the human rights of all people,

---

[56] See e.g. Charlotte Bunch, "Women's Rights as Human Rights: Toward a Re-Vision of Human Rights," *Human Rights Quarterly* 12 (1990), 487-92. There is an attempt to remedy the omission in UN General Assembly, "Declaration on the Elimination of Violence against Women," February 23, 1994 (A/RES/48/104), which of course lacks the force of international law.

[57] UN Office of the High Commissioner for Human Rights, "Ratifications and Reservations" (http://www2.ohchr.org/english/bodies/ratification/index.htm) (consulted November 2, 2008).

can there be HR w/o violation of it that
caused it to be an HR?

188   INTERNATIONAL CONCERN

applied without discrimination to women as well as to men. According to this view, there are no "human rights of women" *per se*. The reason to consider the rights of women to be a subject suitable for a dedicated treaty and implementation process is the historical fact that discrimination against women has been such a pervasive feature of most human societies that special measures are needed to eliminate it.

But the nondiscrimination view cannot be the whole story. One way to see why is to consider the criticism of international human rights doctrine as embracing a distinction between the "public" and "private" spheres that works to the detriment of women.[58] This distinction pertains to the human rights of women in various ways, but most importantly by distinguishing certain kinds of threats to basic interests to which women are more or differently vulnerable than men. These include threats of abuse that typically occur within the household, such as domestic violence, exploitation of domestic labor, arbitrary deprivation of property, and the subordination of the will and limitation of choice resulting from acceptance of traditional conceptions of the household division of labor. It is of fundamental importance to recognize that the contingent structure of social life can produce circumstances in which women's interests are vulnerable to different threats than those of men. These threats, however, are not confined to the household. They can occur elsewhere as well—for example, in employment relations (e.g. as sexual harassment), criminal justice (as a systematic failure to prosecute rape), and in the legal treatment of prostitution.[59] The idea of a distinction between public and private calls attention to the phenomenon of special vulnerability but it would be a mistake to infer that this phenomenon only occurs in the sphere of the household.

Still, with a few exceptions primarily associated with reproduction, the interests of women which are subjects of distinctive vulnerability are perfectly general—they are mainly interests in physical security and personal liberty. This might seem to be a reason to resist the idea that the human rights of women should be treated as a special subject, but this, too, would be a mistake. As I observed earlier, human rights are not best conceived as

---

[58] For example, Hilary Charlesworth and Christine Chinkin, *The Boundaries of International Law: A Feminist Analysis* (Manchester: Manchester University Press, 2000), 232; Susan Moller Okin, "Feminism, Women's Human Rights, and Cultural Differences," *Hypatia* 13 (1998), 36. I am grateful for illuminating conversations on this subject with Susan Okin.

[59] Dorothy Q. Thomas and Robin S. Levi, "Common Abuses against Women," in *Women and International Human Rights Law*, ed. Kelly D. Askin and Dorean M. Koenig (Ardsley, NY: Transnational, 1999), i. 139-76.

open-ended protections of basic interests, but rather as protections against standard or predictable types of threats. The human rights of women are properly considered matters of special concern because certain important interests of women are subject to gender-specific forms of abuse. Some examples identified in the CEDAW are prostitution and trafficking, discrimination in employment against women on grounds of maternity, and unequal rights within the family.[60] Forms of gender-based violence such as rape and "dowry murder" occurring both within and outside the household, which were not specifically identified in the CEDAW, belong on this list as well. These forms of abuse are patterned in that similar abuses are predictable under relevantly similar circumstances, and they are systematic in that the circumstances in which they occur are embedded in features of societies and cultures which are more-or-less resistant to change. The patterns of subordination sustained by these features of societies help to explain why women typically face certain kinds of threats to their interests not also typically faced by men. This is why, although there may be only a few human rights that can be seen as protections of interests belonging distinctively to women, the "human rights of women" regarded as a special subject of concern has a wider domain.

It is worth remarking that recognition of a special class of women's human rights would be problematic if one took a stringent view of the idea that human rights should be "universal" in the sense of being claimable by everyone. It is hard to see how this idea can be reconciled with the thought that the interests of women require different (even if overlapping) forms of international protection to those of men. The question is whether there is a good reason to adopt a stringent view of the universality of human rights. One could feel compelled to do so by the traditional conception of natural or fundamental rights: if one construed human rights on that model, it might appear incoherent to hold that there could be a "human" right that could only be claimed by a proper subset of humanity. If, however, one regards human rights functionally, as elements of a practice whose purpose is to elevate certain threats to urgent interests to a level of international concern, then the conceptual objection can be sidestepped. The pertinent questions about the status of women's human rights are normative: they concern the importance of the threatened interests, the severity of the threats, and the feasibility and costs of protecting against them by means of human rights.

[60] CEDAW, arts. 6, 11, 16.

These normative questions return our attention to the reasons why women's human rights might be regarded as a hard case. As I said, these reasons involve the degree of deference that a doctrine of human rights owes to existing social moral codes. This problem arises in other areas of human rights as well, but nowhere as sharply as in connection with the human rights of women. To take these seriously—and here I limit myself, for the moment, to the rights actually specified in contemporary human rights doctrine—is to contemplate not only large-scale changes in policy and social practice but also in prevailing social norms in some of the world's societies. The persistence of social practices such as female genital cutting, the use of female infanticide as a means of sex selection, suttee, and the like, is often taken as evidence of this.[61] But the point could be made as persuasively with examples that are less dramatic but more pervasive, like the forms of unequal treatment of men and women found in laws governing inheritance, marriage, and divorce, the failure of legal systems to criminalize domestic violence (and of governments to prosecute it effectively), and allowance of practices of child betrothal and marriage. In each case there is a likelihood of conflict between the requirements of human rights doctrine and gendered norms found in the moral outlooks and patterns of social life that prevail in some existing societies. It is significant that in many of these societies the traditional norms are contested, a fact to which we shall return.[62] Nevertheless, there is no plausible argument that women's human rights are culturally neutral or that they state a standard for law and policy equally acceptable from all major moral-political points of view.

The non-neutrality of women's human rights may generate doubt about whether these rights are suitable to serve as grounds of international political action. There are issues of both principle and practice. External efforts to promote the human rights of women would constitute interference in longstanding and deeply embedded cultural practices, some of which may be resistant to local regulation by law, to implement norms that may not be widely accepted within the culture itself. The issue of principle is whether interference of this kind is objectionable for reasons analogous to those that arise in cases of unwarranted paternalism. There is also an issue of practice, which would arise even if one believed there were no question of principle.

---

[61] As, for example, in the account given by Talbott, *Which Rights Should be Universal?*, ch. 5.
[62] For the case of Muslim societies, see Ann Elizabeth Mayer, "The Islam and Human Rights Nexus: Shifting Dimensions," *Muslim World Journal of Human Rights* 4 (2007): 1-27 (http://www.bepress.com/mwjhr/) (consulted July 26, 2008).

It is whether there are any feasible steps open to the international community or its agents that would induce states to adopt policies reasonably likely to accomplish the transformations of cultural belief and practice necessary to secure women's human rights. Either way, the status of at least some women's rights as bona fide human rights would be in question.

Beginning with the matter of cultural difference, we should consider what follows from the fact that women's rights are not culturally neutral. It does not obviously provide a reason to doubt that these rights belong in a catalog of human rights. In each of the cases listed earlier the interests protected are some combination of those in physical and material security and in the exercise of an elemental capacity for self-direction. The importance of these interests seems to be perfectly general. We see this by considering that their importance would be conceded in any culture if the beneficiaries of the protections were men. The generic reasons that explain why the protection of these interests is important also explain why their protection is as important for women as for men. (If there are gender-specific elements in the justification of these protections, they involve the salience of the threats protected against, not the underlying interests themselves.)

Perhaps, however, the likelihood of conflict with traditional norms justifies a more limited caution about women's human rights. Someone might believe, for example, that although the equal protection of such "core" interests as those in physical security, material subsistence, and elementary self-direction is a legitimate aim of human rights practice, it would not be legitimate to seek to advance a broader equality of status for women. This might be regarded as a specifically liberal aspiration.[63] But even in this modified form the position is difficult to defend. The force of the argument from the equal importance of the underlying interests extends considerably beyond these "core" protections. Consider, for example, the treatment of women in laws governing marriage, divorce, and inheritance. The liberty interests involved in marriage and divorce law and the security and subsistence interests involved in laws governing property-holding and inheritance do not differ in nature or urgency by gender. The same might

---

[63] "[W]omen's human rights and women's equality are different, albeit sometimes overlapping, issues, and ... we need to consider them separately if we want to avoid making human rights a synonym for all the political values that we Western liberals treasure." David Miller, "Introduction to Susan Moller Okin," *Sex Rights: Oxford Amnesty Lectures 2002*, ed. Nicholas Bamforth (Oxford: Oxford University Press, 2005), 82.

be said about the interests protected by rights of political participation, access to education, and employment. In each case the weight of argument is borne by the reasons that explain why the protected interests should be taken to be important together with pragmatic judgments about the kinds of threats to which these interests are normally vulnerable. The only role played by the value of equality is to urge that cases that are not relevantly different should be treated alike.

It might be said that the urgency of the protected interests is not the feature whose variation allows public policy to treat women differently than men in (at least some of) the respects in which human rights doctrine requires equal treatment. Perhaps the relevant feature is the desirability of the particular forms of protection that might be provided against threats to these interests. This, it might be said, is influenced by contingent charac- teristics of a society and its culture. So, for example, although it might be granted that there are no gendered differences in the importance of the interest in self-direction, a society's conventions may be such that it is not necessary, say, to ensure equal access for men and women to (every type of) employment in order to protect this interest: perhaps some careers are widely regarded as demeaning for women, and others for men, so that the interest in self-direction is sufficiently protected by ensuring access to careers differently by gender. On these facts, insisting that law and policy should not differentiate on the basis of sex might seem to be an instance of trying to impose a distinctively liberal, and in this case inappropriate, mechanism for the protection of an admittedly common human interest.[64]

The difficulty is that this line of reply is only plausible if one assumes that the social conventions that make differential treatment seem unobjection- able are accepted by everyone, or if not, that social institutions make it possible for dissenters to avoid the restrictions they impose. Writing about the discriminatory practices of religious groups, for example, Michael Ignatieff holds that if these groups "determine that women should occupy a subordinate place within the rituals of the group, and this place is accepted by the women in question, there is no warrant to intervene on the grounds that human rights considerations of equality have been violated."[65] If this

---

[64] The gender role differentiation found in some interpretations of Islamic law is sometimes defended in this way. For discussion, see Mashood A. Baderin, *International Human Rights and Islamic Law* (Oxford: Oxford University Press, 2003), 58–64, 133–53.

[65] Michael Ignatieff, *Human Rights as Politics and Idolatry* (Princeton, NJ: Princeton University Press, 2001), 19.

were true in our example, then perhaps nobody's prospects would be limited by the existing inequalities and, *a fortiori*, a failure to ensure equal access for men and women to all careers would not actually be objected to by anyone. (Of course, it could also be said that a regime of equal employment rights would not be objectionable to anyone either, since it would not interfere with anyone's ability to follow tradition in the choice of career.) But in the cases of practical interest—for the most part, those involving differential treatment by gender in laws and public policies governing access to essential opportunities and services—it is not plausible that either part of the assumption will be satisfied: disagreement is likely about the conventions that are supposed to justify unequal treatment and dissenters are likely to face serious costs if they seek to avoid the limitations imposed by these conventions.[66] This is a familiar observation in reflection about the moral significance of cultural differences, but it deserves particular emphasis in connection with the human rights of women. Where the laws or customary norms validate differential treatment of men and women, one is more likely to find significant disagreement within the culture about the justification of these norms rather than general acceptance.[67] If there is dispute about the interpretation of existing conventions or if people entertain aspirations inconsistent with them, then the rationale presented for unequal treatment is no longer persuasive. It cannot be defended, at any rate, as the consensus view of the culture in question or as a practice from which dissenters have a realistic possibility of exit.

The largest and most important region of the human rights of women consists of protections of interests of equal generic importance to members of both sexes. With respect to these rights, the argument from the equal importance of the underlying interests seems to me dispositive against

[66] I pass over the important further fact that even when there seems to be agreement, it may only be explicable as a matter of adaptive belief under conditions likely to distort judgment. This of course was Mill's assessment of women's beliefs about gender roles in his time. *The Subjection of Women* [1869], in *Essays on Equality, Law, and Education* [*Collected Works of John Stuart Mill*, xxi], ed. J. M. Robson (Toronto: University of Toronto Press, 1984), ch. 1, paras. 10-11. See also Martha Nussbaum, *Women and Human Development: The Capabilities Approach* (Cambridge: Cambridge University Press, 2000), 136-42, and the sources cited there.

[67] Though the likelihood varies some from one society to another. For example, among conservative Islamic states feminist activism has been more pronounced in Iran than in Saudi Arabia or Afghanistan. For an account of the wide range of views about political and legal reform found among women activists in contemporary Iran, see Hamideh Sedghi, *Women and Politics in Iran: Veiling, Unveiling, and Reveiling* (Cambridge: Cambridge University Press, 2007), 245-71; and, more generally, Ziba Mir-Hosseini, "Muslim Women's Quest for Equality: Between Islamic Law and Feminism," *Critical Inquiry* 32 (2006): 629-45.

concerns for cultural deference in the formulation of human rights doctrine. This is a special case of the more general position I defended earlier about the relevance of considerations of international toleration to the grounds and extent of human rights (§ 23). But it may be, here as in the general case, that concerns about cultural deference have a different orientation: not to the grounds of human rights but to the availability of permissible and potentially effective forms of international action to implement them.

This is the second problematic issue. The human rights of women seek not only to disallow certain forms of conduct by the state and to mandate changes in law and policy, but also to change patterns of belief and conduct in the surrounding society and culture. The resulting structure of first-level responsibilities is complex. For example, effective measures to eliminate violence against women in the household would most likely require not only the establishment of criminal penalties for domestic abuse but also changes in law enforcement and in the administration of various social services. Protection against rape would require not only criminal legislation but also the elimination of discriminatory practices in the investigation and prosecution of offenses. The elimination of abuses associated with prostitution would require not only the detection and prosecution of trafficking, debt slavery, and related practices but also measures aimed at changing social norms that justify the treatment of prostitutes as persons undeserving of legal protection. In each case the various responsibilities are related: changes in law and administration are unlikely to be successful in securing their objectives without corresponding changes in background beliefs and social practices.[68]

The question to which these examples call attention is whether there are strategies of action available to outside agents in cases of domestic-level failure which have reasonable prospects of success without being objectionably intrusive. It would be easy to suppose not. Change in patterns of belief that are well established in a culture, or for that matter in culturally sanctioned habits of legal and administrative practice, is a slow, complex process. It is not well understood, and the epistemic barriers facing outside agents seeking to influence it are substantial. Moreover, the means of influence available may seem crude and not well suited to the task. The inference is that a government's failure to comply with those elements of women's human rights doctrine that require efforts to bring about substantial cultural change does not supply a reason for action by outside agents because there is

---

[68] Thomas and Levi, "Common Abuses against Women," 139–76.

no plausibly effective strategy of action for which it could be a reason. But if this is correct, then these elements do not satisfy one of our schematic conditions for justifying human rights: they are not appropriately matters of international concern.

Is the inference correct? I do not believe it can be dismissed. It is difficult to conceive of any plausibly effective strategy of international or transnational action that could induce a recalcitrant government to undertake policies with a reasonable chance of modifying "social and cultural patterns of conduct of men and women... which are based on the idea of the inferiority or the superiority of either of the sexes or on stereotyped roles for men and women" (CEDAW, art. 5(a)). Indeed, it is not even clear what would count as doing so. This, of course, is not to say that the social and cultural changes in question are unimportant. But human rights are supposed to be matters of international concern, and if there are no feasible means of expressing this concern in political action, then perhaps to this extent women's human rights doctrine overreaches.

On the other hand, it is important to take into account the respects in which human rights practice has developed beyond the juridical paradigm envisioned by the framers. As I observed earlier, human rights have come to function not only as legal standards and as objectives for foreign policy, but also as political values that inform and motivate action by nongovernmental group agents with both indigenous and external participants (§ 6). This is particularly significant with respect to women's human rights. The relevant agents are more likely to be nongovernmental organizations and social movement activists rather than international organizations or other states. These agents may function as "translators," interpreting the meaning of the provisions of human rights doctrine for local circumstances, rather than as independent political actors. The forms of political action open to them more likely involve discursive interaction and political communication and mobilization rather than the threats and incentives typical of conventional kinds of political interference. And the distinction between local and outside agents does not have the same significance it would have in the conventional cases.[69]

---

[69] This is made clear in Sally Engle Merry's anthropological study, *Human Rights and Gender Violence: Translating International Law into Local Justice* (Chicago: University of Chicago Press, 2006), esp. ch. 7. Compare Talbott, *Which Rights Should be Universal?*, 108-10. See also Margaret E. Keck and Kathryn Sikkink, *Activists beyond Borders: Advocacy Networks in International Politics* (Ithaca, NY: Cornell University Press, 1998), 165-98.

These facts bear on both of the problems we identified. The first concern triggered by a recognition of the depth and degree of change called for by women's human rights is that the international actions that would be required for success would likely be objectionably intrusive: they might threaten a society's capacity for self-determination and subject individuals to the threat of coercive sanctions. But the forms of contestation just mentioned would not be vulnerable to such an objection: they succeed (when they succeed) by engaging a society's capacities for self-determination rather than by overruling them, and they influence conduct by offering information and persuasion rather than by imposing sanctions. The second problem is that the aims of women's human rights may be beyond the reach of any feasible strategies of action available to outside agents. For example, there may be little that any external agent can do to change the conduct of a government that resists adopting measures aimed at inducing comprehensive changes in conventional beliefs. For this reason, human rights doctrine may overreach in embracing an open-ended entitlement to social and cultural change. But this is plainly a special case. Most human rights of women are open to the same range of protective and remedial action by outside agents as most other civil and political rights, so the problem about feasibility in the special case need not be especially troubling for women's human rights as a class.

Each of the cases we have considered illustrates a distinct problem that can arise in explaining why the protection embodied in a human right should count as a matter of international concern. These problems involve the basis and strength of the responsibilities of external agents to act when a society's own government fails to protect a human right, the extent to which an international practice can plausibly aim for specific institutional protections of important generic interests, and the nature and degree of the accommodation to moral diversity that should be exhibited by a practice claiming universal reach. As I noted at the beginning, these problems are not unique to the cases we have discussed; they represent different ways the idea that human rights are matters of international concern might influence and constrain our thinking about the content and conduct of the public practice. We appreciate the practice's normative complexity by working through the implications of this idea.

8

Conclusion

TOGETHER with the legal prohibition of aggressive war and the establishment of an institutional framework for collective security, the articulation of a doctrine of international human rights is among the most ambitious elements of the settlement of World War II. This doctrine, progressively elaborated in a series of international covenants and conventions, supplies the norms of an increasingly elaborate global practice. I have tried to present a reasonably sympathetic analytical account of the idea of human rights as it exists within this practice, together with a description of the kind of justification that human rights, so conceived, should be capable of.

The main constructive argument is this. We understand international human rights better by considering them *sui generis* rather than as instantiations of one or another received idea. Human rights are the constitutive norms of a global practice whose aim is to protect individuals against threats to their most important interests arising from the acts and omissions of their governments (including failures to regulate the conduct of other agents). The practice seeks to achieve this aim by bringing these aspects of the domestic conduct of governments within the scope of legitimate international concern. Human rights are in this way revisionist appurtenances of a global political order composed of independent states. I summarized these features of human rights in a two-level model. The practice is emergent. In the absence of authoritative global institutions capable of monitoring the performance of governments, reconciling conflicts among norms, determining and applying sanctions, and coordinating the provision of assistance, "international concern" is expressed unsystematically, primarily by means of various forms of political action carried out by whichever agents are capable and appropriately placed and have sufficient reason to act. These agents include states acting unilaterally and in combination, international organizations, and a variety of other actors.

With this conception of the nature and aims of human rights in mind, I proposed a schema to identify and organize the considerations it seems reasonable to take into account in reflection about what ought to be the contents of the public doctrine. These are considerations that follow from a grasp of the general purpose and role of human rights within the global practice. They relate to the importance of the interests that might be protected, the advantage of protecting these interests by means of policies that might be adopted by states, and the character and weight of the reasons for action available to external agents in cases in which states fail to protect the interests in question. Among other things, the schema shows that these reasons are likely to be diverse. Their content and force depend upon the importance of the interests threatened, the nature and sources of the violation, and the character of the relationship, if any, between the potential beneficiaries, other actors in the noncompliant state, and the potential agents. Relatedly, the repertoire of strategies of action that might be open to these various agents is heterogeneous, ranging from the legal to the political and from the coercive to the persuasive and consensual. We observed both kinds of complexity in the cases we took up in the last chapter. One inference is that, although it would be a mistake to identify international human rights with principles of domestic social justice, it is also an error to conceive of them as a "moral minimum," understood as a body of norms that apply among all persons in all historical circumstances. We might say that international human rights occupy a middle ground between these ideas. They are critical, public standards distinguished by their special role as elements of the global normative order we inhabit today.

28. Residues of skepticism

We began with the observation that the discourse of human rights evokes various kinds of skepticism. I have not attempted to refute these positions seriatim. Instead, I have tried to describe a conception of human rights that is compatible with the international practice as we observe it and can be given an interpretation that explains the practice's normative appeal and helps orient critical reflection about its contents and reach. The hope is to replace conceptions of human rights that invite skepticism with one that is more sympathetic to the aims and conduct of the existing practice without sacrificing a capacity to criticize it. Now that we have such a conception on hand, the main lines of reply to the skeptics should be clear.

Some kinds of skepticism are primarily conceptual. They start from what they take to be an independently plausible idea of universal human rights and hold that for one or another reason some or all of the human rights of international doctrine cannot be accommodated within it. One example is the skeptical view that turns on the belief that it is internal to the concept of a right that there should be an institutional capacity for authoritative adjudication and enforcement. Another is that which arises from supposing that human rights, like natural rights, should be justifiable in relation to features possessed by human beings "as such." In both cases we reply by showing that the existing practice embodies a different conception than the one adopted by the skeptic and is addressed to different problems.

Other kinds of skepticism are primarily normative. They express themselves in doubt that human rights should guide political action, either because (some) violations are such that they cannot be prevented or remediated by any strategy realistically available to international or transnational agents or because no such agent would have sufficient reason to carry out any strategy that has a reasonable probability of success. To some extent these kinds of skepticism can be countered by showing that they, too, depend on received ideas of human rights at odds with that implicit in the practice. This is true, for example, of views that treat human rights as grounds of claims for the immediate enjoyment of the substance of a right. It is also true of views holding that human rights must be sufficiently urgent that violations could warrant coercive intervention as a preventive or remedial measure. Human rights conceived according to the two-level model are more elastic in both dimensions. Here, as before, the effect of exhibiting a conception of human rights more in keeping with the existing practice is to raise the question why we should accept the received view as a basis for criticizing the practice's content and reach. Why not regard such a criticism as dogmatic?

The more challenging forms of normative skepticism question whether outside agents typically have sufficient reason to act when human rights are violated by governments. In some cases it may seem, for example, that considerations about the interests of potential beneficiaries are insufficient to explain why any particular agent could have a responsibility to act. Alternatively, it may seem objectionable for outside agents to bring human rights to bear in societies where their requirements are incompatible with religious and moral beliefs widely held in the local culture.

Beginning with the first of these, it is true that the discourse of human rights is sometimes excessively beneficiary-oriented. It is usually easier to explain why the enjoyment of some particular right would be a good thing for beneficiaries than to articulate a plausibly sufficient reason for outside agents to act when a government violates the right or fails to remove obstacles to its enjoyment. As I have argued, in the general case a reply to the first question may not be enough for the second. But it is hardly clear that no other reply to the second question is possible. In some cases, conditions of "strong beneficence" will explain why outside agents have particularly weighty reasons to act; in others, appeal to features of an existing or historical relationship between the potential beneficiary and contributor may be in order. If one regards human rights as middle-level norms designed for a certain kind of practice, the fact that different kinds of reasons to protect an interest will be available in different circumstances does not argue that the protection is unsuitable as the subject of a human right. The pertinent question is whether reasons of an appropriate kind can be given to explain why outside agents should act to protect any particular right in the various circumstances in which governments might be expected to threaten or fail to protect it. Without offering a comprehensive reply, I have tried to show why the prospects of a satisfactory account are better than they would appear if one were to adopt one or another of the received conceptions.

In the alternative, the question is why an apparent conflict with local norms should discredit a value as a ground of international action if the value satisfies the substantive justifying conditions of a human right. The bare fact of a conflict does not argue that a protection is ineligible as a human right; the examples of a racist political culture and an oppressively patriarchial society make this clear. On reflection, the objection to acting to protect human rights where they conflict with local norms often seems to be an objection to certain forms of action rather than to its generic aims—for example, to the use of coercive means in an attempt to bring about changes in a society's prevailing norms. In cases of this kind, however, other forms of action are typically also available to various agents, and these are likely to survive the objection that they are impermissibly intrusive, particularly when there is division within the society in question and the activities of these agents take place in association with members of the society itself.

These considerations suggest that, once we have on hand a practical conception, what began as a temptation to generalized skepticism resolves into one or another more specific concern about matters such as the importance of the interests protected by a right, the nature of the historical and contemporary relationship of the victims and the potential agents, and the propriety of protecting the threatened interest by the means likely to be available. What began as a problem about the practice becomes a problem within it. I have tried to address these concerns at a general level in connection with each element of the schema and as they arise specifically for the cases considered in the last chapter. As that discussion illustrates, a consequence of understanding human rights as I have proposed here is that the question whether any particular protection belongs in an international doctrine of human rights must be treated as a substantive problem of political morality. This means that, in any comprehensive theory of human rights, each distinct protection would require separate consideration. I have not tried to do that here. The residue of skepticism is the suspicion that there are some putative human rights (like the supposed right to democratic institutions, perhaps) for which an adequate justification cannot be given. This suspicion is almost certainly correct. But if the bulk of the existing doctrine survives this form of critical scrutiny, the suspicion need not be debilitating for the practice. Indeed, its expression would be constructive.

29. Pathologies

These kinds of skepticism are largely theoretical. There is also a more political kind of skepticism that arises from reflection about the fact that the practice of human rights has developed and operates in a global context with large inequalities of political power. The significance of this fact can be obscured by an excessive concentration on the legal instruments and institutions of the human rights system, which convey an impression of greater autonomy from the political context than in fact exists. What matters, it might be said, is not the discursive practice abstracted from its context but the practice as it actually operates, influenced as it must be by the global distribution of power. But regarded in this perspective, the practice may not appear to be progressive or even benign; instead, it may seem to function primarily as a mechanism by which powerful actors advance their strategic interests—that is, as an instrument of domination rather than liberation. It might even be contended that human rights legitimate a global political-economic structure that generates forces anti-pathetic to the values human rights are supposed to protect.[1]

It is tempting to reply that what provokes criticism is the public misuse of a normative idiom rather than the principles expressed in that idiom or the idiom itself. If this is true, as it frequently is, then as a matter of political theory the criticism might seem to hold little interest. But to reply this way would miss the point of the criticism. Human rights is by design a public doctrine and the fact, if it turns out to be a fact, that it attracts systematic misuse in ways that set back the purposes the practice aims to advance would be something we should not ignore.[2]

The political critique recalls what is sometimes said about the counter-intuitive consequences of the application of progressive doctrines of international law advanced in the last age of empire. In the later nineteenth century, of course, there were several actual or aspiring empires, whereas today there is, for the moment, at most only one. Moreover, the form and substance of empire were different; indeed, the idea of empire may no longer be very illuminating as a characterization of the structure of global power. But the analogy might be suggestive nonetheless. In the earlier period, international law was widely considered to be a progressive force within a global political structure in which power was unequally distributed. Legal norms were, among other things, mechanisms by which the consequences of this inequality could be regulated. Many of the international lawyers of the time were critics of the colonial policies of the European governments. They held, for example, that under the principle of sovereignty colonial powers had actually to occupy territory to dispose political authority legitimately, and that they were obligated do so in the interests of its inhabitants. They understood the doctrine of the "standard of civilization" as a means by which these powers could carry out a responsibility to encourage the development of the rule of law and law-based administration, which they believed to be essential for any progressive, modern society. In retrospect, however, as Martti Koskenniemi observes, progressive international lawyers found that

---

[1] See e.g. Tony Evans, *The Politics of Human Rights*, 2nd edn. (London: Pluto Press, 2005), ch. 2. I am grateful to Leif Wenar for helping me to see the force of this kind of skepticism.

[2] For a similar view and a more extensive survey of the pathologies of human rights, see David Kennedy, *The Dark Side of Virtue: Reassessing International Humanitarianism* (Princeton, NJ: Princeton University Press, 2004), 3–36.

their ideas often "turned out to have consequences that were the exact opposite of [their] expectations" and that by contributing to the justification of imperialistic policies they had unwittingly "legitimized some of the worst injustices in the history of modernity."[3]

Some people believe the same is true of human rights. According to one critic, for example, "human rights, and the relentless campaign to universalize them, present a historical continuum in an unbroken chain of Western conceptual and cultural dominance over the past several centuries." The claim is not that the idea of human rights is insupportable (the same author writes of "the basic nobility of the human rights project"). The objection is rather that the doctrine and international machinery of human rights tend to be used as instruments of domination by the strong and predominantly Western states that were its principal authors. The practice, intended to correct for pathologies of the states system, is itself pathological.[4]

The critical position combines several elements best considered separately. These concerns are prone to overstatement, but none should be dismissed: each calls attention to a distinct pathology to which the practice of human rights is vulnerable. I comment briefly about three of these.

The most familiar concern is that measures purportedly aimed at protecting uncontroversially important interests may in fact impose a parochial system of political and moral values on societies to which those values are alien. Human rights are vehicles of "moral imperialism." The way this is usually put combines empirical and normative claims: first, that human rights are in some significant sense Western in content and origin and lack a foundation in the world's other moral cultures; second, that when outside agents take action to enforce human rights, they express an arrogant and therefore objectionable disregard of the moral beliefs and ways of life of the ostensible beneficiaries of their action.

There are two common lines of reply. The first is to note that the empirical claim is inflated: it is plainly not the case, for example, that human rights to physical security, the essentials of personal liberty, and basic material goods like adequate nutrition and health care derive from parochially Western concerns. However one understands the normative significance of differences among the moral outlooks prevailing in various

---

[3] Martti Koskenniemi, *The Gentle Civilizer of Nations: The Rise and Fall of International Law 1870–1960* (Cambridge: Cambridge University Press, 2001), 3, 110, and, more generally, ch. 2.

[4] Makau Mutua, *Human Rights: A Political and Cultural Critique* (Philadelphia: University of Pennsylvania Press, 2002), esp. chs. 1-2; quotations at pp. 15 and 10.

cultures, these differences are not so extensive as to impeach the entire human rights enterprise. The second is to observe that it is not objectionably arrogant to aim to protect interests that the intended beneficiaries have reason to regard as urgent, even if they do not actually do so. It might, of course, be reasonable to object to the means chosen to protect the threatened interests; as I observed earlier, the use of coercive means faces an especially high threshold of justification. But in these cases the objection would be to the means, not to the aims, of the protective action.

Whereas, for reasons presented earlier, the first of these responses seems to me correct, the second has parallels with the nineteenth-century "standard of civilization" that we ought not to ignore. Then, international lawyers believed it to be obvious that the capabilities of any society would be enhanced, and the prospects of individual lives made better, with the introduction of what were historically specific institutional forms—written legal codes, individual rights of petition, routinized, rule-based systems of public administration, and so forth. But the attempt to introduce these forms did not reliably produce the outcomes that were anticipated; often, for example, it bred corruption and created opportunities for oppression by colonial governors and their local clients. The error might be said to have been not philosophical but practical: as Koskenniemi puts it, it was a failure to see that "institutions do not carry the good society with themselves. The same types of government create different consequences in different contexts."[5]

The value of the historical analogy is to suggest a more perspicuous interpretation of the idea of "moral imperialism" than is usually assumed and one to which the second response rehearsed earlier is not sufficient. Part of the critique of the uses of international law in the nineteenth century was that the colonial societies on which certain institutional forms were imposed were not suited for them, in part because these forms lacked a grounding in the local culture, in which they therefore behaved in unpredicted and sometimes undesirable ways. In this respect, the "moral imperialism" of that century might be characterized as a form of overreaching. The objection today is that this is also true of human rights. Or if not of human rights generally, then of parts of human rights practice.

It is implausible to apply this critique to human rights doctrine as a whole but it is not implausible to think it might apply to rights that prescribe specific institutional protections for predictable threats to important

[5] Koskenniemi, *The Gentle Civilizer of Nations*, 176–7.

interests. To sustain such a critique, one need not deny that the interests that would be protected or advanced by these measures, if they were successful, are ones that the intended beneficiaries have reasons to care about. The burden of the critique rests on other considerations: on the one hand, about the compatibility of the institutional remedy with widely accepted moral and political values in the culture together with the epistemic difficulties faced by outside agents in making judgments about this and, on the other, about the availability of strategies likely to succeed in protecting the right without bringing about unacceptable incidental harms. Where cautionary considerations of these kinds are apt, we may indeed have reason to regard human rights doctrine as over-extended.

A second concern involves the danger of a more conventionally political subversion of the human rights enterprise. Public appeals to human rights can be used to justify measures that are actually intended to secure some national foreign policy objective.[6] There is, of course, one sense in which this could be tautologically true: if a major power were to include the protection of human rights among its foreign policy objectives, then political action justified by human rights considerations would also advance the interests of the acting power. What troubles people, however, is not this kind of case, but rather one in which human rights considerations are invoked in order to mobilize support for foreign policies that seek a national security objective distinct from the protection of human rights.

Here, again, we might be tempted to seek analogies in the nineteenth century. Possibly the most repellent comparison is the formation by the Belgian King Leopold of the Congo Free State, elaborately justified in humanitarian terms but in fact the occasion of a destructive system of wealth extraction that may have brought about as many as 10 million deaths.[7] The difficulty with the analogy is that no significant recent instance of action to protect human rights resembles this case in the hypocrisy of the appeal to humanitarian considerations or the ruthlessness of the pursuit of interest. The most prominent recent cases—for example, the humanitarian interventions

---

[6] Chris Brown argues, for example, that "the enforcement of human rights is determined, in practice, by the foreign policy objectives of the major powers." "Universal Human Rights: A Critique," in *Human Rights in World Politics*, ed. Tim Dunne and Nicholas J. Wheeler (Cambridge: Cambridge University Press, 1999), 115.

[7] Roger Anstey, *King Leopold's Legacy: The Congo under Belgian Rule, 1908–1960* (London: Oxford University Press/Institute of Race Relations, 1966), ch. 1. The death toll is speculative; see Adam Hochschild, *King Leopold's Ghost* (Boston: Houghton-Mifflin, 1998), 225–33.

in the Balkans—are more accurately seen as motivated by a mixture of aims including both security interests and a desire to protect human rights. It seems clear that the latter was genuine for at least some of those who participated in and supported the decisions in question.[8] This fact suggests a reply to the concern about subversion: someone might say that mixed motives are normal in politics and that the presence of considerations of interest does not make the pursuit of humanitarian aims any less important.[9]

This is true, but it does not fully meet the concern. The problem is not simply that strategic and humanitarian considerations might both be present in either the motivation or the justification of foreign policy. It is that in one or another way the presence of the first is likely to distort or corrupt the second. When strategic and humanitarian motives are mixed, for example, one might fear that strategic interests would shape judgments about the range of alternatives available and bias the balancing of goods and harms for those affected. The effect of appeals to considerations about human rights, even when genuine, would be to mobilize support for policies that would be less likely to improve respect for human rights than alternative measures that might have been adopted but were not. (The case of a policy that would bring about a setback to the human rights of its ostensible beneficiaries is the limiting case.)

This criticism resembles the political realists' critique of "idealism" in foreign policy. The realists accepted that "idealist" principles were sincerely accepted by those who professed them; their critique did not turn on representing idealism as hypocrisy. Instead, they held, as a historical thesis, that the self-conscious attempt to act on principle under the circumstances typical of decision-making in foreign affairs impairs judgment in the choice of policy. Among other things, it encourages misperception of the political and social conditions of other societies and causes overconfidence in the capacity of foreign policy to bring about internal change.[10] The problem about human rights and strategic interests is in a way the reverse—it

[8] I do not count the US intervention in Iraq in 2003 as a case of humanitarian action, but there is no doubt that authentic concern about the human rights abuses of the regime of Saddam Hussein influenced some who supported it.

[9] See e.g. Michael Walzer, "The Argument about Humanitarian Intervention," in *Thinking Politically: Essays in Political Theory*, ed. David Miller (New Haven, CT: Yale University Press, 2007), 243–4.

[10] George Kennan observes both phenomena in his critique of American foreign policy before World War II. *American Diplomacy 1900–1950*, expanded edn. (Chicago: University of Chicago Press, 1984 [1951]). I have discussed this critique in *Political Theory and International Relations*, rev. edn. (Princeton, NJ: Princeton University Press, 1999), 185–91 (Afterword, 1999).

involves the distortion of calculations of principle by considerations of interest. But it seems equally realistic to believe that it is a likely possibility.

What follows about human rights? The politically skeptical view is that the likelihood of distortion is so great, and the damage that would be done as a result so substantial, that we should not recognize human rights violations as justifications of unilateral political action (or anyway coercive action).[11] Otherwise, even if it were nobody's intention, human rights would function in practice as a mechanism for the advancement of the strategic objectives of strong powers at the expense of the interests of vulnerable populations.

The plausibility of such a view depends on two suppositions. The first is that respect for human rights would be greater in the counterfactual world in which unilateral protective action was generally agreed to be unacceptable than in a world in which it was treated as allowable *in extremis*. The second is that human rights practice must remain decentralized, so that, for the most part, any decisions to take action to protect human rights will continue to be made unilaterally by one or a few states with the capacity to act. The first supposition is speculative and it is hard to know what would count as evidence for it, so for the moment I remain agnostic. (It is worth observing, however, that the skeptic cannot avoid defending some form of this counterfactual.) The second supposition is more readily disputable. The decentralization of human rights practice is the result of political choices that might have been different. It is not hard to imagine an international regime combining a mechanism for approval of unilateral protective efforts with a capacity to apply incentives to encourage fidelity to the efforts' purposes.[12] Though the difficulties involved in enacting such a regime cannot be denied, it is a clear political possibility whose achievement would remove much of the force of the skepticism we are considering.

A third concern is that inequalities of power are likely to generate inconsistencies in the application of human rights norms. The contrast between the intervention in Kosovo and the failure to intervene in Rwanda, even though the harms that might have been prevented in the latter case were much greater, is a case in point. There was a failure to bring force to

[11] I mean to include as "unilateral" those actions carried out by alliances and "coalitions of the willing."

[12] The inference is developed, with an illustration of such a process, in Allen Buchanan and Robert O. Keohane, "The Preventive Use of Force: A Cosmopolitan Institutional Proposal," *Ethics and International Affairs* 18 (2004): 1–22. See also Allen Buchanan, *Justice, Legitimacy, and Self-Determination* (Oxford: Oxford University Press, 2004), ch. 11.

bear on human rights violations in proportion to their urgency and extent. Another illustrative contrast is that between the prosecution of officials of relatively weak states for their roles in human rights abuses (for example, the Chilean dictator Augusto Pinochet) and the absence of similar proceedings against the officials of any strong country. It may appear that the only officials likely to be held accountable for violations are those of weak countries and that officials of strong states are practically invulnerable to enforcement of the same norms.[13] Here, again, inconsistencies in enforcement may seem repugnant.

In a system where there are no agreed international institutions to enforce human rights or to regulate the efforts of other agents to do so, inconsistencies like these may be unavoidable. The question is whether there is something objectionable about them. One might think not. About the contrast between Bosnia and Rwanda, for example, one might say: of course it would have been better to intervene in Rwanda than to abstain. But the fact that there should have been intervention in Rwanda, but was not, is not a reason why there should not have been intervention in Kosovo or, where justified, elsewhere. It is irrational to allow concern about inconsistency to impede action to protect human rights where there is both capacity and will; to do so, one might say, would sacrifice the interests of human beings for an abstraction.[14] There is a parallel reply to the objection to the prosecution of officials of weak states.

In the past I have been inclined to accept this reply as sufficient, but now it seems too quick. Human rights is a public practice. I have described it as "emergent" in the sense that the practice has primitive and only intermittently effective machinery for enforcement. Nevertheless, the human rights system has accumulated a measure of moral authority and, however inadequate it may be, an international capacity to act. The trouble with selective enforcement is that it may tend to undermine the authority of human rights principles themselves and such international means of enforcement as we possess.

This, of course, is an empirical conjecture that might turn out false. But suppose it turns out true. It is important to be clear about the implication. Inconsistency is not inherent in the idea and practice of human rights; it is an artifact of the global distribution of political power and the weakness

---

[13] Geoffrey Hawthorne, "Pinochet: The Politics," *International Affairs* 75 (1999), 255–6.

[14] Walzer, "The Argument about Humanitarian Intervention," 239.

of global institutions capable of regulating its effects. After the Kosovo intervention, the Secretary General of the UN called on the international community to reach a consensus on the principle that massive human rights violations should be checked and on a multilateral process for deciding how and when to act.[15] Here, as before, concerns about a pathological tendency of human rights practice are reasons to favor the development of such a process, which might reconcile what seems to be an incompatibility between the effectiveness and the legitimacy of humanitarian action.[16]

The pathologies I have described are genuine political possibilities. When they are realized, the practice of human rights is corrupted and its effectiveness most likely diminished. But the existence of these possibilities is not a reason to reject the human rights project itself: one can recognize them without disparaging the emancipatory potential of a practice of human rights. Realizing that potential is a task for international collaboration at both global and regional levels. There is room for disagreement about the prospects of success of such an effort, but one should resist the temptation to skepticism on the grounds that any such effort is doomed to fail. That temptation seems to me more often to reflect a refusal to take seriously the possibilities of political action than a realistic judgment about the alternatives actually open to us.

30. Human rights and global normative order

I have described the practice of human rights as part of the global normative order. I conclude with a comment about the nature of such an order and what it means to say that human rights are part of it.

The "global normative order" is the body of norms that are more-or-less widely accepted as regulative standards for conduct in various parts of global political space. Some of the norms are law-like—for example, those established by treaty and those embodied in longstanding patterns of international customary practice. Others are better conceived as background norms or principles—they are widely although not unanimously accepted as

---

[15] Kofi Annan, "Two Concepts of Sovereignty," *Economist*, Sept. 18, 1999, 49.

[16] It would be artificially constraining to think that such a response would best occur at the level of global institutions. The prospects for legitimate and effective mechanisms for humanitarian intervention may be greater within regions. See James Kurth, "Humanitarian Intervention after Iraq: Legal Ideals vs. Military Realities," *Orbis* 50 (2006): 87–101.

publicly available, critical practical standards to which agents can appeal in justifying and criticizing actions and policies proposed or carried out (or not) by governments. Human rights as I have characterized them are one kind of background norm.

Human rights, of course, are also embodied in international treaty law. According to some commentators, some human rights—perhaps those articulated in the 1948 declaration—have also become part of customary international law by virtue of their acceptance in the international legal practice of states.[17] Why, then, describe them as background norms rather than simply as legal (or proto-legal) rules? There are several reasons. First, the content of the norms—that is, their requirements for the agents to which they apply—is not settled by referring to the so-called "sources" of international law. To the extent that these norms can be seen as legally binding, their legal character may influence judgments about their content, but it will not be dispositive. Given an understanding of the discursive functions of human rights, we can still ask whether there is a justification for taking this or that value to have the normative force of a human right in practical reasoning about conduct in global politics. Similarly, the nature and weight of our reasons to comply with any particular norm are not settled by determining whether it is properly considered to be a rule of law. This, of course, is true of legal rules in municipal legal systems as well, but the less well-developed character of international law means that the question of the obligation to comply must turn more substantially on background considerations of the kind discussed earlier. Third, whatever may be thought about law in general or international law in particular, it is not even facially plausible that the principles of a public normative order should be in some way available (for example, in an authoritative statute or code) in a form sufficiently explicit to allow them to be applied uncontroversially to any but the simplest cases. One should expect there to be space for reasonable disagreement among the members of a discursive community about the basis and detailed contents of its norms and about their application to particular cases. Indeed, as I have stressed, one function of these norms is to organize disagreement. It is a familiar temptation to think of public principles as if they are settled, private decision rules; this is a mistake at the domestic level and even more so at the global. These principles are components of public life, elements of a system

---

[17] See e.g. Theodor Meron, *Human Rights and Humanitarian Norms as Customary Law* (Oxford: Clarendon Press, 1989), ch. 2. Jack L. Goldsmith and Eric A. Posner take a skeptical view in *The Limits of International Law* (New York: Oxford University Press, 2005), 132–3.

of critical discourse in which agents expect each other's practical reasoning to be influenced by the considerations they frame and justify by appeal to the norms but in which they do not normally expect the inferences drawn to be clear-cut or uncontested.

As we observed in the last section, one kind of skepticism about human rights derives from recognizing that both its doctrine and practice occur within a global order characterized by wide disparities in power. What might be added here is that, even if skepticism can be resisted, one's understanding of the nature and roles of the practice's public norms may be affected by this recognition. Writing about international law in general, Martti Koskenniemi observes that, when we combine an awareness of the openness of legal rules to contrasting interpretations with an understanding of the prevailing differences in political power among states, we come to see that engagement in controversy about international law's requirements can be a "hegemonic technique"—a process of "articulating political preferences into legal claims that cannot be detached from the conditions of political contestation in which they are made."[18] The idea is that actors seek to advance their interests by proposing advantageous interpretations of legal rules and principles for the resolution of conflicts. In the presence of politically significant inequalities of power, states that have substantially greater influence in the international institutions and practices in which normative conflict takes place will tend to prevail, and by doing so will shape the prevalent understandings of the law. Law is thereby bent to the advantage of the stronger powers.

It does not follow, however, that there is no basis for regarding some interpretations of legal rules as more reasonable than others. By availing themselves of the resources of law, states acknowledge each other as members of a legal community and submit to a certain normative discipline. As Koskenniemi observes, "Engaging in legal discourse, persons recognise each other as carriers of rights and duties who are entitled to benefits from or who owe obligation to each other not because of charity or interest but because such rights or duties belong to every member of the community *in that position*."[19] Similar observations apply to the norms of the global order more broadly conceived, and particularly to human rights. What is different in the case of global background norms is that the arenas of contestation are more

---

[18] Martti Koskenniemi, "International Law and Hegemony: A Reconfiguration," *Cambridge Review of International Affairs* 17 (2004), 198.

[19] Ibid. 214 (emphasis in original).

diverse. The global normative order finds expression in many different settings with varying degrees of structure and formality. The agents who participate in these arenas are more diverse as well, consisting not only of the representatives of states and international organizations but also of individuals, nongovernmental groups, and other corporate actors. So controversy about the content and application of the norms may appear even more likely and the prospects of agreement about its proper resolution in any individual case more remote. Nevertheless, as in the case of law, agents accept a certain normative discipline by availing themselves of the resources of the practice of human rights. We appreciate this discipline by looking at the functions the idea of human rights performs within the practice and the commitments one undertakes by engaging in it.

These observations help to explain why the idea of a human right is not best understood as a fundamental moral idea in the way that some people conceive of "natural" or "fundamental" rights. Human rights operate at a middle level of practical reasoning, serving to consolidate and bring to bear several kinds of reasons for action. Their normative content is to some extent open-ended and their application is frequently contested. If we understand human rights as the constitutive norms of an emergent global practice with its own characteristic purposes, neither fact should be surprising.

These observations also explain why the aspirations of a theory of human rights should be in one way modest. To think of human rights as I have suggested is to accept that we should understand their nature and requirements as responses to contingent historical circumstances. So it is probably a mistake to expect to discover a basis for human rights in one or a few clear moral ideas, to formulate a canonical list of rights, or to devise a single authoritative means for bringing them to bear on practical choices. What a theory of human rights might rather hope to accomplish is to clarify the uses to which they may be put in the discourse of global political life and to identify and give structure to the considerations it would be appropriate to take into account, in light of these uses, in deliberating about their content and application. It would seek to interpret the normative discipline implicit in the practice. Such a theory would not, so to speak, stand outside the practice; it would be continuous with it.

Works Cited

Alston, Philip. "Conjuring up New Human Rights: A Proposal for Quality Control." *American Journal of International Law* 78 (1984): 607–21.

[——] UN Commission on Human Rights, 53rd session. *Final Report on Enhancing the Long-Term Effectiveness of the United Nations Human Rights Treaty System*, by Philip Alston, independent expert (E/CN.4/1997/74), March, 27 1996.

—— and James Crawford, eds. *The Future of UN Human Rights Treaty Monitoring*. Cambridge: Cambridge University Press, 2000.

—— "Reconceiving the U.N. Human Rights Regime: Challenges Confronting the New U.N. Human Rights Council." *Melbourne Journal of International Law* 7 (2006): 185–224.

American Anthropological Association, Committee on Human Rights. "Declaration on Anthropology and Human Rights" [1999], http://www.aaanet.org/stmts/humanrts.htm (consulted September 2, 2008).

——, Executive Board. "Statement on Human Rights." *American Anthropologist*, ns 49 (1947): 539–43.

Angle, Stephen C. *Human Rights and Chinese Thought*. Cambridge: Cambridge University Press, 2002.

An-Na'im, Abdullahi A. *Toward an Islamic Reformation: Civil Liberties, Human Rights, and International Law*. Syracuse, NY: Syracuse University Press, 1990.

—— "Universality of Human Rights: An Islamic Perspective." In *Japan and International Law: Past, Present and Future*, ed. Nisuke Ando. The Hague: Kluwer Law International, 1999, 311–25.

—— *Islam and the Secular State: Negotiating the Future of Shari'a*. Cambridge, MA: Harvard University Press, 2008.

Annan, Kofi. "Two Concepts of Sovereignty." *Economist*, Sept. 18, 1999: 49.

Anstey, Roger. *King Leopold's Legacy: The Congo under Belgian Rule, 1908–1960*. London: Oxford University Press Institute of Race Relations, 1966.

Ashford, Elizabeth. "The Demandingness of Scanlon's Contractualism." *Ethics* 113 (2003): 273–302.

Baderin, Mashood A. *International Human Rights and Islamic Law*. Oxford: Oxford University Press, 2003.

Baehr, Peter R. *The Role of Human Rights in Foreign Policy*, 2nd edn. Houndmills: Macmillan, 1996.

Barry, Brian. "Is Democracy Special?" In *Democracy, Power, and Justice: Essays in Political Theory*. Oxford: Clarendon Press, 1989, 24–60.

Beitz, Charles R. *Political Theory and International Relations*, rev. edn. Princeton, NJ: Princeton University Press, 1999.

—— "Human Rights as a Common Concern." *American Political Science Review* 95 (2001): 269–82.

—— "What Human Rights Are." *Daedalus* 132/1 (winter 2003): 36–46.

—— "Human Rights and *The Law of Peoples*." In *The Ethics of Assistance: Morality and the Distant Needy*, ed Deen Chatterjee. Cambridge: Cambridge University Press, 2004, 193–214.

—— "Protections against Poverty in the Practice of Human Rights." In *The Theory and Politics of Socio-economic Human Rights*, ed. Thomas Pogge. UNESCO, forthcoming.

Benhabib, Seyla. *Another Cosmopolitanism*. New York: Oxford University Press, 2006.

Best, Geoffrey. "Justice, International Relations and Human Rights." *International Affairs* 71 (1995): 775–99.

Bjornlund, Eric C. *Beyond Free and Fair: Monitoring Elections and Building Democracy*. Washington, DC: Woodrow Wilson Center Press, 2004.

Brandom, Robert. "Freedom and Constraint by Norms." In *Hermeneutics and Praxis*, ed. Robert Hollinger. Notre Dame, IN: University of Notre Dame Press, 1985, 173–91.

—— *Articulating Reasons: An Introduction to Inferentialism*. Cambridge, MA: Harvard University Press, 2000.

Brett, Annabel S. *Liberty, Right and Nature: Individual Rights in Later Scholastic Thought*. Cambridge: Cambridge University Press, 1997.

Brown, Chris. "Universal Human Rights: A Critique." In *Human Rights in World Politics*, ed. Tim Dunne and Nicholas J. Wheeler. Cambridge: Cambridge University Press, 1999, 103–27.

Brown, Philip Marshall. "The New York Session of the Institut de Droit International." *American Journal of International Law* 33 (1930): 126–8.

Brownlie, Ian. *Principles of Public International Law*, 5th edn. Oxford: Clarendon Press, 1998.

—— and Guy S. Goodwin-Gill, eds. *Basic Documents on Human Rights*, 5th edn. Oxford: Oxford University Press, 2006.

Brucken, Rowland M. "A Most Uncertain Crusade: The United States, Human Rights and the United Nations, 1941–1954." Ph.D. dissertation, Ohio State University, 1999.

Buchanan, Allen. "Charity and Justice." *Ethics* 97 (1987): 558–75.

—— *Justice, Legitimacy, and Self-Determination: Moral Foundations for International Law*. Oxford: Oxford University Press, 2004.

—— and Robert O. Keohane. "The Preventive Use of Force: A Cosmopolitan Institutional Proposal." *Ethics and International Affairs* 18 (2004): 1–22.

Bueno de Mesquita, Bruce, George W. Downs, and Alastair Smith. "Thinking Inside the Box: A Closer Look at Democracy and Human Rights." *International Studies Quarterly* 49 (2005): 439–57.

Bull, Hedley. "Society and Anarchy in International Relations." In *Diplomatic Investigations*, ed. Herbert Butterfield and Martin Wight. London: George Allen and Unwin, 1966, 35–50.

—— *Justice in International Relations*. The Hagey Lectures. Waterloo, Ontario: University of Waterloo, 1984.

—— *The Anarchical Society* [1977], 3rd edn. New York: Columbia University Press, 2002.

Bunch, Charlotte. "Women's Rights as Human Rights: Toward a Re-Vision of Human Rights." *Human Rights Quarterly* 12 (1990): 486–98.

Burgers, Jan Herman. "The Road to San Francisco." *Human Rights Quarterly* 14 (1992): 447–77.

Caney, Simon. "Human Rights, Compatibility and Diverse Cultures." In *Human Rights and Global Diversity*, ed. Simon Caney and Peter Jones. London: Frank Cass, 2001, 51–76.

Carothers, Thomas, ed. *Promoting The Rule of Law Abroad: In Search of Knowledge*. Washington, DC: Carnegie Endowment for International Peace, 2006.

—— "How Democracies Emerge: The 'Sequencing' Fallacy." *Journal of Democracy* 18 (January 2007): 12–27.

Charlesworth, Hilary, and Christine Chinkin. *The Boundaries of International Law: A Feminist Analysis*. Manchester: Manchester University Press, 2000.

Chesterman, Simon. *Just War or Just Peace? Humanitarian Intervention and International Law*. Oxford: Oxford University Press, 2001.

China, Information Office of the State Council. *Human Rights in China*. Beijing: Information Office of the State Council, 1991.

Clapham, Andrew. "Defining the Role of Non-Governmental Organizations with Regard to the UN Human Rights Treaty Bodies." In *The U.N. Human Rights Treaty System in the 21st Century*, ed. Anne F. Bayefsky. The Hague: Kluwer Law International, 2000, 183–94.

—— *Human Rights Obligations of Non-State Actors*. Oxford: Oxford University Press, 2006.

—— *Human Rights: A Very Short Introduction*. Oxford: Oxford University Press, 2007.

Cohen, Joshua. "Minimalism about Human Rights." *Journal of Political Philosophy* 12 (2004): 190–213.

—— "Is There a Human Right to Democracy?" In *The Egalitarian Conscience: Essays in Honour of G. A. Cohen*, ed. Christine Sypnowich. Oxford: Oxford University Press, 2006, 226–48.

Collier, Paul. *The Bottom Billion: Why the Poorest Countries Are Failing and What Can be Done about It*. Oxford: Oxford University Press, 2007.

Commission to Study the Organization of Peace. "International Safeguard of Human Rights" [Fourth Report of the Commission, sec. III]. Repr. in *International Conciliation*, 403 (September 1944): 552–75.

Cranston, Maurice. *What Are Human Rights?* Rev. edn. London: Bodley Head, 1973.

Craven, Matthew C. R. *The International Covenant on Economic, Social, and Cultural Rights: A Perspective on its Development.* Oxford: Clarendon Press, 1995.

Cullity, Garrett. *The Moral Demands of Affluence.* Oxford: Clarendon Press, 2004.

Davenport, Christian, and David A. Armstrong II. "Democracy and the Violation of Human Rights: A Statistical Analysis from 1976 to 1996." *American Journal of Political Science* 48 (2004): 538–54.

Diamond, Larry. *Developing Democracy: Toward Consolidation.* Baltimore: Johns Hopkins University Press, 1999.

Donnelly, Jack. "International Human Rights: A Regime Analysis." *International Organization* 40 (1986): 599–642.

—— "The Social Construction of International Human Rights." In *Human Rights in Global Politics*, ed. Tim Dunne and Nicholas Wheeler. Cambridge: Cambridge University Press, 1999, 71–102.

—— *Universal Human Rights in Theory and Practice*, 2nd edn. Ithaca, NY: Cornell University Press, 2003.

Drèze, Jean, and Amartya Sen. *Hunger and Public Action.* Oxford: Clarendon Press, 1989.

Dworkin, Gerald. "Paternalism." *Monist* 56 (1972): 64–84.

Dworkin, Ronald. *Law's Empire.* Cambridge, MA: Harvard University Press, 1986.

Epstein, David L., Robert Bates, Jack Goldstone, Ida Kristensen, and Sharyn O'Halloran. "Democratic Transitions." *American Journal of Political Science* 50 (2006): 551–69.

Evans, Tony. *The Politics of Human Rights*, 2nd edn. London: Pluto Press, 2005.

Farmer, Paul. *Pathologies of Power: Health, Human Rights, and the New War on the Poor.* Berkeley: University of California Press, 2005.

Feinberg, Joel. *Social Philosophy.* Englewood Cliffs, NJ: Prentice Hall, 1973.

Filártiga v. *Peña-Irala*, 630 F.2d 876 (1980).

Finch, George A. "The International Rights of Man" [Editorial Comment]. *American Journal of International Law* 35 (1941): 662–5.

Finnis, John. *Natural Law and Natural Rights.* Oxford: Clarendon Press, 1980.

Foot, Rosemary. *Rights beyond Borders: The Global Community and the Struggle for Human Rights in China.* Oxford: Oxford University Press, 2000.

Fox, Gregory H. "The Right to Political Participation in International Law." *Yale Journal of International Law* 17 (1992): 539–608.

Franck, Thomas M. "The Emerging Right to Democratic Governance." *American Journal of International Law* 86 (1992): 46–91.

Frost, Mervyn. *Ethics in International Relations.* Cambridge: Cambridge University Press, 1996.

Geddes, Barbara. "What do We Know about Democratization after Twenty Years?" *Annual Review of Political Science* 2 (1999): 115–44.

Geuss, Raymond. *History and Illusion in Politics.* Cambridge: Cambridge University Press, 2001.

Glendon, Mary Ann. *A World Made New: Eleanor Roosevelt and the Universal Declaration of Human Rights*. New York: Random House, 2001.

—— "The Forgotten Crucible: The Latin American Influence on the Universal Human Rights Idea." *Harvard Human Rights Journal* 16 (2003): 27–39.

Goldsmith, Jack L., and Eric A. Posner. *The Limits of International Law*. New York: Oxford University Press, 2005.

Goodale, Mark. "Ethical Theory as Social Practice." *American Anthropologist* 108 (2006): 25–37.

—— and Sally Engle Merry, eds. *The Practice of Human Rights: Tracking Law between the Global and the Local*. Cambridge: Cambridge University Press, 2007.

Grant, Ruth, and Robert O. Keohane. "Accountability and Abuses of Power in World Politics." *American Political Science Review* 99 (2005): 29–43.

Green, Michael J. "Institutional Responsibility for Global Problems." *Philosophical Topics* 32 (2002): 79–95.

Greer, Steven. *The European Convention on Human Rights: Achievements, Problems, and Prospects*. Cambridge: Cambridge University Press, 2006.

Griffin, James. *On Human Rights*. Oxford: Oxford University Press, 2008.

Gross, Leo. "The Peace of Westphalia, 1648–1948." *American Journal of International Law* 42 (1948): 20–41.

Hafner-Burton, Emilie M., and Kiyoteru Tsutsui. "Human Rights in a Globalizing World: The Paradox of Empty Promises." *American Journal of Political Science* 110 (2005): 1373–411.

—— —— "Justice Lost! The Failure of International Human Rights Law to Matter Where Needed Most." *Journal of Peace Research* 44 (2007): 407–25.

Halperin, Morton H., and Kristen Lomasnay. "Guaranteeing Democracy: A Review of the Record." *Journal of Democracy* 9 (1998): 134–47.

Hart, H. L. A. "Are There Any Natural Rights?" *Philosophical Review* 64 (1955): 175–91.

—— *The Concept of Law*. Oxford: Clarendon Press, 1961.

—— "Legal Rights." In *Essays on Bentham*. Oxford: Clarendon Press, 1982, 162–93.

—— *Essays in Jurisprudence and Philosophy*. Oxford: Clarendon Press, 1983.

Hawthorne, Geoffrey. "Pinochet: The Politics." *International Affairs* 75 (1999): 253–8.

Hegel, G. W. F. *Elements of the Philosophy of Right* [1821], trans. Allen Wood. Cambridge: Cambridge University Press, 1991.

Herbst, Jeffrey. "Political Liberalization in Africa after Ten Years." *Comparative Politics* (2001): 357–75.

Hobbes, Thomas. *Leviathan* [1651], ed. E. Curley. Indianapolis: Hackett, 1994.

Hochschild, Adam. *King Leopold's Ghost*. Boston: Houghton-Mifflin, 1998.

Holcombe, Arthur. *Human Rights in the Modern World*. New York: New York University Press, 1948.

Humphrey, John P. *Human Rights and the United Nations: A Great Adventure*. Dobbs Ferry, NY: Transnational, 1984.

Ignatieff, Michael. *Human Rights as Politics and Idolatry*. Princeton, NJ: Princeton University Press, 2001.

—— "Human Rights, Sovereignty, and Intervention." In *Human Rights, Human Wrongs: The Oxford Amnesty Lectures 2001*, ed. Nicholas Owen. Oxford: Oxford University Press, 2002, 53–88.

International Commission on Intervention and State Sovereignty. *The Responsibility to Protect*. Ottawa: International Development Research Centre, 2001.

James, Aaron. "Constructing Justice for Existing Practice: Rawls and the Status Quo." *Philosophy and Public Affairs* 33 (2005): 281–316.

Johnson, M. Glen. "A Magna Carta for Mankind: Writing the Universal Declaration of Human Rights." In *The Universal Declaration of Human Rights: A History of its Creation and Implementation*, ed. M. Glen Johnson and Janusz Symonides. Paris: UNESCO, 1998, 19–76.

Jones, Peter. *Rights*. New York: St Martin's Press, 1994.

—— "International Human Rights: Philosophical or Political?" In *National Rights, International Obligations*, ed. Simon Caney, David George, and Peter Jones. Boulder, CO: Westview, 1996, 183–204.

—— "Human Rights and Diverse Cultures." In *Human Rights and Global Diversity*, ed. Simon Caney and Peter Jones. London: Frank Cass, 2001, 27–50.

Joseph, Sarah, Jenny Schultz, and Melissa Castan. *The International Covenant on Civil and Political Rights*, 2nd edn. Oxford: Oxford University Press, 2004.

Julius, A. J. "Nagel's Atlas." *Philosophy and Public Affairs* 34 (2006): 176–92.

Kant, Immanuel. "On the Common Saying: That May Be Correct in Theory, But It Is of No Use in Practice" [1793]. In *Practical Philosophy*, trans. Mary J. Warnock. Cambridge: Cambridge University Press, 1996, 279–309.

—— "Toward Perpetual Peace" [1795]. In *Practical Philosophy*, trans. Mary J. Warnock. Cambridge: Cambridge University Press, 1996, 317–51.

Karl, Terri Lynn. "Dilemmas of Democratization in Latin America." *Comparative Politics* 23 (1990): 1–21.

Keck, Margaret E., and Kathryn Sikkink. *Activists beyond Borders*. Ithaca, NY: Cornell University Press, 1998.

Kelly, Erin. "Human Rights as Foreign Policy Imperatives." In *The Ethics of Assistance: Morality and the Distant Needy*, ed. Deen Chatterjee. Cambridge: Cambridge University Press, 2004, 177–92.

Kennan, George. *American Diplomacy 1900–1950* [1951], expanded edn. Chicago: University of Chicago Press, 1984.

Kennedy, David. *The Dark Side of Virtue: Reassessing International Humanitarianism*. Princeton, NJ: Princeton University Press, 2004.

Kent, Ann. *China, the United Nations, and Human Rights*. Philadelphia: University of Pennsylvania Press, 1999.

Kingsbury, Benedict, Nico Krisch, and Richard B. Stewart. "The Emergence of Global Administrative Law." *Law and Contemporary Problems* 68 3–4 (2005): 15–61.

Koskenniemi, Martti. *The Gentle Civilizer of Nations: The Rise and Fall of International Law 1870–1960*. Cambridge: Cambridge University Press, 2001.

—— "International Law and Hegemony: A Reconfiguration." *Cambridge Review of International Affairs* 17 (2004): 197–218.

Krasner, Stephen D. "Structural Causes and Regime Consequences: Regimes as Intervening Variables." In *International Regimes*, ed. S. D. Krasner. Ithaca, NY: Cornell University Press, 1983, 1–22.

Kurth, James. "Humanitarian Intervention after Iraq: Legal Ideals vs. Military Realities." *Orbis* 50 (2006): 87–101.

Kymlicka, Will. *Multicultural Citizenship*. Oxford: Clarendon Press, 1995.

Langlois, Anthony J. *The Politics of Justice and Human Rights: Southeast Asia and Universalist Theory*. Cambridge: Cambridge University Press, 2001.

Lauren, Paul Gordon. *The Evolution of International Human Rights*, 2nd edn. Philadelphia: University of Pennsylvania Press, 2003.

Lauterpacht, H. *International Law and Human Rights*. New York: Praeger, 1950.

Li Buyun. "International Protection of Human Rights and the State Sovereignty." In *Constitutionalism and China*. Beijing: Law Press, 2006, 447–60.

Locke, John. *Two Treatises of Government* [1690], ed. Peter Laslett. Cambridge: Cambridge University Press, 1988.

Luard, Evan. *Human Rights and Foreign Policy*. Oxford: Pergamon, 1981.

McDonald, Margaret. "Natural Rights." *Proceedings of the Aristotelian Society*, NS 47 (1946–47): 225–50.

McFaul, Michael. "The Fourth Wave of Democracy and Dictatorship: Noncooperative Transitions in the Postcommunist World." *World Politics* 54 (2002): 212–44.

Manin, Bernard, Adam Przeworski, and Susan C. Stokes. "Elections and Representation." In *Democracy, Accountability, and Representation*, ed. Adam Przeworski, Susan C. Stokes, and Bernard Manin. Cambridge: Cambridge University Press, 1999, 29–54.

Mansfield, Edward D., and Jack Snyder. *Electing to Fight: Why Emerging Democracies Go to War*. Cambridge, MA: MIT Press, 2005.

Maritain, Jacques. *Man and the State*. Chicago: University of Chicago Press, 1951.

Martin, Rex. *A System of Rights*. Oxford: Clarendon Press, 1993.

Marx, Karl. "On the Jewish Question" [1843]. In *Karl Marx: Selected Writings*, ed. Lawrence Simon. Indianapolis: Hackett, 1994, 1–26.

Mayer, Ann Elizabeth. "The Islam and Human Rights Nexus: Shifting Dimensions." *Muslim World Journal of Human Rights* 4 (2007): 1–27 [e-journal], http://www.bepress.com/mwjhr/ (accessed July 26, 2008).

Meron, Theodor. *Human Rights and Humanitarian Norms as Customary Law*. Oxford: Clarendon Press, 1989.

Merry, Sally Engle. *Human Rights and Gender Violence: Translating International Law into Local Justice*. Chicago: University of Chicago Press, 2006.

Mill, J. S. *On Liberty* [1859]. In *Essays on Politics and Society I* [*Collected Works of John Stuart Mill*, xviii], ed. J. M. Robson. Toronto: University of Toronto Press, 1977, 213–310.

Mill, J. S. *Considerations on Representative Government* [1861]. In *Essays on Politics and Society II* [*Collected Works of John Stuart Mill*, xix], ed. J. M. Robson. Toronto: University of Toronto Press, 1977, 371–577.

—— *Utilitarianism* [1861]. In *Essays on Ethics, Religion, and Society* [*Collected Works of John Stuart Mill*, x], ed. J. M. Robson. Toronto: University of Toronto Press, 1969, 203–59.

—— *The Subjection of Women* [1869]. In *Essays on Equality, Law, and Education* [*Collected Works of John Stuart Mill*, xxi], ed. J. M. Robson. Toronto: University of Toronto Press, 1984, 259–340.

Miller, David Hunter. *The Drafting of the Covenant*. New York: G. P. Putnam's Sons, 1928.

Miller, David. "Group Rights, Human Rights and Citizenship." *European Journal of Philosophy* 10 (2002): 178–95.

—— "Introduction to Susan Moller Okin." In *Sex Rights: Oxford Amnesty Lectures 2002*, ed. Nicholas Bamforth. Oxford: Oxford University Press, 2005, 79–82.

—— *National Responsibility and Global Justice*. Oxford: Oxford University Press, 2007.

Miller, Richard. "Beneficence, Duty and Distance." *Philosophy and Public Affairs* 32 (2004): 357–83.

Mir-Hosseini, Ziba. "Muslim Women's Quest for Equality: Between Islamic Law and Feminism." *Critical Inquiry* 32 (2006): 629–45.

Moody-Adams, Michele M. *Fieldwork in Familiar Places: Morality, Culture, and Philosophy*. Cambridge, MA: Harvard University Press, 1997.

Moravcsik, Andrew. "The Origins of Human Rights Regimes: Democratic Delegation in Postwar Europe." *International Organization* 54 (2000): 217–52.

Morsink, Johannes. *The Universal Declaration of Human Rights: Origins, Drafting and Intent*. Philadelphia: University of Pennsylvania Press, 1999.

Mower, Glenn. *Human Rights and American Foreign Policy*. New York: Greenwood Press, 1987.

Mulligan, Casey B., Ricard Gil, and Xavier Sala-i-Martin. "Do Democracies Have Different Public Policies than Nondemocracies?" *Journal of Economic Perspectives* 18 (2004): 51–74.

Mutua, Makau. *Human Rights: A Political and Cultural Critique*. Philadelphia: University of Pennsylvania Press, 2002.

Nelson, John O. "Against Human Rights." *Philosophy* 65 (1990): 341–8.

Nickel, James W. "Is Today's International Human Rights System a Global Governance Regime?" *Journal of Ethics* 6 (2002): 353–71.

—— "Poverty and Rights." *Philosophical Quarterly* 55 (2005): 353–71.

—— *Making Sense of Human Rights*, 2nd edn. Malden, MA: Blackwell, 2007.

Nolde, O. Frederick. *Freedom's Charter: The Universal Declaration of Human Rights*. Headline Series, 76, July 20, 1949. New York: Foreign Policy Association, 1949.

Normand, Roger, and Sarah Zaidi. *Human Rights at the UN: The Political History of Universal Justice*. Bloomington: Indiana University Press, 2008.

Nowak, Manfred. *An Introduction to the International Human Rights Regime*. Leiden: Martinus Nijhoff, 2003.

Nussbaum, Martha C. "Human Rights Theory: Capabilities and Human Rights." *Fordham Law Review* 66 (1997): 273–300

—— *Women and Human Development: The Capabilities Approach*. Cambridge: Cambridge University Press, 2000.

—— "Capabilities and Human Rights." In *Global Justice and Transnational Politics*, ed. Pablo De Greiff and Ciaran Cronin. Cambridge, MA: MIT Press, 2002, 117–49.

—— "Capabilities as Fundamental Entitlements: Sen and Social Justice." *Feminist Economics* 9 (2003): 33–59.

Oberdiek, Hans. *Tolerance: Between Forbearance and Acceptance*. Lanham, MD: Rowman and Littlefield, 2001.

Okin, Susan Moller. "Feminism, Women's Human Rights, and Cultural Differences." *Hypatia* 13 (1998): 32–52.

—— "Poverty, Well-Being, and Gender: What Counts, Who's Heard?" *Philosophy and Public Affairs* 31 (2003): 280–316.

O'Neill, Onora. *Bounds of Justice*. Cambridge: Cambridge University Press, 2000.

—— "The Dark Side of Human Rights." *International Affairs* 81 (2005): 427–39.

Orend, Brian. *Human Rights: Concept and Context*. Peterborough, Ontario: Broadview Press, 2002.

Pagden, Anthony. "Human Rights, Natural Rights, and Europe's Imperial Legacy." *Political Theory* 31 (2003): 171–99.

Parry, Clive, ed. *Consolidated Treaty Series*. Dobbs Ferry, NY: Oceana, 1969.

Patten, Alan. "Should We Stop Thinking about Poverty in Terms of Helping the Poor?" *Ethics and International Affairs* 19/1 (2005): 19–27.

Pauwelyn, Joost. "Human Rights in WTO Dispute Settlement." In *Human Rights and International Trade*, ed. Thomas Cottier, Joost Pauwelyn, and Elisabeth Bürgi Bonanomi. Oxford: Oxford University Press, 2005, 205–31.

Pechota, Vratislav. "The Development of the Covenant on Civil and Political Rights." In *The International Bill of Rights: The Covenant on Civil and Political Rights*, ed. Louis Henkin. New York: Columbia University Press, 1981, 32–71.

Philp, Mark. "Delimiting Democratic Accountability." *Political Studies* 57 (2009): 28–53.

Pico della Mirandola, Giovanni. *On the Dignity of Man* [1486], trans. Charles Glenn Wallis. Indianapolis: Hackett, 1998.

Pogge, Thomas. *World Poverty and Human Rights*. Cambridge: Polity, 2002.

Postema, Gerald J. " 'Protestant' Interpretation and Social Practices." *Law and Philosophy* 6 (1987): 283–319.

Przeworski, Adam, Michael E. Alvarez, Jose Antonio Cheibub, and Fernando Limongi. *Democracy and Development: Political Institutions and Well-Being in the World, 1950–1990*. Cambridge: Cambridge University Press, 2000.

Ratner, Steven R. "Corporations and Human Rights: A Theory of Legal Responsibility." *Yale Law Journal* 111 (2001): 443–545.

Rawls, John. *Political Liberalism*. New York: Columbia University Press, 1996.

—— *A Theory of Justice* [1971], rev. edn. Cambridge, MA: Harvard University Press, 1999.

—— "The Idea of Public Reason Revisited." In *The Law of Peoples*. Cambridge, MA: Harvard University Press, 1999, 129–80.

—— *Justice as Fairness: A Restatement*. Cambridge, MA: Harvard University Press, 2001.

—— *The Law of Peoples*. Cambridge, MA: Harvard University Press, 1999.

Raz, Joseph. *The Morality of Freedom*. Oxford: Clarendon Press, 1986.

—— *Practical Reason and Norms* [1975], 2nd edn. Princeton, NJ: Princeton University Press, 1990.

Renteln, Alison Dundes. *International Human Rights: Universalism Versus Relativism*. Newbury Park, CA: Sage, 1990.

Rich, Roland. "Bringing Democracy Into International Law." *Journal of Democracy* 12 (2001): 20–34.

Risse, Mathias. "How Does the Global Order Harm the Poor?" *Philosophy and Public Affairs* 33 (2005): 349–76.

Rodrik, Dani. *One Economics, Many Recipes: Globalization, Institutions, and Economic Growth*. Princeton, NJ: Princeton University Press, 2007.

—— and Romain Wacziarg. "Do Democratic Transitions Produce Bad Economic Outcomes?" *American Economic Review* 95 (2005): 50–5.

Roosevelt, Eleanor. "The Promise of Human Rights." *Foreign Affairs* 26 (1948): 470–7.

Roosevelt, Franklin D. Annual Message to Congress, January 6, 1941. *The Public Papers and Addresses of Franklin D. Roosevelt, 1940 Volume: War—And Aid to Democracies* [vol. ix], comp. Samuel I. Rosenman. New York: Macmillan, 1941, 663–78.

[Roosevelt, Franklin D., and Winston S. Churchill]. The Atlantic Charter, August 14, 1941. *The Public Papers and Addresses of Franklin D. Roosevelt, 1941 Volume: The Call to Battle Stations* [vol. x], comp. Samuel I. Rosenman. New York: Harper Brothers, 1942, 314.

Rorty, Richard. "Human Rights, Rationality, and Sentimentality." In *On Human Rights: The Oxford Amnesty Lectures 1993*, ed. Stephen Shute and Susan Hurley. New York: Basic Books, 1993, 112–34.

Ross, Michael. "Is Democracy Good for the Poor?" *American Journal of Political Science* 50 (2006): 860–74.

Roth, Brad R. *Governmental Illegitimacy in International Law*. Oxford: Clarendon Press, 1999.

Russell, Ruth B., and Jeannette E. Muther. *A History of the United Nations Charter: The Role of the United States, 1940–1945*. Washington, DC: Brookings Institution, 1958.

Sachs, Jeffrey. *The End of Poverty: Economic Possibilities for Our Time.* New York: Penguin, 2005.

Scanlon, T. M. *What We Owe to Each Other.* Cambridge, MA: Harvard University Press, 1998.

—— "Human Rights as a Neutral Concern." In *The Difficulty of Tolerance: Essays in Political Philosophy.* Cambridge: Cambridge University Press, 2003, 113–23.

—— "Preference and Urgency." In *The Difficulty of Tolerance: Essays in Political Philosophy.* Cambridge: Cambridge University Press, 2003, 70–83.

—— "Rights, Goals, and Fairness." In *The Difficulty of Tolerance: Essays in Political Philosophy.* Cambridge: Cambridge University Press, 2003, 26–41.

—— "Value, Desire, and Quality of Life." In *The Difficulty of Tolerance.* Cambridge: Cambridge University Press, 2003, 169–86.

Schlesinger, Stephen C. *Act of Creation: The Founding of the United Nations.* Boulder, CO: Westview Press, 2003.

Schmitz, Hans Peter. "When Networks Blind: Human Rights and Politics in Kenya." In *Intervention and Transnationalism in Africa: Global–Local Networks of Power*, ed. Thomas M. Callaghy, Ronald Kassimir, and Robert Latham. Cambridge: Cambridge University Press, 2001, 149–72.

Searle, John R. *The Construction of Social Reality.* New York: Free Press, 1995.

Sedghi, Hamideh. *Women and Politics in Iran: Veiling, Unveiling, and Reveiling.* Cambridge: Cambridge University Press, 2007.

Sen, Amartya. "Democracy as a Universal Value." *Journal of Democracy* 10 (1999): 3–17.

—— *Development as Freedom.* New York: Knopf, 1999.

—— "Elements of a Theory of Human Rights." *Philosophy and Public Affairs* 32 (2004): 315–56.

Sengupta, Arjun. "The Human Right to Development." *Oxford Development Studies* 32 (2004): 179–203.

Seybolt, Taylor B. *Humanitarian Military Intervention: The Conditions for Success and Failure.* Oxford: Oxford University Press, 2007.

Shue, Henry. *Basic Rights*, 2nd edn. Princeton, NJ: Princeton University Press, 1996.

Simmons, A. John. *The Lockean Theory of Rights.* Princeton, NJ: Princeton University Press, 1992.

—— "Human Rights and World Citizenship: The Universality of Human Rights in Kant and Locke." In *Justification and Legitimacy: Essays on Rights and Obligations.* Cambridge: Cambridge University Press, 2001, 179–96.

Simmons, Beth. *Mobilizing for Human Rights: International Law in Domestic Politics.* New York: Cambridge University Press, 2009.

Simpson, A. W. B. *Human Rights and the End of Empire: Britain and the Genesis of the European Convention.* Oxford: Oxford University Press, 2001.

Singer, Peter. "Famine, Affluence, and Morality." *Philosophy and Public Affairs* 1 (1972): 229–43.

Skinner, Quentin. *The Foundations of Modern Political Thought.* Cambridge: Cambridge University Press, 1978.

Slaughter, Anne-Marie. *A New World Order.* Princeton, NJ: Princeton University Press, 2004.

Sobek, David, M. Rodwan Abouhard, and Christopher G. Ingram. "The Human Rights Peace: How the Respect for Human Rights at Home Leads to Peace Abroad." *Journal of Politics* 68 (2006): 519–29.

Sohn, Louis B. "How American International Lawyers Prepared for the San Francisco Bill of Rights." *American Journal of International Law* 89 (1995): 540–54.

Steiner, Henry J. "Political Participation as a Human Right." *Harvard Human Rights Yearbook* 1 (1988): 77–134.

Stone, Julius. *International Guarantees of Minority Rights.* London: Oxford University Press, 1934.

Sunstein, Cass R. *Legal Reasoning and Political Conflict.* New York: Oxford University Press, 1996.

Talbott, William J. *Which Rights Should be Universal?* Oxford: Oxford University Press, 2005.

Tan, Kok-Chor. *Toleration, Diversity, and Global Justice.* University Park: Pennsylvania State University Press, 2000.

Tarrow, Sidney. *The New Transnational Activism.* New York: Cambridge University Press, 2005.

Tasioulas, John. "Human Rights, Universality and the Values of Personhood: Retracing Griffin's Steps." *European Journal of Philosophy* 10 (2002): 79–100.

Taylor, Charles. "Conditions of an Unforced Consensus on Human Rights." In *The East Asian Challenge for Human Rights*, ed. Joanne R. Bauer and Daniel A. Bell. Cambridge: Cambridge University Press, 1999, 124–44.

Thomas, Daniel C. *The Helsinki Effect.* Princeton, NJ: Princeton University Press, 2001.

Thomas, Dorothy Q., and Robin S. Levi. "Common Abuses against Women." In *Women and International Human Rights Law*, ed. Kelly D. Askin and Dorean M. Koenig. Ardsley, NY: Transnational, 1999: i. 139–76.

Thompson, Dennis F. *John Stuart Mill and Representative Government.* Princeton, NJ: Princeton University Press, 1976.

Tierney, Brian. *The Idea of Natural Rights.* Atlanta: Scholars Press, 1997.

Tuck, Richard. *Natural Rights Theories.* Cambridge: Cambridge University Press, 1978.

Twiss, Sumner B. "A Constructive Framework for Discussing Confucianism and Human Rights." In *Confucianism and Human Rights*, ed. W. Theodore de Bary and Tu Weiming. New York: Columbia University Press, 1998, 27–54.

UN Committee on Economic, Social and Cultural Rights, 5th Session. *Report on the Fifth Session*, suppl. 3, annex III, *General Comment 3 (1990), The Nature of States Parties' Obligations.* Economic and Social Council Official Records, 1991 (E/1991/23), 83–7.

UN Economic and Social Council, 2nd Session. *Report of the Commission on Human Rights to the Second Session of the Economic and Social Council* (E/38/Rev. 1), May 21, 1946.

UN Economic and Social Council, Commission on Human Rights, 2nd Session. *Proposal for a Declaration of Human Rights Submitted by the Representative of the United States* (E/CN.4/36), November 26, 1947.

UN Economic and Social Council, Commission on Human Rights, 2nd Session. *Summary Record of the Twenty-Sixth Meeting* (E/CN.4/SR.26), December 3, 1947.

UN Economic and Social Council, Commission on Human Rights, 2nd Session. *Draft Report of the Working Group on Implementation* (E/CN.4/53), December 10, 1947.

UN General Assembly, 5th Session. *Resolution 421* [*Draft International Covenant on Human Rights and Measures of Implementation: Future Work of the Commission on Human Rights*] (A/1620), December 4, 1950.

UN General Assembly, 41st Session. *Resolution 41/128* [*Declaration on the Right to Development*] (A/RES/41/128), December 4, 1986.

UN General Assembly, 48th Session. *Resolution 48/104* [*Declaration on the Elimination of Violence against Women*] (A/RES/48/104), February 23, 1994.

UN General Assembly, 60th Session. *Resolution 60/1* [*2005 World Summit Outcome*] (A/Res/60/1), October 24, 2005.

UN General Assembly, Third Committee. *96th–100th Meetings*, Official Records (A/C.3/SR 96–100), October 7–12, 1948.

UN Human Rights Commission, Subcommission on the Promotion and Protection of Human Rights. *Norms on the Responsibilities of Transnational Corporations and Other Business Enterprises with Regard to Human Rights*, August 26, 2003 (E/CN.4/Sub. 2/2003/12/Rev. 2).

UN Human Rights Committee. *General Comment Adopted by the Human Rights Committee under Article 40, Paragraph 4, of The International Covenant On Civil and Political Rights: Addendum, General Comment 25 (57)* (CCPR/C/21/Rev.1/Add.7), August 27, 1996.

UN Office of the High Commissioner for Human Rights. "Ratifications and Reservations." http://www2.ohchr.org/english/bodies/ratification/index.htm (consulted November 2, 2008).

UNESCO. *Human Rights: Comments and Interpretations*. London: Allan Wingate, 1949.

Vattel, Emerich de. *The Law of Nations* [*Le Droit des gens*] [1758], trans. Charles G. Fenwick. Washington, DC: Carnegie Institution, 1916.

Vincent, R. J. *Human Rights and International Relations*. Cambridge: Cambridge University Press, 1986.

Waldron, Jeremy. "Can Communal Goods be Human Rights?" In *Liberal Rights: Collected Papers 1981–1991*. Cambridge: Cambridge University Press, 1993, 339–69.

Waltz, Susan. "Universalizing Human Rights: The Role of Small States in the Construction of the Universal Declaration of Human Rights." *Human Rights Quarterly* 23 (2001): 44–72.

Walzer, Michael. *Thick and Thin: Moral Argument at Home and Abroad*. Notre Dame, IN: University of Notre Dame Press, 1994.

—— *On Toleration*. New York: Yale University Press, 1997.

Walzer, Michael. "The Argument about Humanitarian Intervention." In *Thinking Politically: Essays in Political Theory*, ed. David Miller. New Haven, CT: Yale University Press, 2007, 237–50; 1st edn. 1951.

Weissbrodt, David, and Muria Kruger. "Norms on the Responsibilities of Transnational Corporations and Other Business Enterprises with Regard to Human Rights." *American Journal of International Law* 97 (2003): 901–22.

Wells, H. G. *The Rights of Man—or What are We Fighting for?* Harmondsworth, Middlesex: Penguin, 1940.

Wertheimer, Alan J. *Exploitation*. Princeton, NJ: Princeton University Press, 1996.

Williams, Bernard. "The Standard of Living: Interests and Capabilities." In *The Standard of Living*, ed. Amartya K. Sen. Cambridge: Cambridge University Press, 1987, 94–102.

—— "Internal Reasons and the Obscurity of Blame." In *Making Sense of Humanity*. Cambridge: Cambridge University Press, 1995, 35–45.

—— "In the Beginning Was the Deed." In *In the Beginning Was the Deed*. Princeton, NJ: Princeton University Press, 2006, 18–28.

—— "Human Rights and Relativism." In *In the Beginning Was the Deed*. Princeton, NJ: Princeton University Press, 2006, 62–74.

World Bank. *World Development Report 2006: Equity and Development*. Washington, DC: World Bank, 2005.

Index

Printed in the USA
CPSIA information can be obtained
at www.ICGtesting.com
JSHW050819110923
48251JS00003B/50